WEB VIDEO

MAKING IT **GREAT**, GETTING IT **NOTICED**

JENNIE BOURNE with DAVE BURSTEIN

WEB VIDEO: MAKING IT GREAT, GETTING IT NOTICED

Jennie Bourne with Dave Burstein

Peachpit Press
1249 Eighth Street
Berkeley, CA 94710
510/524-2178
Fax: 510/524-2221

Find us on the Web at: www.peachpit.com
To report errors, please send a note to errata@peachpit.com
Peachpit Press is a division of Pearson Education

Senior Editor: Karyn Johnson
Developmental Editor: Stephen Nathans-Kelly
Production Coordinator: Kate Reber
Copyeditor: Kimberly Wimpsett
Proofreader: Liz Welch
Composition: Kim Scott, Bumpy Design
Indexer: FireCrystal Communications
Interior Design: Charlene Charles-Will and Kim Scott
Cover Design: Charlene Charles-Will
Cover Images: Alison Folland and Michael Goduti in the Hillman Curtis short film "Bridge"

ISBN-13: 978-0-321-55296-9

ISBN-10:   0-321-55296-2

9 8 7 6 5 4 3 2 1

Printed and bound in the United States of America

I dedicate this book to my coauthor and partner, Dave Burstein,
who taught me that many rules are made to be broken.

Acknowledgments

Writing *Web Video: Making It Great, Getting It Noticed* would have been impossible without the help of many people who shared their stories and helped me understand some of the technology behind Web video. They include interviewees and advisors Andrew Baron, Barry Braverman, Joanne Colan, Roxanne Darling, Kathleen Graham, Fritz Grobe and Stephen Voltz of Eepybird, Jen Grogono, Larry Jordan, Dina Kaplan, Philip Nelson, Aza Raskin, Steve Rosenberg, Yaron Samid, Ken Schneiderman, Jay Smooth, Michael Szpakowski, Ben Waggoner, Carletta Joy Walker, Jamie Wilkinson, and Josh Wolf.

My beautiful friend Mai Ly modeled for me, fed me, walked with me, and listened when I needed an ear. Photographer Al Holston took gorgeous photographs for this book. Dave Burstein is helping to build the book's Web site. Thanks to Kathleen Mandis and Simon Quellen Field who got me started writing at their Birdfarm, as well as many others who worked behind the scenes to make sure I had what I needed to make it the best book I could write. A list of credits is also included at the end of the book. If I've left anyone out, please forgive me—your help has not gone unnoticed.

Special thanks to Karyn Johnson who championed this book and made it great, as well as the amazing team at Peachpit: Stephen Nathans-Kelly, developmental editor; Kate Reber, production editor, who worked magic with the illustrations that make this book special; Charlene Charles-Will, design manager who brought imagination and style to designing both the cover and the book's interior; Kim Scott, who handled layout and composition; and Hillman Curtis, who let us use stills from one of his videos for the cover.

Special thanks also go to my coauthor and partner, Dave Burstein. He says we're still together after all these years because although he seems like a nice man, he's really a bad boy at heart. Before I met Dave, I tried to do things by the book. This made many things tedious and a lot less fun. It made learning how to use video equipment and software frustrating and sometimes impossible.

Now I know that to make great Web video you have to take chances and have fun while you learn. Trust your instincts, give yourself time to fall in love with making Web video, and know it's OK to make mistakes.

CONTENTS

INTRODUCTION

STEP UP YOUR GAME

I wrote this book to help you make great video for the Web. I love watching the stories of people's passion and their lives, but not always the quality of the images and sounds on the Web. This book will show you how to make video that communicates your ideas and looks and sounds great. Like you, I bring who I am and what I know to making Web video. For me that's film school, experience working on feature films and network news shows, a decade as a reporter and radio journalist, a few years teaching college, and experience building a network and a studio for tech-talk TV on the Web.

I've learned that the best videomakers aren't afraid to share their point of view and that telling a good story is the key to good video. And I've found that passion for your topic and enthusiasm for sharing it keeps viewers coming back for more.

It takes practice to make Web video that looks and sounds great. This book contains projects throughout that are designed to help you understand what works online and why. You'll learn how to make short videos, practice shooting for the Web, and learn how to put your video online. Each project will bring you closer to creating your own unique Web video style.

To produce high-quality Web video, you'll also need to learn about video compression, the technology that makes it work, and the business that makes it possible. Low-cost bandwidth and hosting companies willing to carry the costs make distribution free for producers but give hosts control over the quality viewers see. You can take control by choosing the right host and learning how to format your video for the Web.

Whether your goal is to get famous or to make the world a better place, improving the way your video looks and sounds will make it better and get it noticed. You might even make a little money along the way.

Producing for Web Audiences

Connecting with your audience is essential. I'll help you identify and reach the right people for your topic and your style. The biggest Web audience so far is people watching short, funny clips. That's changing. As viewers get faster broadband connections, many are watching full episodes of their favorite TV shows online. Hollywood is moving to the Web, and the competition is getting tougher. That's why it's so important to improve the quality of the video you produce.

Here's a sample of what you'll learn about Web video and what makes it different from video produced for other media: Shooting for the Web means less motion and more focus on the subject. Learning to light for the Web also is important because compression changes the way your video looks online. On the small screen, subtle details can get lost, so you'll shoot more close-ups. Editing Web video involves more cuts and fewer effects, and you'll learn ways to make the editing process smoother. Before you upload your video to the Web, you'll want to choose a host that will give you the help you need and put your video out in the best quality you can afford.

I've met some of the best videomakers. Many have agreed to be part of this book through a series of interviews. Over the next nine chapters, you'll meet Andrew Baron, who created Rocketboom, one of the Web's great successes; Dina Kaplan, whose Blip.tv hosts and finds advertisers for some of the best Web TV shows; Barry Braverman, who shoots feature films, TV documentaries, and video for the Web; Larry Jordan, a veteran producer and Final Cut Pro trainer; and Kathleen Grace, producer of the hit dramatic series *The All-for-Nots*. In addition to the interview segments of each chapter, you'll also find these Web video experts and other useful resources on the book's Web site (www.webvideobook.tv).

Making a Web Video Pay

As I was finishing up this book, Dave Burstein, who assisted with the research and writing, invited me to a party for a Web tech/culture show called *Diggnation* (www.diggnation.com; **FIGURE 1**).

When we got there, I was astonished to see hundreds of people lined up around the block (**FIGURE 2**). More than 600 fans crowded inside to meet hosts Kevin Rose and Alex Albrecht (**FIGURE 3** and **FIGURE 4**), who raised $8 million to finance their production company, Revision3.

FIGURE 1 *Diggnation* invited fans to meet offline.

FIGURE 2 Fans line up to watch *Diggnation* being taped.

ON Networks, another Web video shop you'll read about in Chapter 9, *Making It Pay*, raised $12 million to produce Web video shows. Meanwhile, the major networks are spending hundreds of millions of dollars on the Web. It's an exciting, growing field with remarkable opportunities.

Developing your audience and getting to know them are the first steps to making Web video pay off. Advertisers love large audiences. Statistics collected by your video host tell them how popular your video is; in this book, you'll learn how to use them. Social networking sites will help you get the word out about your video. After you develop a large following, hosts like Blip.tv will help you find advertisers. Sharing revenues with your video hosts or posting advertising on your Web video page can also pay off.

FIGURE 3 Kevin Rose and Alex Albrecht, hosts of *Diggnation* and founders of Revision3.

FIGURE 4 Your audience makes your show a hit. *Diggnation*'s fans turned out by the hundreds to meet the show's hosts at a meetup in Brooklyn.

Producing video for the Web isn't just about creating and uploading your own shows. There are an increasing number of jobs in Web video. I'll tell you where to look and give you tips on networking to make the connections you'll need to start a Web video career.

What's in the Book?

Now that you know about some of the broader topics that will be covered in the book, here is a quick snapshot of the contents for each chapter:

Chapter 1, *Making Great Web Video*. The task of making Web video look good and sound great starts with a good story. This chapter informs you of the production skills you'll need to get your project started and developed for the Web. Jump right in and learn the steps to making Web video with the end-of-chapter project.

Chapter 2, *Shooting for the Web*. The chapter explains why taking your camera off automatic will improve the quality of your video, how to frame your shots for the small screen, how to budget camera movement for when it works best, which equipment you'll need, and how to get the most out of that equipment.

Chapter 3, *Shooting Events and Interviews*. Shooting events and interviews "Web style" involves attitude and an eye toward the unusual. Included in this chapter are tips for single-camera shooting on location and advice on working with available lighting and recording sound from a professional board. You'll learn lighting tricks to give your interview guests a star-quality glow using equipment you can carry. You'll also learn microphone techniques to keep noise low and sound quality high.

Chapter 4, *Videoblogs, How-to Videos, and News*. In this chapter, you'll discover how to make yourself and your subjects look good on camera. You'll receive tips for working solo, learn about using screen direction and continuity to build sequences for how-to videos, and discover how to shoot with editing in mind. At the end of the chapter, you'll use what you've learned to create news packages and profiles.

Chapter 5, *TV Techniques for Better Web Video*. Here you'll get practical tips for multicamera shoots. You'll learn about live three-camera switching on a budget, setting up lighting for green screens, compositing, and using equipment that makes keying easy. You'll also get the inside scoop on shooting a dramatic series for the Web and how to build a set for your productions.

Chapter 6, *Editing and Post-Production*. It's important to edit your footage, keeping the Web's short attention span in mind. You'll learn to streamline the post-production process and stay organized while you edit. I'll give you advice on using editing software, as well as step-by-step instructions for editing video shot for multicamera and green screen.

Chapter 7, *Uploading Video to the Web*. This chapter guides you on choosing the best host for your Web video and knowing which features to look for to make delivering your video easy for you and a great experience for your viewers. Included is a reference to the best formats for online video and formulas for compressing it for popular hosts.

Chapter 8, *Getting Your Video Noticed*. After you've uploaded your video, I'll share secrets for taking your video viral. You'll learn how to use social networking to get your video noticed and how to work effectively with the press to promote your video. Finally, you'll learn to adopt a distribution plan that will grow with your success.

Chapter 9, *Making It Pay*. Now that all's been said and done, you'll learn how to make advertisers take notice. This includes discovering how to make subscription plans work and adding Google AdSense to your video Web page. You'll learn to approach revenue sharing with your video host and also get tips on finding a job in Web video.

Additional Resources

Throughout the book, you'll see an icon with the label "On the Web." Join my online community at www.webvideobook.tv to get access to files that will help you with the projects you'll find at the end of each chapter in the book. Some of the interviews that appear throughout the book will be included there in audio or video form. You'll also find equipment reviews and a forum where you can bring your questions and exchange ideas with other Web videomakers.

At the end of the book is a list of resources that you may find useful in helping you learn more about Web video.

CHAPTER 1

MAKING GREAT WEB VIDEO

1 MAKING GREAT WEB VIDEO

What makes video a hit on the Web? The best Web video producers craft compelling stories people want to watch using solid production values. They've mastered the technology that makes the Web a unique video delivery medium, and they know how to make video work on the Web.

Many successful Web video producers let their personalities show. They aren't afraid to show what they think, but perhaps even more important is their relationship with their viewers. They know who's watching, and they listen carefully to what they have to say. This is the first step toward using the power of the Web, its tools, and its communities to fuel the viral buzz around their video and get it noticed.

NOTE Using standard techniques well is important but don't be afraid to take chances. Your experiments with unconventional camera angles and unusual locations for interviews won't always work but when they do, your work will be more creative and more interesting to your viewers.

Today's Web video producers are also creating new ways of working. Although many shoot the video themselves or work in small teams with limited budgets, the work they produce has become so wildly popular with viewers that professionals from TV and other media are scrambling to learn how to make their commercial efforts on the Web as successful.

This book will help you create high-quality original video for the Web. You'll learn techniques and strategies from the best in the business. You'll meet producers and read about the amazing work they've created as Web video evolves into a professional medium with its own style. You'll learn about new tools and techniques to make your work better and how a career in Web video can pay off.

Things Change Fast on the Web

Many early Web video creators understood the Web first and learned about video later. Bad compression often masked poor-quality video, and high production values were thrown out the window as inexpedient.

Because early compression algorithms could mangle even the best video, some inexperienced producers assumed it didn't matter if their sound wasn't good, if they didn't use tripods, or if they used a cheap mic (or no mic at all).

Today, the tools and technology are better, and audiences expect more. Using consumer gear and home movie shooting styles are OK if you're just getting started, but keep in mind that Web video today is more competitive than ever. To get your ideas out to viewers you'll need more technical skills and a plan to help you manage all the details of a more complex production. Video that looks and sounds really great doesn't have to be out of reach even if you didn't go to film school or don't own professional gear.

Producing Web video starts with a great idea. *Rocketboom* producer Andrew Baron started with little related experience in video and built one of the most recognized and imitated shows on the Web. His stage was simple: a smart pretty actress behind an anchor desk that consisted of a table and a map on the wall behind her (**FIGURE 1.1**).

FIGURE 1.1 *Rocketboom*'s host Joanne Colan on set in front of the show's famous map. Andrew Baron started *Rocketboom* with a good idea and prosumer equipment, creating an irreverent news show that became a runaway hit.

The secret was smart, irreverent writing and an amazing team. Host Joanne Colan's deadpan delivery pokes fun of the limited tools they use to roll in footage, and audiences love it.

Your idea doesn't have to be complicated—as the success of *Rocketboom* shows— but putting it on paper will help you focus it. Defining your project clearly will also help you determine what resources you'll need to bring your idea to life and give you a head start on bringing together the equipment and talent you'll need on camera.

During post-production, you'll edit for the Web audience's short attention span and voracious appetite for new content. You'll keep the bottom line in mind as you market your work and put it out for the world to see.

Keeping Your Viewers in Mind

The key to success on the Web is keeping your viewers in mind during every stage of production. Web audiences are sophisticated. They know the difference between amateur video shot with a digital still camera and high-quality footage shot in high definition (HD). They may not care when they're watching for only five minutes during their lunch break or on their phones, but when the video is longer or they need to show it on a large monitor as part of a presentation, they're likely to be more critical.

Web video—whether it's produced for corporate or educational use or designed for commercial entertainment—should look and sound polished (**FIGURE 1.2**).

FIGURE 1.2 VideoJug, ExpoTV, and other how-to sites are delivering some of the best and most watched video on the Web.

To improve the quality of your video, borrow techniques from the pros, but use pro-sumer gear that's not as expensive as the professional equipment used for broad-cast TV and that doesn't require such a steep learning curve to master. Your video will look and sound better, and you'll still be able to keep the focus on your content.

Great Web video begins with captivating pictures and good sound. Then you'll need to find creative ways to use images to tell your story and edit in a way that keeps your audience interested.

What Makes Web Video Different

Attention is the most important commodity on the Web. Thinking about how to capture your audience's imagination begins during pre-production, and it doesn't stop when you turn off the camera, or even when you're in the editing room.

Getting video noticed and making it popular without big advertising or marketing budgets are two of the hallmarks of successful Web video that commercial entities are trying desperately to copy.

You Can't Always Control What Your Audience Will See

The fundamental technical difference between Web video and broadcast video is that Web video is heavily compressed. Under-standing your audience's bandwidth limitations is often as impor-tant as understanding their tastes. The speed of their Internet connections will determine how your video looks to your viewers.

NOTE Web video differs dramatically from DVD-Video; although DVD-Video is also compressed, the platform is standardized. All DVD players have essentially the same capabilities, and their ability to deliver video to a TV is never in question. Because there are many dif-ferent formats for Web video it is more like a moving tar-get. The speed of a viewer's Internet connection plays a role in the quality she sees.

Compressing your video so it can travel over the Internet can change the way your video looks to viewers. Understanding the basics of compression is the first step toward making your video look and sound good. Keeping in mind that you'll eventually com-press your video will also save you time. When you know what will and won't work on the Web, you'll make different choices while shooting and editing.

Making sure viewers can view your video the way you want them to see it is an ever-present concern. Although most viewers have high-speed Internet connections, some do not.

Knowing who's in your audience makes it easier to anticipate their needs. College students, for example, routinely have access to broadband, but many campuses restrict video that must be downloaded to be viewed. Older audiences may still be on dial-up connections, so they'll need lower-resolution files that work at slower speeds or the option to download your video before watching it.

Viewers can make or break the success of your video by linking to it, recommending it, or blogging about it. To create an effective plan for marketing and distributing Web video, you'll need to understand what your audience is looking for. Understanding what they want is the key to getting more viewers to watch your work.

The need to compress your video for the Web and the power of your audience to help it spread across the Internet affect the entire production cycle and help to define your approach to producing for the Web. Keeping these issues in mind as you shoot, as well as lighting your scenes and editing your video with the Web platform in mind, will make your job easier and your results more satisfying when you're ready to upload your video to the Web.

Producing for a Web-Savvy Audience

The Internet democratizes video production and distribution. Anyone with access to the Web and a video camera can produce for the Web. The result is a wonderfully diverse, creative, and idiosyncratic video medium where original ideas flourish and producers seldom hide their points of view.

Some successful Web video productions are as polished as commercial TV, while others pay less attention to production and focus on getting their content out fast to an online community.

NOTE Delivering high-quality images is only the visible part of the improvements in the fast-changing technology of video on the Web. Video hosting companies can now monitor your viewers, track who is watching, and tell you how long they watch. To play at this level, you'll want to keep the quality of your video high. This opens the door for more support from advertisers who need these statistics to track effectiveness.

To keep your audience coming back for more, you'll need to make your productions provocative, take chances, and wow them. That might mean adopting an innovative graphic style, shooting in front of a green screen, or finding unique locations and topics for your video. Simply copying standard production techniques from traditional TV just doesn't work. Web video is a new medium. Success is largely determined by whether you capture your audience's imagination with video that shows them something different.

Now that advertisers and sponsors are on board, Web video quality standards are changing. An increasing number of Web video viewers have broadband connections, making it possible for them to watch full-length TV dramas on the Web in a quality that still looks great full-screen (**FIGURE 1.3**).

Make up your mind to produce great video, and you'll be right in step with what's happening on the Web. As you learn what works on the Web, you'll create your own way of doing things (**FIGURE 1.4**). By next year, people will be studying your style for clues how to take their videos viral.

FIGURE 1.3 The Move player from Move Networks protects TV networks' copyrighted video and consists of a downloadable player that delivers excellent quality even at full-screen.

FIGURE 1.4 Expotv.com features videos created by viewers: Most speak straight to the camera and show off a product and its features. In the video pictured here a regular contributor extols the virtues of an advanced Canon video camera.

Production Values and Goals

Using professional approaches to production and advanced technology to deliver video to the Web can help make your original Web video look great. But don't let your ideas get lost in the process. Producing glossy video that looks like TV takes a lot of time and effort. But remember, if your video doesn't bring new ideas and new perspectives to viewers it won't work with Web audiences. Use high-quality production values while keeping your production goals in mind. Not all traditional approaches to video production apply, but those that do can improve the quality of your work and its appeal on the Web.

You'll use the technologies of production to realize your vision. Even if you won't be shooting and editing your own work, understanding the tools and technology that make Web video work will help you communicate with professionals on your production team, and it will also help you work with them to craft video that people will want to watch, at a level of quality that doesn't get in the way of your message.

It really takes a team to create the best work. Even if you're a team of one, there's no getting around the fact that careful production, good editing, and strong writing generate loyal audiences. Later in this book you'll learn about distribution and marketing because it doesn't matter how good your video is if nobody gets to see it.

Building a Team to Make Better Video

Many Web video producers have their hands full shooting solo, at times even interviewing from behind the camera. This means producers take on multiple roles. At different times during production you'll need to create priorities based on the role you take on. You'll end up thinking like a videographer, sound person, lighting person, interviewer, and production assistant as you take on these roles.

Few people are good at everything. Each of these roles involves a craft that many people specialize in and often spend a lifetime getting good at. Tackling them all at once limits what you're likely to achieve with your production. Although a videographer needs to keep the needs of an editor in mind while shooting, it's very difficult to be objective about footage you've shot when you're in the editing room. When you work with other skilled people, you'll always learn something, and working in a team will improve your work.

On the other hand, working solo is a great training ground for a producer because it forces you to learn everything it takes to make a production work. Walking a mile in several different pairs of shoes gives you perspective and empathy. Since you'll also be your own production manager, keeping track of your production's budget and schedule, you'll know what's really needed and what's optional, making it easier to stay within your budget.

Watching the Web

It's almost possible today to cancel your subscription to cable and watch the Web. Soon the dream of watching the Web like we watch TV will be a reality. The Web offers viewers more control over what viewers watch and when. New tools like the Miro player make it easy to download and watch the video already available (**FIGURE 1.5**). RSS feeds make it easy for your viewers to create channels or line-ups that include your work and publish them for the world to watch.

On the Web your video offering can appear side by side with dramas from ABC and with tech documentaries from the Discovery Channel. These programs are often produced with higher budgets and more experienced technical staffs. If you're going to stack your video up against this kind of programming, you'll want to make it look as good as you can.

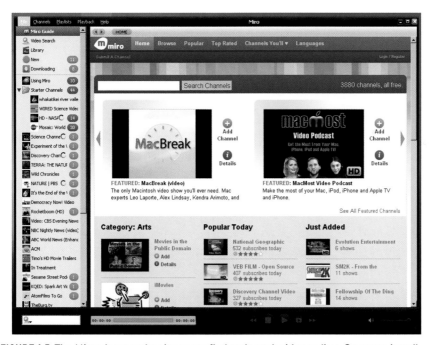

FIGURE 1.5 The Miro player makes it easy to find and watch video online. Once you install the free player on your computer, it acts like a digital video recorder or TiVo for Web video.

Getting Started in Web Video

DJ Jay Smooth, DJ, Radio Host and Producer of the hip-hop music site Illdoctrine.com

Jay Smooth got his start in radio, where he became a popular on-air host and learned to record, edit, and mix sound. Ten years ago he took his passion for hip-hop to the Web and created one of the first blogs to serve the hip-hop music community.

Today he produces and hosts *Ill Doctrine* (**FIGURE 1.6**), a Web-based video program at http://illdoctrine.com/. For Smooth, good sound matters more than pictures. He uses his skills as a sound editor to shape his program and then fine-tunes it to make the picture work. This type of editing, called a *radio cut*, is common in projects where the information comes first.

FIGURE 1.6 DJ Jay Smooth put what he learned from radio to work when he launched his video blog Illdoctrine.com.

Smooth has a distinctive visual style that includes constantly changing camera angles and focal lengths over the course of his commentaries that typically last about three minutes. "I wanted to spice up the visuals as much as I could," he says.

But his style is also born of necessity. Smooth works solo using a Hi8 digital video camera he bought on eBay mounted on a tripod. He has to work hard to meet his own critical standards for sound because he's using his camera's built-in microphone. Bypassing tape, he records a few sentences directly to the hard drive of his laptop and then checks to see how it came out before continuing (**FIGURE 1.7**). The jump cuts come naturally when he cuts together footage from several different takes during editing.

He's tailored his video style to the realities of Web-viewing habits. "I feel like you have to set your work up to be interrupting itself," he says, "so the people will keep paying attention to it."

FIGURE 1.7 Smooth's straight-to-video capture setup.

Accustomed to talking over an audio bed in radio, he scores his talks for *Ill Doctrine* with music. The effect is mesmerizing. "I wanted to set myself apart from the million people on YouTube who are just sitting there talking in their rooms," he says. He also wanted viewers to know he was making the effort to give them something to watch.

> *Once you've carved out a space in a community, you don't have to do that much. Everyone is watching in their RSS aggregators, and if you're doing good work, it will get linked up.*

Another innovation also comes from facing technical limitations head-on. Working without lights, his video often lacks contrast and definition, so he plays with it in Sony Vegas, the editing package he has used for editing sound. He switches the footage to black and white and changes the color palette or orientation of the shots in counterpoint to the music.

Smooth also creates artistic thumbnails for his videos. He says people are more likely to click something that's visually interesting and mysterious.

Web-savvy, Smooth uses social networking tools to promote his video. "After I make a video, I Twitter about it. I might try to find some message boards that relate to it and post there, especially if it's hip-hop related," he says. "You can get a lot of traffic from that."

But he cautions that Web audiences can be easily alienated by constant self-promotion. "I Stumble it in StumbleUpon.com, and I add it to Digg.com, which is like buying a lottery ticket. Usually nothing will come of it," he admits, "but you've got to give it a shot. If a couple of regulars vote for it during the first few minutes, it can build up a momentum. Once in a while you'll get lucky."

Smooth also uses his reputation in hip-hop music to promote his work. "I know a lot of hip-hop bloggers," he says. "Once in a while I'll e-mail and let them know there's a new post out there." He says, "Once you've carved out a space in a community, you don't have to do that much. Everyone is watching in their RSS aggregators, and if you're doing good work, it will get linked up."

He's gotten lucky several times. A handful of his short, funny, visually compelling videos set to music gained popularity and spread quickly across the Web. Smooth is a member of the small fraternity of vbloggers getting paid for the work they produce. His work appears regularly on a Web site, XXLMag.com, popular with the hip-hop music community.

Although Smooth is exploring other partnerships, he's realistic about his prospects for making a living doing Web video. The people in a position to pay haven't figured out how to make it pay off for them, he says. Until they do, there will be fewer opportunities.

Jay Smooth's Tips for Niche Videoblogging

Figure out what you're passionate about, and focus on that as narrowly as possible.

Create a schedule for your posts and stick with it.

Say things you think are true, and say them as briefly as possible.

Stick with it. Keep on producing after the first couple of weeks when the honeymoon is over. That's when it really becomes a grind to keep on producing, but you have to work through that.

As a producer, you'll want to work with the best talent possible both in front of and behind the camera. Often that won't be you. You'll also be keeping your eye on the bottom line. To keep your costs low, learn enough about your craft to satisfy your own high standards or work with talented beginners. Keep in mind that it takes more time to work with inexperienced crew members, and they may make expensive and time-consuming mistakes. Keeping an eye on the schedule and budget is the way professionals know when they're getting into trouble or need to take a different approach.

> **TIP** A good site for hiring Web video professionals is http://mandy.com.

Sometimes it might seem easier to just jump in and get started without knowing what you're getting into. Most people start this way but soon discover it's easy to get overwhelmed if you're not organized. Without at least a simple written plan, it's more difficult to communicate your vision to the people you're working with.

Use a plan to help figure out how to reach your goals. You'll get better at doing the things you enjoy and hire people to do the rest with referrals from other producers and from Web-based crew lists.

Working with Skilled Professionals

Hiring a professional when you have the budget can be a great learning experience. But expertise isn't enough; look for creativity and a cooperative spirit in the people you pay to work with you. People who enjoy their work and are glad to get the job are more pleasant to work with and often do a better job.

On the other hand, the industry is full of competent hacks. These experts know their craft but can be difficult to work with and uninspired in their performance. You'll recognize them because they keep their eye on the clock and tell you a lot of what you want to do is impossible or expensive. You don't need that. Instead, look for someone who's excited about your project, knows her trade well, and will work within your budget.

Working with someone who has experience can save you time and make your work better. But sometimes you just won't have the money. Keep your standards high, and look for creative ways to get the help you need. One way is to trade services with students or video producers. The Web is great for making these types of connections.

Low budget doesn't have to mean low quality. Learn as much as you can about professional techniques for lighting, shooting, and sound. You don't have to go to film school to become a great Web video producer, but trial and error is a painful teacher. One of the best ways to learn video production is to volunteer to work on productions without pay. But make sure you work with someone who has experience to share. A good rule of thumb is if you're going to work for free, make sure the people you're working with have at least 10 years' experience.

If you want to be a producer with a big hit on the Web, start with something you're good at. It might be writing, raising money, shooting, or interviewing. Create a simple project. Put together your team and the money and equipment you need to produce it. Don't forget about transportation and feeding your crew. First focus on making your video good and getting it on the Web where people can see it and give you feedback. The second half of this book shows you how to market your video to get your video noticed—another important part of your work as a producer.

Use What You Know

Professional photographer Ken Schneiderman (**FIGURE 1.8**) created a short video to introduce friends to his puggle Louie (**FIGURE 1.9**). Using a still camera, he captured the action in one unedited shot and added titles and music using Apple iMovie. The video looks at Louie from Schneiderman's perspective. Looking down on the small dog increases the "cute" factor.

He shot the video using a digital point-and-shoot camera (Canon D9), edited it, and sent it out to friends and family in about an hour using iMovie. "I love the idea of being able to tell a story with sound, music, and both still photographs and moving images," says Schneiderman, whose next project will be interviewing family members and editing the footage with stills and music.

FIGURE 1.8 Still photographer Ken Schneiderman made his first Web video with a point-and-shoot still camera. His dog Louie is an experienced model who has appeared in Vogue magazine.

FIGURE 1.9 *Canine Frustration* was filmed in one unedited shot.

Schneiderman's skill as a still photographer helped make his first video project a success. He counsels others new to video to put some thought into framing their shots. "Being conscious about how the perspective you shoot from affects the video is the most important thing," he says.

As a still photographer, Schneiderman always looks at a scene before he looks through the camera. "You can figure out 90 percent of what you need to know before you look through the lens," he says and that includes framing, lighting, how close or far away you need to be, what lens you'll use, and the height of the camera.

"With my dog I opted to shoot it from my perspective because it was funny," he says. "I could have gotten on the ground, and that would have been interesting as well. Everything you do is going to matter in the end in terms of creating an artistic product."

Because many people shooting video use available light, I asked Schneiderman how to make the best of the light at hand. He stressed the importance of paying attention to the quality of light. "Is it hard light, soft light, is it overcast? Is it the magic hours, the wee hours of the morning, or late afternoon that's a beautiful soft kind of daylight that has a punch to it? These are things to notice," he says.

Just because you're new to video doesn't mean you aren't bringing useful skills to the table. Follow Schneiderman's example and start with a simple project that takes advantage of something you already know to get started.

Start with a Great Idea

Great Web video starts with an interesting idea. Producer Brian Conley set out to show the world what life is really like in Iraq through the eyes of people who live there. The result is the acclaimed Web news program *Alive in Baghdad* (**FIGURE 1.10**).

FIGURE 1.10 Brian Conley's *Alive in Baghdad* is a weekly news program on the Web, produced by Iraqi journalists. Sky News and the BBC have licensed the show's broadcasts, and now the team has expanded with *Alive in Mexico*.

Or perhaps you've found a way to create a fountain of Diet Coke and Mentos candy that mimics the dancing waters at Las Vegas's Bellagio Hotel (**FIGURE 1.11**)—like other producers of a runaway hit Web video. Fritz Grobe and Stephen Voltz had the foresight to put their video of the Diet Coke and Mentos fountain on Revver, a site that pays producers for revenue it generates from ads. More than 5 million viewers watched the video, which featured geysers of Diet Coke in a choreographed display. The producers earned more than $40,000 by sharing revenues 50/50 with Revver.

Each Web genre has specific demands and production needs. Some mimic TV formats such as news and talk shows, often with a twist, a new approach, or a new point of view. Others are unique to the Web, like the growing library of short, visual how-to and educational videos showing up on many popular sites. There are also dramas, documentaries, and oral histories you'd never see on TV.

Content producers are constantly creating new styles of presentation on the Web. Some recent styles include stories told in 10-seconds (**www.tensecondfilms. com**). Others mimic the shooting conditions of the Lumiere brothers' 1895 shorts: 60-second maximum, fixed camera, no audio, no zoom, no edit, no effects (**www. solitude.dk**).

Even advertisers are jumping in creating short videos with story lines, high-quality production values, and loads of product placement.

FIGURE 1.11 This legendary viral Web video found an audience of 5 million and earned its producers $40,000.

Plan for Success

Sometimes shooting for the Web is more demanding than other kinds of video because you'll also need to keep compression in mind. All the pre-production that takes place before you point the camera and press Record is invisible. Although many Web video producers take an improvisational or documentary-style approach and clean up their footage later, producing without at least a simple plan ends up taking more time and energy, not less.

Pre-production begins with thinking about your shoot in advance and making sure you have the equipment you need and an idea for how you want to capture your subject on tape. This type of preparation is actually more liberating than limiting. It takes care of the basics so you can improvise while shooting, which is how you'll get some of your most memorable and creative stuff.

Full-scale pre-production includes creating a script and a storyboard and then preparing a budget that outlines the staffing and equipment needed to do the job at hand. But it can also be as simple as sitting down before your shoot, thinking about what you'll need, and then asking someone involved to fill in the blanks about the kind of lighting and sound you'll find on location or whether there is anything you should know about the event or the venue to better prepare.

You'll also want to think about how you plan to use the video and who will be watching it. Your approach will be very different if you're trying to replicate the experience of being there for your viewers than if you're reviewing or critiquing the event.

During production you'll shoot video and record sound. Post-production includes getting your video out of your camera, editing the video (piecing it together and adding titles, effects, and sounds), and encoding and compressing it for uploading to the Web, where it can be marketed and distributed.

The exercise at the end of this chapter will take you through all these steps very quickly.

When you get to Chapter 5, *TV Techniques for Better Web Video*, you'll learn that the more resources that go into your production, the more time you'll need to put into planning. For now I'll remind you that shooting video for the Web requires a plan and attention to details, from remembering the adapter that lets you plug your headphones into your camera to getting permission to shoot before you show up at a venue.

Managing Your Production

Effective production planning is one of the most important lessons in this book. Working for a Hollywood production manager taught me a lot about managing and coordinating all the resources productions require. (I also got to meet Sylvester Stallone.) Although you'll be planning on a much smaller scale than a Hollywood movie, planning is no less important when producing video for the Web.

Whether you're working solo or in a small team, communication is important. If you have a client or are working for someone else, pre-production starts with interpreting your assignment.

Ask Questions

If you're shooting something simple such as an event, pre-production starts with getting the details, such as where you'll be shooting and what kind of control you'll have over the situation. Ask questions during this phase. Will you have access to a sound feed directly from the system? Will you have any say in the lighting? The answers will help shape your approach to the project.

Plan Your Shots

You'll also want to think in advance about the kind of shots you want to get. Even if you don't create a traditional storyboard, making a quick sketch of your project can help you think about it in visual terms and end up with all the shots you think you'll need.

Early in my career I worked as a film editor. On big productions, directors looked at the footage shot each day. Often, the editor who prepared the footage for screening would mention that there was a gap in the continuity—like a character has a hat on in one scene but not in the next—or suggested an additional shot that would make editing easier.

You won't often have the luxury of coming up with additional coverage, so I'll say it again even though I know you're tired of hearing it: planning will improve the quality of your beginning efforts. Experienced camera people—particularly those who shoot news and documentaries—know how to cover a story because they've been doing it every day for years. Soon you will too.

Until it's old hat, you'll want to make a shot list. How do you know which shots to include? One way to think about the shots you'll need when you're starting out is to look at the competition. The Web makes that easy, but you can also watch TV and rent movies for inspiration. Even before you understand the visual language of video, you'll start to appreciate certain kinds of shots and interesting approaches to shooting a subject.

Check Out the Location

When I have time and access, I check out a location before I go to shoot. That way I know what equipment to bring and what conditions to expect. It also gives me a chance to talk with staff sound technicians and electricians about my needs and get to know them before any problems arise and before the pressure is on. You can hold up your end by bringing the cables and connectors you need and making it easy for any staff member to help you.

A Budget Shapes and Defines Your Project

It's up to you to educate the people you work with. They aren't aware of all that goes on behind the scenes; they're depending on you to tell them. Putting your budget and shooting schedule in writing often helps. Otherwise, you'll often find yourself making do with less when with foresight you could have had the equipment you need.

Set a schedule and create a way to work that gives you lead time and a realistic budget to work with. Learn to say no nicely and ask for what you need to do the job. This is a little more complicated than it might seem. There are lots of ways to approach any job. A small prosumer camera (**FIGURE 1.12**) may be all you need to get the job done, but it might make the interview seem less important to a busy executive used to having a large lens pushed in his face for a sound bite. Lighting takes time and makes a project more expensive, but the results are much better.

TIP It's tempting to play it by ear and find a way to pull off production spontaneously. A word of warning: if your employer gets accustomed to you pulling off miracles without the budget or equipment you need, she'll expect miracles each time.

FIGURE 1.12 Sony's HVR-A1U prosumer camera has professional microphone inputs with phantom power and manual controls for focus and exposure, but many settings can be accessed only through its touch screen.

Put It All Together

For any job you'll need to think about the following:

▶ Budget

▶ Schedule

▶ Skill level

▶ Staffing

▶ The desired outcome

Interviewing your clients is a good way to assess the scope of freelance Web video jobs. One good strategy is to say something like "I'll be glad to take a look at what it will take to do that for you." Then ask two or three questions to focus the assignment, followed by a commitment to get back to the prospect with a ballpark budget and timeline in a reasonable time. This may be by the end of business if the request comes before noon, or the next day if it doesn't.

Decide how you'll shoot a job, whether you'll need a crew, and what equipment you'll need. Conditions don't have to be perfect for a shoot to yield very good footage, and you don't need to have a lot of equipment to get excellent results, but you'll sometimes need to be very creative with what you have. If you don't have lights, for example, you can position an interview subject across from a window or take her outside to a quiet place you've identified in advance.

Producing on a Budget

Some of the most beautiful video online was originally produced for TV or film and then carefully encoded, formatted, and edited to work on the Web. Web producers can learn a lot from these professionals who bring technical talent and traditional production values to the Web.

Although the results from big budgets can be spectacular, it doesn't have to cost a lot to make compelling Web video. One of the wonderful things about the Web is that you can produce on a modest budget, giving you control over what you're doing. You don't have to compromise your work based on the notes from the studio execs.

Create your own style. Once you master the basics of shooting Web video, you'll develop your own way of doing things. That's when the rebel in you will come in handy. Sometimes by breaking the rules you can come up with a really cool new way of doing things, a breakthrough innovation. Sometimes this happens anyway— a happy accident when you don't have a clue what you're doing—but don't expect it to happen very often.

The equipment you'll need to make high-quality Web video is getting cheaper and better every year. Prosumer HDV camcorders, mini-steadicams, tripods, professional-quality microphones, and low-power on-camera lights are now inexpensive enough for independent producers to afford. Versatile nonlinear editing and encoding software and powerful multiprocessor computers make post-production possible on a tight budget.

Web video gear is also getting easier to use, which makes it possible for creative producers with modest experience, minimal budgets, and maximum inspiration to produce work with high-quality production values that looks and sounds great online.

15 Minutes to Your Video Online

Sometimes you have a video that's so hot you just have to get it out there fast. It may not be a masterpiece, but you know people will watch.

The good news is, getting your video online is easier than ever. New tools and software streamline the process, and you can easily track your results and get feedback from the people watching.

> **FOR THIS PROJECT, YOU'LL NEED**
> - a computer
> - a video that's one to five minutes long
> - a high-speed Internet connection
> - an account with a video host

Create an Account with a Video Host

Choose a video host that makes it easy to register and get started. Look under the host's help menu for detailed instructions, including which formats you can upload and what settings to use during encoding. **FIGURE 1.13** shows the basic settings for Brightcove.

FIGURE 1.13 The Brightcove.com home page includes a link to the jumpstart guide with instructions for uploading and tutorials.

Beyond YouTube

YouTube made it easy for anyone with a camera and an idea to get a video on the Web. What it lacks in quality it makes up for in convenience by providing a lowest common denominator video experience that most viewers can watch.

Many producers upload their video to more than one host. Tubemogul (www.tubemogul.com) makes it easy to upload to several hosts, and to keep track of your viewer statistics across all the sites that host your videos.

YouTube (www.youtube.com): The largest video site in the United States and Europe. YouTube recently announced it's working to offer a higher-quality video option.

Blip.tv (www.blip.tv): A favorite among independent producers, Blip accepts only shows that have several episodes and produced on a regular schedule. They'll find you advertisers and share revenues with you when your audience gets big enough.

Brightcove (www.brightcove.com): One of my favorites, Brightcove provides free video hosting for small organizations and individuals as well as full-scale services for large companies such as *The New York Times*.

Dailymotion (www.dailymotion.com/us): France's YouTube. It also offers high-definition if you have 2 Mbps broadband; viewers can also download high quality videos to watch later.

Google Video (http://video.google.com): This site has millions of videos. Upload your work here to get it indexed on Google and seen by millions.

AOL (http://video.aol.com): Now owned by Google, AOL has its own video offerings. It partners with Truveo to provide search and other options for Web developers.

Jumpcut (http://jumpcut.com): Here you can do online editing from Yahoo. Upload your video, edit, share, and remix directly from your computer or camera, from the Jumpcut online editor, or from your phone by e-mail.

Metacafe (www.metacafe.com): This site specializes in short-form original entertainment video from both Hollywood and emerging producers. The producer rewards program pays producers for work that generates large audiences.

Ourmedia (http://ourmedia.org): This site has a community focus for creative podcasters and video producers.

Tudoh (www.tudou.com): This is China's largest online video site. It serves 55 million videos each day, which makes it larger than YouTube.

Veoh (www.veoh.com): This revolutionary Internet TV site includes everything from home movies to Hollywood offerings. It offers a VeohTV DVR-style player.

Yahoo Video (http://video.yahoo.com): This site has strong offerings from around the world, including videos featuring unicorns, chipmunks, ninjas, cats, and robots. It also has music videos and news, sports, autos, comedy, TV clips, and movie previews.

Don't forget the social networking sites when it comes time to spread the word about your video:

Bebo (www.bebo.com)

Facebook (www.facebook.com)

MySpace (www.myspace.com)

Get Your Video Out of Your Camera and On to Your Computer

Generally, you'll use editing software to capture your video into your computer. Connect your camera or deck to your computer using the FireWire or USB cables that came with your camera.

Inexpensive software such as iMovie or Windows Movie Maker can quickly capture your video to your computer and add simple titles and transitions. You can even edit and add titles in some cameras.

Get started with what you have on hand. Later in the book, I'll show you how a non-linear editing package such as Apple Final Cut Pro or Adobe Premiere Pro will save you time and give you more options.

Don't forget to add key words during uploading to the Web (**FIGURE 1.14**).

FIGURE 1.14 Brightcove's upload interface requires key words.

Choose a Format

Each host works with a limited number of video formats. Choosing the right one can speed up your work and deliver your video to viewers at a higher quality. If you haven't picked a host, start with a .wmv, .avi, .mov, or .mpg file. Some hosts also accept .flv or Flash Video files.

Following your host's recommendations for format, file size, and settings will help your video to look its best once it's on the host's server.

Upload Your Video

Once you've set up an account, uploading is easy. Depending on your host's requirements, you may have to limit the size or length of your video and choose a player and controls. Most free sites limit quick uploads to 100 MB or 10 minutes. If you have a Web site or blog, you may want to include a watermark in your video or a URL in your titles. That way, if your video gets away from you, viewers will still know its source.

Add a title and keywords that make your video visible to search engines. Don't skip this step no matter how much of a rush you're in. I find it helpful to think about the best keywords ahead of time and type them into a text note on my computer. That way, all I have to do during upload is cut and paste them.

Create a Thumbnail Image

Some hosts like YouTube create thumbnails automatically; others allow you to choose a frame from your video that helps tell your story.

You'll need Photoshop or other image editing software to edit and size your thumbnail to the video host site's dimensions. Remember this thumbnail helps to promote your video. Make it interesting visually so people will want to click on it (**FIGURE 1.15**).

FIGURE 1.15 Use the visual power of thumbnails to make your video stand out.

Copy the URL or embed code to include your video on your Web page or blog. If you need an RSS feed (a feature that allows you to notify your audience automatically when you update your blog or other content), choose a host that makes it easy. Most will also supply an embed code to make it easy to link to your video from a Web page (**FIGURE 1.16**).

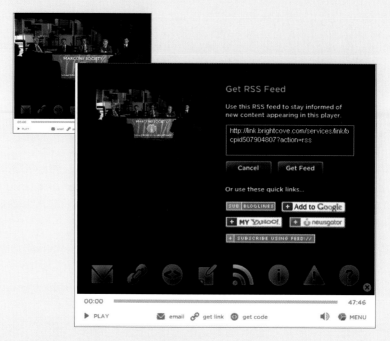

FIGURE 1.16 Brightcove's player makes it easy for viewers to subscribe to an RSS feed of your Web video and lets them link to it from their Web site.

Get the Word Out

Start with friends and family. Paste a link to your video into an e-mail and invite friends to watch. If you're a member of My Space or another social networking site, create a posting and invite people to watch. As you learn later in Chapter 8, *Getting Your Video Noticed*, this generally works better if you're already an active member of a Web community.

> **NOTE** Check out the tools page at Digg (http://digg.com/tools/) for information about how to add Digg to your Web page.

Webizens seldom respond well to being marketed to. They will respond, however to an interesting video on a topic they've already expressed interest about. Follow Jay Smooth's lead in this chapter and share your video with people who are already interested in your subject. Once you're an active part of a Web community you'll have other options, including exchanging links with bloggers, and other web video producers. You can't fake this. Exchange links with people who know you and like your work. Adding referral tools such as Digg and del.icio.us on your video Web page will help viewers who like your work to share it with others.

Check Out Who's Watching

Monitoring your video's success with viewers is the first step toward making it pay off financially. Many hosts and sharing sites include tools for monitoring how popular your video is with viewers. Once you get your video online, you'll want to track how many people are watching.

Tubemogul is a site that allows you to do just that. In addition to allowing you to upload your video simultaneously to most of the major Web video and social networking sites (AOL Video, Blip.tv, Brightcove, Crackle, Dailymotion, Google Video, Metacafe, MySpace, Revver, StupidVideos.com, Veoh, Yahoo Video, and YouTube), it also offers you tools that can help you manage marketing and advertising campaigns. Use it to track views, comments, and ratings. Reporting tools help you make sense of the data and even respond to viewer comments efficiently (**FIGURE 1.17**).

FIGURE 1.17 Tubemogul delivers a wealth of tracking data on the popularity and success of your Web videos.

Unless your video includes a scandal du jour or naked celebrities, don't expect it to go viral without a little extra push. Picking a provocative name for your video, one that includes the word "secret" or "never before seen" is one strategy. Another is to write a description that make viewers think "I don't want to miss this," such as "ice skating turtle," or "The real Paris." You'll find strategies for taking your video viral in Chapter 8, *Getting Your Video Noticed*.

CHAPTER 2

SHOOTING FOR THE WEB

© Mimk42, Sloth92, and joycevdb at Dreamstime.com

2 SHOOTING FOR THE WEB

Producing high-quality video for the Web requires a combination of subterfuge and skill. It's not enough to shoot good video and put it online. To get the best-quality Web video, you have to shoot with the Web in mind. Video that would look spectacular on your 50-inch plasma or on a movie screen often doesn't work on the Web because compression takes a toll on the quality of the video.

Put away any thoughts that video shot for the Web doesn't have to be "that good." In some ways, it has to be better to run the gauntlet of lowest-common-denominator free Web hosting and come out looking good. You can do several things to make your video look better on the Web:

▶ Pay careful attention to exposure with compression in mind.

▶ Compose your shots for the small screen.

▶ Light with compression for the Web in mind.

▶ Restrict unnecessary camera movement.

▶ Use a tripod or brace to stabilize your camera.

▶ Pace your footage for attention-getting dramatic impact.

Framing your shots for the small screen is one of the many strategies to keep in mind when shooting for the Web. Details can get lost when wide-angle shots are shrunk to fit Web formats. Lighting and exposure for Web video are also crucial. Video shot by a professional that meets all the standards for broadcast TV or DVD can end up looking like it takes place in a twilight world after it's compressed and formatted for the Web.

You can make your video look spectacular on the web. It takes work and an understanding of compression but it's definitely worth the effort. If you have any doubts, go to a network TV Web site and look at one of their online shows or promos to get a sense of what's possible. What you see uploaded by amateurs to YouTube is no indication of the state of the art. If you shoot, light, and expose for the Web; are careful with compression; and choose a host committed to delivering the best quality possible. I guarantee you'll like the results.

In this chapter, you'll learn about these and other strategies for making your video look great on the Web. You'll also learn about the equipment you'll need and how learning to use your camera's manual controls can make it easier to shoot great Web video.

You'll shoot a short interview with supporting B-roll for this chapter's project, and edit a simple package.

Making Video Work on the Web

Many Web video producers work solo. *Preditor* is an insider term that describes those intrepid producers who produce, shoot, and edit projects for reality TV and other budget-minded media. Some Web video producers take this a step further, acting as talent, uploading their own video, and sometimes even creating their own Web sites.

NOTE Whenever possible, take along someone to help out. Even if that person is just a friend and not a professional, there are a dozen ways they'll be able to help you during a shoot.

Even if you don't plan to become a professional videographer, learning a bit about camera work, lighting, sound, and the other details of producing for the Web will make your video look better online. When you do pick up a camera—whether to shoot an interview that just can't wait or to capture an important event on tape—you'll better understand how to make your footage work for the Web.

You'll also recognize and appreciate the skills of the professionals you hire when you can afford paid help. Understanding what it takes to make video look good online will make you a better producer because an insider's view of production will help you plan and budget realistically for your projects.

Don't Forget the Fundamentals

Knowing the fundamentals will make your work better. Shooting for continuity and varying your shots will make video easier to edit, which is even more important when shooting for the Web since you're likely to be dealing with quick turnaround times and will need to speed up the post-production. Many Web video producers get into video because they have a great idea and find a way to get it on video. But there are some video-shooting basics such as shooting for continuity and varying your shots that become even more important when shooting for the Web. There are lots of books that teach you how to shoot good video. You'll find a list of my favorites in the appendix, including one by "video shooter" Barry Braverman, whom you'll hear from later in this chapter.

But I know you'd rather grab a camera and go than read a pile of books, so I'm including some basics along with the critical techniques that will make your video look and sound better online. These fundamentals, such as white balancing your camera, are critical production skills you'll want to keep in mind if producing for the Web is your first experience with video.

The Gear You'll Need

It's easy to get wrapped up in lust for the latest equipment. I understand your pain. I too become paralyzed with lust for the latest gear. But beware of getting caught up in marketing propaganda when you're choosing a video camera or other gear. Instead, look for features. There will always be a newer and better camera, a faster computer, and better lights. There's no question that working with excellent equipment is a pleasure. Professional gear offers control over your shooting that isn't possible with consumer gear. It also takes more skill to operate. But better equipment alone won't improve the quality of your Web video.

You'll need a camera that has a microphone input, a place to plug in your headphones, and a screw mount on the bottom for your tripod. Many manufacturers offer both consumer and professional equipment. Consumer cameras are cheaper and some of them are very good, but in most cases they won't have all the features or controls you'll need to do professional Web video work.

NOTE SD cameras produce an image that's 720 or 640 pixels wide and 480 pixels high (720 by 480 or 640 by 480). These are the resolutions associated with standard old-school TVs. HD cameras capture images that are 1920 by 1080 or 1280 by 720 (width times height), which correspond to the HDTVs that are found in more and more consumers' homes these days.

When you start shopping for cameras, you'll notice that they fall into several categories. Some describe who would use them: consumer, prosumer, and professional. Others, such as palmcorder, handheld, and shoulder-mount, describe something about how you work with them. Terms such as *interlaced* and *progressive* and *standard definition* (SD) and *high definition* (HD) refer to the format of video the camera shoots.

Get a camera that shoots in HDV or another HD format (such as AVCHD, DVCPRO, or XDCAM) if you can. Although it may be some time before it becomes practical to deliver true HD (720 or 1080 horizontal-line) video on the Web, buying a camera that can shoot HDV has several benefits. HDV is a highly compressed HD format designed to democratize high-definition video production and to provide a smooth transition from the ubiquitous standard-definition DV format to the brave new world of HD. All HDV-capable cameras will let you output DV when you need to, and you'll be ahead of the game when you need better-quality footage as part of your projects. Some Web video shops including Ted.com and ON Networks only work in high-definition.

Because of the way HDV video is compressed to store high-definition video in the same number of bits as standard-definition DV, it's very demanding for a computer to process. Although that can slow down the editing process, shooting HD for SD (or lower resolution) delivery can give you flexibility during post-production. If you need to crop something out of a frame or zoom in on a shot to vary a sequence during editing, starting out with a much bigger video frame and zooming in on a section of the image won't cause pixelation in an HD frame as it would with an SD source.

Working with a Consumer Camera

If you have a camera that doesn't have advanced features, don't run out and buy a new one right away. Push your camera to its limits, learn what it can do, and borrow or rent more advanced cameras before making a substantial investment in a new one. You can do a lot with a small consumer camera—perhaps even enough to pay for your next camera.

Be on the lookout for accessories that will help you get more out of your current camera but remain useful with your next one. These include good-quality microphones, headphones, and zoom controllers.

You might be tempted to buy one of the newer-model consumer cameras. Resist that urge. If you're going to plunk down your hard-earned cash for a new camera, save enough to get one with the features you'll need. It will be with you much longer and serve you better. Shy away from the miniature shotgun microphones and 3-watt on-camera lights that can be purchased as accessories for consumer cameras, because they'll seldom serve you well.

One recent consumer hard drive camera, features a hot shoe that powers a short-range Bluetooth microphone. Though the camera has no headphone jack, the mic allows you to plug in headphones to monitor sound. This won't serve your needs if you're doing a lot of shooting under different conditions, but it will get you started.

Many video bloggers use small, light consumer cameras. Sanyo's Xacti CG9 (**FIGURE 2.1**), a pocket-sized camera designed to be used handheld, is a favorite among geeks and video-bloggers. Some models shoot MPEG-4 AVC/H.264 format in 720p; others can be used under water or to shoot stills. A small, light camera has the advantage of being with you when you need it. Consider a camera like the Xacti only if sound is not critical to your video, since it has no microphone input.

FIGURE 2.1 Sanyo's Xacti is a favorite among video-bloggers. When I interviewed Roxanne Darling of *Beachwalks with Rox*, she pulled out her Xacti and started shooting while I was setting up.

Prosumer Cameras

Cameras with more professional features but not quite rugged enough for broadcast work are called *prosumer* equipment. Designed for consumers who want to use professional techniques and for professional event videographers who need compact and lightweight cameras that allow them to be flexible and unobtrusive, these are a cost-effective option when you're starting out. They provide some of the convenience of consumer models such as shooting presets, and they come with a range of features and in different sizes. Prosumer HDV camcorders tend to sell in the $3,000 to $7,000 range and fall between consumer palmcorders and professional shoulder-mount cameras in size and weight. Popular recent prosumer HDV cameras include the Canon XH A1 and XH G1, the Sony HVR-Z7U and HVR-V7U, and the JVC HD110 and HD200. Another widely used camcorder in this category is the Panasonic HVX200, which doesn't shoot in the HDV format but offers HD quality and other similar features at a comparable price and size.

Look for a camera that will let you adjust your focus, white balance, and exposure manually when you need to do so. My small camcorder (**FIGURE 2.2**) has many of the features you'll need to do professional work, but the lens and sound reproduction fall short in comparison to prosumer gear.

You can sometimes get great footage while shooting in automatic mode, but the automatic settings on your camera can also cause problems when your footage is destined for the Web. As you get more skilled and want to shoot under more challenging conditions, you'll appreciate the flexibility and control that the manual controls on your camera can provide.

Small professional cameras such as Sony's A1U that features professional XLR microphone inputs (**FIGURE 2.3**) are compact and light. They give you the features you need but can sometimes be more difficult to operate.

FIGURE 2.2 This tiny camera shoots DV but has a microphone input, headphone jack, a remote zoom option, and tripod mount.

FIGURE 2.3 The Sony A1U has two phantom-powered microphone inputs. Replace the microphone that's included with a real shotgun for better sound.

The Large-Camera Advantage

Small camcorders have a limited amount of space for all the controls that let you make adjustments to your camera (**FIGURE 2.4**). There's another problem. Even though your small professional camera like the Sony A1U, which has a CMOS chip, may be more powerful than a larger one with older technology, some people may take you less seriously with a small camera. A camera closer in size to professional shoulder-mount models signals "professional" and encourages cooperation from some of the people you'll want to interview.

Photo by Al Holston

FIGURE 2.4 The controls on larger prosumer cameras make it easier to access many of the functions you'll want to adjust while shooting, including audio levels, white balance, and exposure. It also includes handy features such as a quick adjustment for backlight and built-in neutral density filters.

Manufacturers of small cameras sometimes compensate by providing a touch-screen LCD that gives you several menus (**FIGURE 2.5** on the next page). Making changes on an LCD screen while you are shooting can be time-consuming, camera-shaking, and frustrating.

Be very critical when you evaluate small cameras. Many have annoying features such as tape compartments that load from the bottom, which forces you to take the camera off the tripod and remove the quick release connecting plate to change the tape (**FIGURE 2.6**). This can create a problem when you're shooting events that last more than an hour.

I don't recommend shooting handheld for the Web, but when you have to work off-tripod, small, light cameras are more difficult to keep stable than heavier models. Although I enjoy the convenience of small cameras, I often find that they're not much lighter than their larger counterparts, and when fully set up for shooting, they're not that much smaller than larger models that are easier to operate. Smaller cameras also have smaller and shorter lenses.

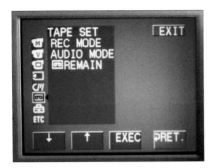

FIGURE 2.5 Here's the LCD on a small consumer DV palmcorder.

FIGURE 2.6 This palmcorder opens from the bottom.

I shoot with a Sony HDR-FX1 (**FIGURE 2.7**). It uses MiniDV tapes and shoots in two modes: DV, standard-definition digital video; and HDV, a highly compressed high-definition format. It's a workhorse, but the professional model, the HVR-Z1U, has a nearly identical body design but additional features such as a built-in XLR microphone input and shotgun shock mount. The Z1U is a better choice if you can afford one.

There will always be new cameras on the market. Some of the newest models, such as the Sony V1U and Z7U (**FIGURE 2.8**), use hard drives and solid state memory cards instead of (or in addition to) tape, providing many advantages, including speeding up editing and reducing the number of moving parts in the camera.

Buy the best camera you can afford and then learn to use all its features. You'll be better off than if you buy the latest gear and don't know how to make it work for you.

FIGURE 2.7 My Sony FX1 shoots both DV and HDV and is small enough to use hand-held but more stable than smaller models.

FIGURE 2.8 The Sony Z7U is one of a new generation of digital video cameras that record without tape.

Get the Most Out of the Camera You Have

Get to know your camera, and make sure you know how to use all its major controls before you need to shoot anything important. Find out what the different buttons do, and practice making adjustments. I learned this lesson the hard way during a project.

When Macintosh inventor Jef Raskin invited me to record a series of interviews with him after discovering he was terminally ill with cancer, Dave Burstein, who worked with me on the project, borrowed a Sony FX1 from a friend. I only had a few hours to learn to use it before I started shooting the next day. Over the three months leading up to Raskin's death, I learned enough about the FX1 that when I had a chance to buy a camera, it was the one I chose. But there were many harrowing moments when my shooting would have been better if I'd known more about my gear (**FIGURE 2.9**).

FIGURE 2.9 Sony hides many of its connections under little doors. The FireWire connector (inset) was so well hidden it took me 20 minutes to find it.

You have to shoot a lot with a new camera for it to become second nature. Shoot as much as you can. After 20–50 hours it will start to feel familiar and you can focus more on what you're shooting than your gear. Shoot birthday parties, tours of your home or a local park, or even your pet's antics to get comfortable with your camera. Then offer to shoot something more demanding for free to get a sense of how your camera works when you're under pressure to deliver. Many not-for-profits, schools, churches, and other small organizations will be happy to take you up on your offer.

If you shoot events or concerts, you'll sometimes find yourself shooting in a darkened room, so you really need to have a feel for your camera and its controls. Practice identifying your camera's controls by touch so making adjustments will be second nature when it's time to shoot. It's also good to carry a tiny powerful flashlight so you can check your settings.

The manual that comes with your camera is a good starting point for identifying the basic parts and functions of your camera. Sometimes the more complicated instructions are poorly translated or just plain confusing, so you'll want to find other sources of information, including other videographers who use the same camera. When I shot Fashion Week in New York with a borrowed camera, a pro helped me adjust my camera to compensate for the fashion show's dramatic lighting.

You can also purchase after-market video tutorials for some cameras. A company called Vortex Media (**www.vortexmedia.com**) produces the Hands-On series for several of the Sony cameras. VASST (**www.vasst.com**) sells DVD tutorials for Sony's XDCam, Panasonic's AGHVX200, the Canon XHA1, and other popular models.

I've identified some of the features and controls you'll want to look for on your camera in the following figures. **FIGURE 2.10** shows the key controls on my Sony FX1. **FIGURE 2.11** shows my camera set up, all ready to work.

FIGURE 2.10 Here are the key components and controls on my well-traveled Sony FX1.

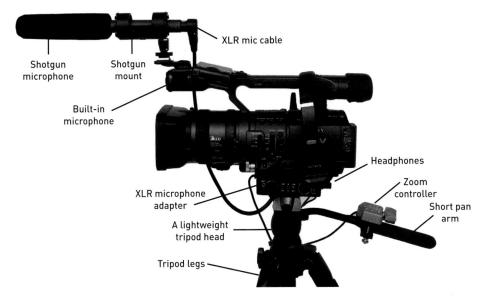

Shotgun microphone

Shotgun mount

XLR mic cable

Built-in microphone

Headphones

XLR microphone adapter

Zoom controller

Short pan arm

A lightweight tripod head

Tripod legs

FIGURE 2.11 Here's my Sony FX1 all set up for a shoot.

Use a Tripod

Use a tripod to stabilize your camera whenever possible. A tripod is a critical part of your shooting gear, so get the best one you can afford. Here's why:

▶ Handheld footage is unsettling for viewers, and the jittery footage is difficult to compress for the Web.

▶ If you do your entire shoot handheld, your arms will get tired and your footage won't look good.

▶ With handheld shooting you'll be limited in the kind of motion you can use.

▶ You have to be a real pro to shoot anything worth watching handheld, especially with a light consumer or prosumer video camera.

The best tripods are sturdy and tall, extending to at least six feet high. Most professional tripods come in two parts: the head and the legs. Start with aluminum legs. If you need your tripod to be compact as well as light, use one that folds up smaller.

Tripods come in stages. If there are only two stages, each section has to be longer to make up the full length of the tripod than if your tripod has three stages. Check the folded length of your tripod if you need to ship it to make sure it will fit into your shipping case.

I prefer flip-lock legs because I find they allow a faster setup. I also use a tripod that allows me to adjust the angle of each leg separately so I can work on uneven surfaces.

If your tripod has spiked metal feet for setting up in dirt or grass, make sure they retract into rubber tips so you can set up safely on smooth surfaces.

Because I often have to carry my own gear, I invested in a carbon-fiber tripod that's very sturdy, very light, very tall, and very expensive (**FIGURE 2.12**). Light tripods are easier to carry, but heavy ones keep your camera more stable.

FIGURE 2.12 Carbon-fiber tripods are strong and light but more expensive than aluminum.

Tripods are rated for the weight of your camera. When you're buying one, keep in mind the weight of your camera fully loaded with a battery and all your accessories attached. My tripod has a hook on the center pole where you can hang your bag to make it heavier and more stable (**FIGURE 2.13**).

FIGURE 2.13 Hook a sandbag or your equipment bag to a light tripod to make it more stable.

Choosing a Tripod

A tripod includes two basic components: the legs and the head. Paying the extra money for a fluid head for your tripod will give you much smoother pan (horizontal) and tilt (vertical) movement by allowing you to adjust the angle and positioning of your camera when it's sitting on top of the tripod. Not all fluid heads are created equal; many manufacturers offering lower-priced products claim their fluid-like heads are full fluid heads. Test any tripod you plan to buy, and ask questions to make sure it works for the size and weight of your camera. Your tripod head should also have an adjustment to compensate and keep your camera in balance as you add accessories to your camera, such as wide-angle and telephoto lenses and shotgun microphones.

Short pan arms are good for tight situations. Longer ones make camera movement almost effortless. I use a Bogen Manfrotto 503 (**FIGURE 2.14**), which has a telescoping pan arm when I'm willing to carry the weight.

FIGURE 2.14 This Miller Fluid head tripod provides stable and smooth support.

When I'm shooting something simple or need to make my gear lighter, I use a lightweight Gitzo. Once I'm shooting, I always wish I'd brought the better head, so if you have to choose, get a good fluid head and suck it up while you're carrying it. You'll get better results (**FIGURE 2.15**).

FIGURE 2.15 Bogen makes affordable, fluid tripod heads for lightweight video cameras.

In most cases, true fluid heads will be more expensive, starting at about $200; the best ones cost in the thousands. Most of the really expensive tripods are designed to hold very heavy professional cameras. If your camera is light, you probably won't need the most expensive models. Look for package deals, but make sure both the head and the legs fit your needs. You should be able to find a good one for about $500. Don't be shy about setting it up and breaking it down several times in the store and bringing along your camera to try it.

Many professional camera operators prefer the professional-style crutch leg tripod, which can travel attached to a spreader and be set up quickly. I find crutch-leg models difficult to carry when I'm working alone. A shoulder strap will make carrying your tripod easier, and a case will protect your investment. Buy an extra plate to connect your tripod to your camera. Keep one on your camera and one in your camera case.

I strongly suggest you invest in a zoom controller for your camera when working with it on a tripod (**FIGURE 2.16**). Check first to make sure your camera has an LANC input; this type of connection is necessary for using zoom control. Many prosumer models have tiny zoom and focus controls that are tiny and difficult to use, especially if you have big hands. A zoom controller gives you control over your camera's zoom, focus, and record functions once your camera is off automatic.

FIGURE 2.16 This VariZoom zoom controller attaches to your tripod's pan handle and puts zoom record and focus controls at your fingertips.

If you're short on cash, consider a lightweight aluminum consumer tripod. Generally, they are much shorter than professional tripods. Avoid buying a very short one. Unless you plan to put it on a table, you'll have to sit down to use it. Instead, get the tallest one you can find, and make sure it's rated to hold the weight you need. Some include a zoom controller built into the handle, which is a plus.

Camera dollies need big wheels to be effective, but if you're shooting in a large facility, they allow you to move from one location to another while remaining fully set up. Buy a collapsible one to make it easy to travel with your gear.

Capturing Good-Quality Audio for Web Video

Most consumer and prosumer video cameras have built-in microphones. They're good for recording traffic noise and the sound of your cameras but not much more. Three microphones will meet most of your audio needs: a shotgun (**FIGURE 2.17**, left), a handheld, and a pair of lavaliers (**FIGURE 2.17**, right). If your talent is careful about handling noise, you can use a short shotgun as a handheld in a pinch.

FIGURE 2.17 On the left is a shotgun microphone without a windscreen. Shotguns are highly directional microphones often mounted on top of cameras. The lavalier microphone on the right has two parts: the mic, which is clipped to the lapel or neckline; and the power supply, which clips to the belt or pocket.

Microphones You'll Need

If you can afford only one microphone, buy a lavalier (or *lav*) clip-on mic. Even an inexpensive one with a mini-plug connector attached will give you better sound than your camera's built-in mic because it will be closer to the source of the sound you want to record.

NOTE For a quick fix if you find yourself without a windscreen, wrap a knitted scarf or the arm of your sweater around your shotgun to mute wind noise.

Inexpensive microphones with mini-plugs attached will plug right into most prosumer cameras. For a little more money you can buy professional microphones with XLR-to-mini adapters and get much better sound. XLR connectors deliver balanced sound which is cleaner and less noisy than the sound from mics with mini-plug connectors.

Even if your camera doesn't have the XLR inputs, you can still use professional microphones. Buy an adapter that fits between your camera and tripod head (**FIGURE 2.18**). The BeachTek adapter (www.beachtek.com) comes in passive models, which do not provide power and work with microphones that contain batteries, and active models, which provide phantom power to microphones. It lets you plug in two professional microphones and one additional auxilliary source with a mini-plug input. It will also give you easy-to-use manual volume controls.

FIGURE 2.18 This BeachTek microphone adapter lets you plug powered professional micro-phones (those with batteries) into a prosumer camera. It also provides volume controls for each of the two microphones and a mini-plug auxiliary input.

Cables and Connectors

Most professional cameras do not have built-in microphones, and many con-sumer cameras don't have microphone inputs. If your camera doesn't have a microphone input, it may have an accessory shoe that lets you plug in a light or microphone from the same manufacturer. You can sometimes find after-market adapters that will let you plug a mini-plug into the hot shoe, but you're better off getting a camera that has a microphone input—preferably one with XLR connectors (**FIGURE 2.19**)—that cuts off the camera's built-in microphone.

Professional microphone connectors include a ground wire that improves the qual-ity of sound. You'll also need high-quality shielded microphone cables (**FIGURE 2.20**) to avoid picking up interference, a short one to connect your shotgun, a 15-to-20-foot cable for your lavalier, and a 30-foot cable to plug into soundboards.

FIGURE 2.19 Professional microphones have XLR connectors. All connections have male and female components. The male connector on this microphone connects to the female receiver on a professional microphone cable.

FIGURE 2.20 Professional microphone cable contains shielding to prevent noise in your audio. Keep it carefully wrapped to prevent breaks in shielding.

You always get the best sound when you get close to the original source of the sound or are plugged into a soundboard, so you may need additional tools such as a longer microphone cable or a boom pole to extend your microphone. Get cable ties or bring along ponytail holders to wrap your cables.

If you plan to use a long cable to connect to a soundboard, make sure you carry gaffer's tape to tape down your cable. Gaffer's tape comes in silver and black. It's very strong and sticky, so it works well on carpets. Although people sometimes confuse gaffer's tape with duct tape, don't make that mistake; unlike gaffer's tape, duct tape can leave a sticky residue and thus will not work well. Large rolls of gaffer's tape are a heavy addition to your kit (**FIGURE 2.21**). Instead, carry along a small roll.

FIGURE 2.21 Besides Gaffers tape, Sharpie pens, and adapters for audio boards are essential parts of my kit.

Wireless microphones can let you work untethered under the right conditions. You'll learn more about going wireless in Chapter 3.

Headphones

Headphones are one of the most important pieces of gear you'll take on a shoot. Buy good-quality headphones that cover your ears. Make sure your headphone's plug matches your camera's headphone jack, or get an adapter (**FIGURE 2.22**).

FIGURE 2.22 Professional headphones that cover your ears help you monitor sound much better than earbuds.

Many people feel awkward about wearing headphones, but they're essential equipment for video producers. Monitoring your sound is the only way to make sure it's free from static, pops, background noise, and interference. Working without headphones is like pointing your camera but not looking at the viewfinder or LCD. You might get something, but it's unlikely to be just right.

I've seen lots of people use small, iPod-style earbuds to monitor sound. They'll work in a pinch if you forget your real headphones, but they're inadequate for professional work. Do yourself a favor. Get a pair of good-quality professional headphones that let you hear what's happening. They'll help you place your microphones more accurately and ward off sound problems.

Tape

If you're shooting to tape (and unless you buy a very recent model that shoots to hard disk or flash media, you will be), get good, pro-quality tape. The cheap stuff is thinner and can get tangled on your camera's heads. When you're finished shooting, don't rewind until you're ready to edit. Leaving tape fast-rewound puts tension on it that can stretch the tape or cause "print-through"—video ghosts and audio echoes—if you leave it that way a long time. Many manufacturers produce tape that has a chip built in for use with consumer camcorders. This tape is designed for titling in camera dissolves, fades, and other in-camera effects. It's usually much more expensive than ordinary DV tape, so don't waste your money unless you plan to edit or add titles in your camera.

When you're done shooting, always click the tab to prevent recording over your footage. And if you rewind your footage during shooting, use your camera's end search, or reposition the tape carefully to make sure you don't record over important footage.

Label your tape. This will save you time and heartache. Create a system to label your tapes before you go out to shoot. When you have a moment, make a note of what's on each tape. I can't stress enough how important this is. Most people learn by painful experience. I've spent hours looking for tapes or trying to find something I've shot and even lost important footage. You don't have to learn this lesson the hard way.

Portable Hard Drives

If your camera shoots tape, one option designed to speed workflow is to attach a portable hard drive and capture video to it at the same time. Several manufacturers make these, including Focus Enhancements, with its popular FS-4 and new FS-5 (**FIGURE 2.23**), but make sure you get one compatible with the editing system you're using. Early models had so many compatibility issues they forced recapture, defeating their purpose.

Check the display on any portable hard drive you're considering. Focus Enhancements' FS-5 includes a display that's a huge improvement over previous models. The best displays make it easy to see the clips on your drive and to name them in a way that works for you. They also offer options that work directly with your editing software.

FIGURE 2.23 Focus Enhancements' new FS-5 is a portable hard disk recorder can be used as a direct-to-edit device for your footage, eliminating the capture process.

Techniques for Better Web Video

Here are my six commandments for great Web video:

1. Avoid unnecessary zooms and pans.
2. Frame shots for small screens.
3. Keep backgrounds simple.
4. Make sure you have enough light.
5. Minimize shake when shooting handheld (if you must).
6. Get good sound.

Most motion picture camera work includes moving the camera in interesting and sometimes complicated ways. Panning, horizontal movement, tilting vertical movement, and dolly shots add visual interest. When you shoot for broadcast, film, and DVD, you can give your moving camera technique almost free rein. But when you shoot for the Web, you'll want to avoid unnecessary camera movement.

Camera movement can help tell a story. But when you're working on the Web, you'll want to budget your camera movement because footage from a camera that is constantly moving, particularly if it's on automatic focus, can be difficult to watch and hard to compress.

I'll explain the particulars of compressing video for the Web in more depth in Chapter 7. For now just keep these issues in mind when planning your shoots and when you're shooting on location. This doesn't mean you won't move your camera at all; that would make it hard to tell a story and bore your viewers. But any moving camera work you include in your edited footage will cost extra time down the line during encoding. Opting for a simple background when there's more motion and reducing the number of colors in the scene are other ways to simplify your shot and make it easier to compress.

Take Your Camera Off Autopilot

All consumer cameras and many prosumer models have a fully automatic mode. You can get pretty good video on automatic if the conditions are right or you're in a hurry. But automatic settings can also mean your video doesn't look or sound as good as it could.

One example is a scene with backlight or something in the frame much brighter than the subject you want to focus on (**FIGURE 2.24**).

Another example is a location where fluorescent lights can't be turned off and add a green glow to your video; in addition, when light conditions are very low, depth of field can shift, leaving part of your frame out of focus.

FIGURE 2.24 This awards ceremony has sconce lights on the wall shining into the camera, a common problem when shooting in hotel ballrooms. Find an angle that avoids these lights and use manual exposure controls for the right exposure for your subject, not the lights.

Automatic white balance, automatic focus, and automatic exposure controls are sometimes helpful but you can do much better using your camera's manual controls. White balancing doesn't take long if you're prepared. Always carry a white balance card to make it easy.

White Balance

Taking time to white balance manually for the lighting conditions you're working with can make a big difference in the quality of your footage.

White balancing is necessary because our eyes see very differently from cameras. We make constant adjustments based on what we know. The camera can't. Depending on the light at your location, a white object can look gray, blue, or even purple. This is called *cool light*. It can also look yellow, orange, or red; this is called *warm light*.

Manual white balance is very simple. Point your camera at a white object or card, and press your camera's white balance button (**FIGURE 2.25**) to establish what white looks like under your current shooting conditions. Your camera will use that setting as a reference. As a result, things that are white look white on your tape. When you get the white right, the other colors will be more accurate.

FIGURE 2.25 With your camera pointed at a white balance card, locate your camera's white balance button, and press it to let your camera know what white looks like where you're shooting.

As you get used to working with your camera, you may want to manipulate your white balance to achieve a certain "look." People tend to look healthier in warm light, so you may want to adjust your camera by telling it that a warm, off-white color is white. There are white balance cards designed specifically for this purpose. Kodak makes some, called *warm cards*. You can also make your own.

You'll also learn to see these subtle differences with your eyes. Your camera may give you the option to create a series of customized settings for the way you shoot. This lets you store your settings for future use.

Most prosumer cameras will also let you set your shutter speed and gain. This can be helpful to get shots otherwise impossible under extreme lighting conditions, but the resulting footage will be grainy and lacking in color and contrast when you see it in the editing room.

If you're stuck without lights shooting in a very dark situation, you can also try using your camera's infrared settings. The footage will come out green, but you can change it to black and white or sepia during post-production, and you'll actually be able to see what's happening. This is not something you'd want to do regularly, but in a pinch it works.

Auto Focus

Auto focus is almost always set at the center of your frame. In some cameras you can change this, but in most you can't. This is a big problem for video that will be shown on the Web because auto focus is constantly adjusting, searching for optimal focus. If you're trying to shoot handheld, this can happen several times in a minute. These constant changes make compressing the video for the Web harder and result in larger files sizes.

You'll have to pay closer attention when you're using manual focus. Sometimes you'll need to zoom in focus and then zoom out again because focus can be hard to see in a wide shot. My camera has a feature called *expanded focus* that lets you quickly zoom into a frame to check focus and then back out again. It can be really helpful.

Auto focus also locks you in to the least interesting shot possible because you must put your subject at the center of the frame to keep her in focus. To get the kind of interesting shots you see on the Sundance Channel and in the movies, take your camera off auto focus. You'll find the most interesting shots use a composition trick called the *rule of thirds*. This, along with minimizing headroom (the amount of space above your subject), can create a much more visually interesting composition than the more obvious keep-the-subject-in-the-middle-of-the-screen approach (see "Frame Your Shots for Visual Interest" later in this chapter for more detail).

Auto Exposure

Everything looks better when you have enough light. Colors pop, faces look more interesting (even if they're lined with character), and details are clearer because your camera's aperture setting also affects focus. That doesn't mean you'll be limited to brightly-lit scenes; high-key, film noir–style sequences also need light to register on tape. Take control over exposure to make your video pop. Low contrast low light footage looks muddy and uninteresting. It has lots of grays and little color. Auto exposure settings allow your camera to determine settings based on the brightest object in the shot. This may or may not be the most important thing in your frame, particularly when you're using available light. This can result in brightly lit backgrounds with poorly lit subjects.

Most people don't use exposure meters with digital video cameras. You can generally see when you have it right. You'll learn to see when your images are too dark. There is less color in the shot, and there's a kind of muddy quality that makes your image look soft and uninteresting.

Amateur videographers, however, are often tempted to shoot under conditions where there just isn't enough light. The result is low-contrast footage that's hard to watch. Don't be fooled by the manufacturer's trick of cranking up the viewfinder LCD screen very bright. Make sure you have enough light.

Viewfinder Settings to Monitor Exposure

Deciding whether you have too much light is a more difficult and common problem. Many cameras have settings to help you know when you have too much light.

Zebra stripe and peaking indicators will alert you visually when you're "blowing out" your shot by letting too much light into your lens to get a quality image. Then you'll need to adjust exposure with manual adjustments or a neutral density filter.

Image Stabilization

Automatic stabilization can make your video look fuzzy or out of focus. It also requires more key frames during encoding and increases your video's file size.

Other options for stabilizing your image include using a tripod or gyroscopic mount like a Steadicam. When you need to shoot handheld, brace yourself and use the resulting shots sparingly.

Audio Limiter

An audio limiter, sometimes called *automatic gain control*, keeps sound from distorting when it's too loud. Loud sound that comes unexpectedly, such as during a rock concert or firefight, can exceed the range for quality, and with quick attack sound it's hard to make manual adjustments in time.

In situations that are more predictable, running a test setting sound levels and monitoring your sound using your camera or mixer's volume or gain controls will give you better-quality sound.

▶ Tell Stories with Images

*Barry Braverman, Veteran Director of Photography and author
of* Video Shooter: Storytelling with DV, HD, and HDV Cameras

" **V**ideo shooter" Barry Braverman says the best
video tells a story in images. He believes the
best strategy for Web video is to shoot almost
entirely in close-up.

What's the most important key to producing great Web video?

Storytelling is your first order of business; good
craft comes from that. If good storytelling is at the center of your piece as it should
be, that drives all other decisions. If you have a compelling story, people will watch
it no matter what it looks like. Audiences will accept bad picture before they'll
accept bad sound. When involved in the storytelling, audiences will accept almost
anything visually.

If you're going to be good at this, you need to develop your eye. That takes shooting. Get a hold of the AFI Top 100 Films [www.afi.com/tvevents/100years/movies.
aspx] and see a movie a week. Watch classic films that understood the language of
cinema and pick up some tips.

How good does video have to be for the Web?

It has to be as good as you can make it. Amateur-looking pictures often communicate the opposite of what you intend. To be competent to shoot and decently
doesn't take that much; to shoot well takes a lifetime of commitment. To shoot
competently, to write competently doesn't have to take an extraordinary amount of
time because the tools are all accessible.

What's the best camera for Web video?

There's much too much emphasis on equipment. In fact, equipment should almost be the last thing you consider. When you're selecting gear, it's really a function of what story are you trying to tell. In a way, that's a more fundamental question than how much you want to spend, because no one camera can serve all your purposes.

The advantage of shooting HD is that the additional fineness in quality and contrast is infused into the standard-definition picture or Web video. The more definition and the more detail that's in the original, the better the Web video is going to look after compression.

Learning how to light will do a lot more for you than buying a camera with four times the native resolution. A poorly lit scene is going to look bad no matter how it's compressed. The more compressed the video, the worse it will look. But shooting competently gives you a leg up on the competition regardless of what niche you find yourself in.

Shoot everything in close-up, and withhold information. The tendency is to show too much and light too much. It's much better to withhold information. Medium shots at eye level are very boring; you want to give somebody a perspective of whatever your subject is that they haven't seen before. A good exercise is to go out with a digital still camera. Shoot your story in a series of still shots.

Isn't that a kind of storyboard?

As much as you can, pre-visualize what your show is going to look like. Ultimately you'll have more success because you're not fishing around for what you want. You know when you've got the shot and move on.

Try an exercise I describe in *Video Shooter*: put a cardboard frame around everything you see for an hour. You'll notice there's a lot of crap in your frame that you never saw before. Also recognize that backgrounds are more important than foregrounds. Whether you're shooting for the Web or for the big screen, audiences are always looking for clues about what you're trying to say. Sometimes you can play on this in your storytelling by having elements in the background that work against your story in the foreground, or unintentionally you can doom your project.

Shooting close-ups becomes even more critical when shooting for the Web because you need to tell the audience what to look at. If you have a landscape, particularly on a small screen, audiences have trouble deciphering where the story is. When using close-ups, you're telling the audience, "Look at this. This is something to look at."

What's the difference between an amateur shooting with a consumer or prosumer camera and a professional?

There are two telltale signs of amateur camera work. One is automatic focus. If you leave the camera on automatic focus, the camera will constantly hunt around for focus, and it's extremely nauseating to viewers and very hard to compress. The other thing is auto exposure, because the camera wants to turn everything into 17 percent gray.

> *The way to tell stories visually is to play against the viewer's expectation.*

The world is not 17 percent gray. So, you need to inform your image-capturing system what is supposed to be in focus, what is supposed to be white, what is supposed to be gray, and what is supposed to be black. Your camera is sort of guessing. There's no way an automatic device can make these assessments.

Knowing when [automatic features] work can be an advantage. For example, when you're going from a brightly lit exterior to an interior, sometimes you can use automatic exposure to make the aperture adjustment. Similarly, you can use automatic focus when the camera is very close and you're shooting something on a turntable because it's difficult to follow focus with these cameras.

You've talked about visual storytelling. How do you use images to tell a story?

Every shot has a story in it. The way to tell stories visually is to play against the viewer's expectation. Years ago I was doing a show for National Geographic. The subject was egrets in the Gulf of Mexico, and some guy from the park service took me out on a boat; we came to this dry spot of land sticking up out of the gulf that was maybe 50 feet across. He said to be careful getting out. I asked why, and he said, "You'll see." As I got out there was a dry area that looked like land covered with shells or rocks.

I have this tripod that goes up about 16 feet. So I set up the camera, and I shot this scene. It was about a 30-second shot when they saw it back at the Geographic. Thirty seconds on one shot is a long time. In the wide shot you see it's all sandy, all stones laying all around. But as you zoom in very slowly you realize you're not looking at stones; you're looking at eggs, and they're hatching.

Over the course of the 30 seconds the shot is resolving itself, and you could tell in the room that people were getting it at different times in that journey. The shot is a journey, and you're bringing the viewer along with you. That shot is a good example; it had a beginning, middle, and end.

If you're a good writer, you tend to be a good shooter because you understand how to give information to the viewer slowly. You make the viewer beg for the information; then they think you're a better shooter. It's the same thing with the stones on the ground in that shot. It's a good shot because audiences are wondering, "Why am I sitting here watching this?" The guy is zooming in on these stones and then people have a sense of discovery and then they see there's a twist. It's not stones. So you're playing all the time on viewer expectations.

All these principles apply across the board, not just to the Web. The thing about Web video is to grab attention. It's more competitive than ever in terms of getting stuff seen because there's so much out there.

And there's so much else going on while they're watching. You've said you shoot a lot handheld. That isn't easy. What's the advantage of using a tripod?

You're going to change cameras every two to three years as they evolve, with higher performance, better definition, and better light sensitivity. A better use of resources is to take a portion of that money and invest in things like lighting, a matte box, and a good tripod, because with a good tripod you're going to see the effect immediately onscreen, and it's the same with lighting.

The tripod makes it easier to control what's in the frame and what's out of the frame. If you're shooting handheld, it's too easy to pick up things you don't intend. The tripod instills a kind of discipline that's very valuable for any filmmaker. It's particularly valuable when using a telephoto lens where the camera needs to be stable and also for shots that contain a lot of detail.

> *...invest in things like lighting, a matte box, and a good tripod...*

When picking up a camera, in general you need to understand that the frame lines are sacred. You violate them for a reason, somebody walks into the shot for a reason, something is in the background for a reason. The tripod allows you to control that.

▶▶

We used to tell people to use a tripod for the Web because it increases redundancy from frame to frame and thereby helps compression. But today's codecs and compressors are so good that I don't see the logic of using a tripod to avoid camera movement. If your story benefits from camera movement, I would say the creative requirements always trump all other requirements.

> *Cameras respond much better when you light a scene with adequate fill.*

You've said knowing how to light is important. What kind of lights are good for Web video?

One mistake amateurs make is they invest in a lot of light. But what you really want is light that's controllable, so I'd much rather have several small instruments than one or two big ones, because when we're lighting, the challenge is to put the light where we want it, as opposed to putting a lot of light all over the place and then spending a lot of time cutting the light with various forms of lighting control such as cutters and cookies.

Buying cheap lighting is not a good investment. The ARRI Arriflex kits are a good investment, and the light is very controllable. For somebody shooting for the Web—especially where you don't have a lot of gear—investing in a small tungsten fresnel kit is important, as opposed to an open-faced kit that throws a lot of light all over the place.

There are some cases where we use open-faced lighting; for example, when we're doing green screen and we want a light, even wash across the green screen. But in general, I very seldom use open-faced lighting anymore.

What about fluorescents?

Fluorescents made for video can be good, but you've gotta go with a higher-quality tube and be wary of a green cast. Fluorescents are fine for Web use; the amount of green in them should not deter anyone from using photo-balanced fluorescents, which come in tungsten and daylight.

I use two HMIs. Little ones can be all you need. You can put them through diffusion, which on a face is very flattering. Or you can bounce them off a card. If you have two, you can bounce one off a card and shoot the other through diffusion. This gives you a very flattering setup anywhere, especially if you're shooting in places such as airports, schools, or public places where you want a very soft look.

Cameras respond much better when you light a scene with adequate fill. So I would urge people to think not so much about lighting but about filling. Filling scenes with good light will instantly produce more professional results. Especially on the Web where you're looking at sizable compression, most compressors work by looking into the shadows and discarding as much information as possible. Filling those shadows with detail will make the compression much more efficient and produce much better-looking images.

Any advice for someone who wants to work for a professional shop?

We're all doing Web videos now even if it's combined with other things. When I was working in India last year, I was not only responsible for Web video, but I was also doing the EPKs for stations with the cast members; I was doing the behind-the-scenes show for HBO, long-form, and the home video DVD part of it as well.

You have to be comfortable working not just for the Web but understanding the other venues in your particular niche, which might include big-screen as well. [That makes it] important to exploit high definition, because not only do your Web videos look better, but you might need that high definition at full resolution for large-screen displays at trade shows, which is a good market for a lot of people, or in education, where you're in a big assembly hall.

So if you intend to produce Web video, it's really a converged marketplace where the emphasis is not just on Web video, but there are often other responsibilities you have to do at the same time. It's an array of skills you need to have because, increasingly, employers are looking for one person to do it all.

> *We're all doing Web videos now even if it's combined with other things.*

When I came up there was an apprentice system. How do people learn today?

People have to show you. I learned when people showed me. Try to work with someone who has experience. If you're going to work for free, a good rule of thumb is to work with someone who has at least ten years' experience. In schools there's an emphasis on teaching tools, but somehow nobody is interested in the craft, or slow to ask about it. I think part of the reason is that so few people can teach craft well. You have to know it, love it, and feel empowered. Don't turn down any opportunity for training, even if it doesn't seem related. It might come in handy down the line.

Frame Your Shots for Visual Interest

Next time you're watching TV or a movie, pay attention to where the subject is in the frame. It doesn't matter whether the frame is standard 4:3 or wide-screen 16:9. You'll find the most interesting shots do not put the subject dead center.

Divide your frame into nine sections—three columns and three rows, like a tic-tac-toe board (**FIGURE 2.26**). Put your subject anywhere but the center section, and you'll get a much more interesting shot.

FIGURE 2.26 Framing your subject in an outer section of your imaginary nine-square grid will keep your shots more interesting.

There's a lot more to keep in mind, such as screen direction and continuity. Even in this post-MTV era, you'll need to learn how to tell a story with images and how to create a sequence that viewers can follow.

Get Help When You Need It

Many people continue to work solo long after it's practical. It's difficult to do every-thing well. Play to your strengths. If you're good at camera work and lighting, get help with sound or interviewing.

Choose the people you work with carefully. I feel more comfortable working alone than with assistants I can't trust to pay attention and bring natural intelligence to the shoot. Good assistants are rare. You'll usually have to train them yourself.

Some jobs you won't be able to do alone. Cultivate good relationships with people you can hire, or exchange services with other video producers by working on their shoots in exchange for their help when you need it.

Big cities like New York, where lots of production takes place, have online lists where people offer their services. Hiring people from these lists is one way to put together a crew, but whenever possible, I find it preferable to work with people I know and trust. Sometimes a production assistant is all you need to provide security and help out when you need something.

Don't Count on Fixing It in Post

When you're producing a video, never assume that mistakes made on location can be fixed in the editing room. Start by recording the best images and the best sound you can create. You can do a lot to fix your mistakes in full-featured editing software, but it's always better to start with really good footage rather than depending on special effects, color correction, and cropping during post-production to compensate for deficiencies of your original footage. Some mistakes simply can't be fixed. Others take too much time and energy to correct or result in fixes so obvious you'll wish you'd taken the time to shoot it right.

Often getting the best video will depend on the lighting or careful exposure. Don't hesitate to put in a little extra effort to improve the quality of your work. It will pay off in the long run.

Good sound is really important. It can function as a voice-over with B-roll or stills and help to tie together a production during editing even if the picture isn't that interesting. So, pay careful attention to levels and microphone placement. Monitoring your sound will let you know when there's a problem in time to correct it.

Keep Editing in Mind While You Shoot

The least interesting way to shoot a lecture or sports event is to set up your camera in a wide-angle shot on a tripod and press Record. In the business, this is called "set it and forget it." The results are almost always really boring and impossible to watch for long. When you want to edit the footage later, this kind of shooting presents a problem unless you did this with a second camera while your first camera roamed and got more interesting shots. You'll have the same problem if you shoot an interview in one long take.

The problem is that the footage is impossible to edit without creating awkward breaks in continuity called *jump cuts*. Jump cuts have become more acceptable than when I was in film school, but they still aren't the best way to tell a story.

Our eyes naturally gravitate to what interests us. Sometimes that's the big picture; during other times it's interesting details that tell more about a situation or a person. You can replicate this experience for your users with a variety of shots. In Chapter 4 you'll learn about continuity, which will help you make sure you're shooting shots that have the visual logic that allows them to be edited together.

Vary Your Shots

For a quick fix, vary your focal length. Start and end any zoom or pan with a static shot. Zoom in or out slowly and then hold your new shot. There are three main shots to alternate: wide shots, where you can see the whole scene; medium shots, usually from the waist up; and close-ups, usually just a face or a large image of what you're shooting.

There are also extreme wide shots, but these are often not good for the small screens and frames associated with Web delivery, and extreme close-ups, which can be extremely unflattering to most of your subjects.

Camera Angles

Changing your angle is a little trickier. You'll have to understand something called the *imaginary line* or the *180-degree rule*, a convention that keeps camera angle changes from confusing your audience (**FIGURE 2.27**).

FIGURE 2.27 If the camera crosses the imaginary line while shooting this scene—that is, from position A to position B—the cars will appear to change direction.

B-roll shots, or *cutaways*, are shots you can stick in to show more about what someone is talking about or more about the person talking. The classic example is cutting from a close-up of someone talking to show her wringing her hands or tapping a foot nervously. Common cutaways include hands, details in a room like the books on a shelf, or a close-up of an object being described.

Before You Go Out to Shoot

Take time to prepare before you head out for a shoot. Check your batteries and whether you have all the right cables in advance so that you have time to correct any problems. If you're renting equipment or borrowing it and aren't sure whether it's had routine maintenance, take a little extra time to check out your equipment before you take it out to shoot something.

The first thing I do to prepare for a shoot is to make sure my camera is working and the batteries are charged. Then I lay out all the equipment I'll need for the job. There are some things I carry just in case I need them, such as an extension cord, extra cables and adapters, and the AC adapter for my camera.

If I'm traveling extra-light, I'll consider these things carefully and leave some of them behind. I generally carry the smallest rolling case I can get away with.

Whether you write everything down or simply keep a mental checklist, you'll want to check that all your equipment is packed and ready. It's also useful to make a note of the locations of the closest electronics equipment stores, RadioShacks, and rental houses if you're working in an unfamiliar location.

Get to the location early so you can be relaxed as you prepare for the shoot. No matter how good you are, you'll be better if you give yourself time to set up. If your shoot is really critical and can't be shot again, you'll also want to carry a backup camera. Sometimes I carry a small prosumer camera. It's light, and the footage it shoots is good enough to use as a second camera to take a wide shot for B-roll when my camera is stuck on a tripod or as backup if the main camera fails.

Transporting Your Equipment

If you're traveling by plane, carry your camera on the plane in your hand luggage. Don't ever ship equipment if you can help it. If you do, make sure that it's in well-padded cases, that you're insured for its full value, and that you have a backup plan that includes a local equipment house and the money to rent the gear you'll need.

For local jobs, a lot depends on how much time I have to get set up on location. If time is short, I'll carry a larger case from Petrol Bags that can handle my camera all set up and ready to go (**FIGURE 2.28**). Then all I have to do is put it on the tripod, white balance, plug into the soundboard, and start shooting.

This saves setup time and lets you hit the ground running. News videographers work this way when shooting fires, hurricanes, felonies in process, sports, and other situations where timing is crucial.

But unless you're shooting breaking news or working for a company that really doesn't understand production, you'll often have more time to prepare. If unrealistic demands are putting you under constant pressure, start looking for another job. That kind of stress will kill you.

Don't struggle to carry your gear when you can do it much more efficiently with a rolling bag or cart. Even if you're traveling by car, you'll need some kind of rolling cart. In New York and many other places, it's not safe to leave equipment in a car. So, make it easy to take it with you.

Checklist for Shooting on Location

I never sleep well the night before a shoot if I haven't checked my gear. These are the essentials I carry for location shoots. Each tool adds weight so when I need to travel light I only include as much as I can carry.

- ☐ Camera
- ☐ Camera batteries
- ☐ Charger or AC adapter
- ☐ Zoom controller (very important for small cameras)
- ☐ Filters
- ☐ Microphones
- ☐ Shotgun with shock-mount and camera adapter short cable
- ☐ Lavalier mic (wired or wireless)
- ☐ Microphone cables
- ☐ AA batteries for microphones
- ☐ Headphones
- ☐ Tripod
- ☐ Tape (always more than you think, and label it in advance)
- ☐ A knife or Leatherman tool (if you're not traveling by plane)
- ☐ A bottle of water
- ☐ White balance card
- ☐ Pen and paper
- ☐ Gaffer's tape

- ☐ A small, powerful flashlight
- ☐ Bungee cords
- ☐ Tripod shoulder strap or case
- ☐ Extra camera plate
- ☐ 30 feet of microphone cable
- ☐ Audio input adapters
- ☐ Hard drive recorders
- ☐ A Sharpie pen
- ☐ $50 in $10 bills, a quarter for phone calls, a dime, and a penny to use as a screwdrivers
- ☐ Fanny pack
- ☐ Camera dolly
- ☐ Audio adapter
- ☐ On-camera light
- ☐ Lights
- ☐ Light stands
- ☐ Reflectors and/or chimeras
- ☐ Extra bulbs
- ☐ Extension cord
- ☐ 3-to-2 adapter
- ☐ A rolling bag

FIGURE 2.28 A larger camera bag is heavier, but it helps to keep gear organized and lets me travel with my camera set up and ready to go. This one, from Petrol Bags, is designed for my camera, is well padded, and has wheels.

I have four modes of carrying equipment for a shoot. Whenever possible, I suggest using a rolling case. No matter how strong you are, save your strength for the shoot. The four modes are as follows (each becoming heavier if you travel with lights):

- ▶ **Ultralight.** My camera in a strong nylon bag carried fully set up under my arm with a tripod over my shoulder.
- ▶ **Light/compact.** My equipment broken down in a small rolling bag. This requires setup time.
- ▶ **Ready/full.** My camera fully set up in a rolling bag large enough to hold it, ready to go ENG style.
- ▶ **Shipping by plane.** I always carry my camera on board in a small suitcase and make sure I have most of the essentials I need with me and ship my other gear in rigid, padded shipping cases.

Camera dollies are a sneaky way move your equipment around conference centers or other large facilities. You'll be fully set up and ready to go (**FIGURE 2.29**). Camera dollies are great. They need big wheels to be effective, but if you're shooting in a large facility, they allow you to move from one location to another fully set up. Buy a collapsible one to make it easy to travel with your gear.

FIGURE 2.29 A camera dolly with big wheels will let you travel over a wider variety of terrains.

Shoot an Interview with B-roll

For this project, you'll shoot a short interview and some B-roll, footage that shows something you'll talk about in the interview. You'll be doing simple editing to produce something news teams call a *cut-and-wrap*, a short video package in which a sound bite from an interview helps your viewer to understand something visual.

You'll shoot a simple interview and combine it with additional footage to create a short visual story. Then you'll create an attention grabbing title for your project.

> **FOR THIS PROJECT, YOU'LL NEED THE FOLLOWING:**
> - Your camera
> - Tape
> - A tripod
> - A lavalier microphone
> - Headphones
> - A computer
> - Simple video-editing software

You'll find examples and sample footage you can download and work with on this book's Web site (**www.webvideobook.tv**). The footage is provided as QuickTime (.mov) and Windows (.avi) files. You'll also find a forum for sharing links to your files on the site's Share page.

Make a simple plan. I'll use footage shot in Central Park when artist Cristo set up his Gates installation (**FIGURE 2.30**) and a comment from someone looking at it.

© Mimk42, Sloth92, and
joycevdb at Dreamstime.com

FIGURE 2.30 For this project, pick a visual subject like Cristo's installation in New York City's Central Park. Vary your angles and focal lengths to add visual interest to your shots.

For this assignment you'll be traveling ultralight. Plan to shoot outside so you'll have plenty of light. Check your equipment; make sure your batteries are charged and your microphone is working. Label your tape. Set up your camera, but wait until you're where you want to shoot before you put it on the tripod.

First, shoot your visuals. You're going to shoot them twice: once with your camera on automatic, then again after you white balance and set your exposure and focus manually. You'll compare the two in the editing room.

You'll need about a minute of footage that shows something interesting. Take the time to look at your shot. Make it visually interesting. Get rid of anything you don't want to see by framing your shot differently or changing angles. Poles that appear to grow out of people's heads and large brightly colored signs that interfere with your shot are called *felons* because they break into the frame (like the other kind of felons that break into your house or car). Take the time to look closely at your shot, and you'll see the felons before you're in the editing room.

Frame your shot so you can really see the subject. Try to show something about your subject in one shot. If you need to, start with a medium shot and then zoom in to a close-up to show detail. Your aim is to create a short piece of footage that shows something about your subject. To do this effectively, you need to know what you want the footage to show. My wide shot of the Gates installation says, "This installation is really huge, and a lot of people are out looking at it." It also says that it's a gray windy winter day.

When you set up your interview, pay attention to what's going on in the background. Keep your background as simple as possible to keep the audience's attention focused on the speaker. Ask your subject two or three questions you've prepared in advance. Make sure they're open-ended questions that can't be answered yes or no. You're looking for a *sound bite*, a short interesting statement that helps your viewer understand your topic. Sometimes you'll have to ask a few questions before your subject relaxes. Take your time; you'll know the answer you want when you hear it. Sometimes it just doesn't work out. When that happens, thank them and move on to someone else.

As a part of your setup, do a sound test. Listen with your headphones to make sure there isn't background noise that prevents you from hearing what your subject is saying. This might include nearby construction, wind, traffic noise, or someone talking, shouting, or playing a boom box nearby. If you can't hear what the person is saying, wait until the noise passes or change locations and find a quieter setting. It helps to shoot your interviewee in a location where you can see what she's talking about in the background, but it's better to be able to hear her.

Before you start the interview, compose your shot using the rule of thirds. Then press Record on your camera and let it get up to speed. Continue rolling for about 20 seconds before you ask the first question. This will give you what's called *room tone* on your tape—the sound of your location without dialogue (even when it's an outdoor shooting location). Get in the habit of doing this. It will help you later in editing. Having audio from your shooting environment will give you an authentic aural backdrop if you have to re-record and dub any sound bites in the studio.

When you're done shooting, rewind and check your footage to make sure you have what you need. If there are problems, shoot again.

Capture your footage to your computer and look at it. Then decide on the order for the two pieces of footage you choose. Take the time to come up with a provocative title, one you think will make someone want to watch. I'll use the Gates of Heaven in New York City. Use your editing software to add a title.

Export your edited project as a Windows (.avi) or QuickTime (.mov) file. Before you upload it to your video host, think about who is the intended audience for your video. Be sure to add key words during upload that will make sense to your audience and will also help viewers to find it. When you add your key words, think like a tabloid headline writer—try to come up with things that are both true and would make people want to watch.

Next, create a short description of your video, and copy it to a text file on your computer along with your key words so you can cut and paste when you're ready to upload.

Most free hosts take a few hours to get your video into the system. Wait for about four hours and then search Google and your host's site for your key words. Some hosts like YouTube won't let you choose the key frame that represents your video. Make sure the one chosen works for you or experiment by uploading a slightly different version to get better results.

CHAPTER 3

SHOOTING EVENTS & INTERVIEWS

3 SHOOTING EVENTS AND INTERVIEWS

Web audiences are fickle. If you don't grab their attention during the first 15 seconds, they're likely to click away. As a result, Web video producers are highly motivated to keep things fresh, and they're always developing interesting new ways to capture the magic of the events they shoot. You'll want to study the most popular offerings on YouTube and other video hosts to get a sense of what appeals to viewers, adopting some of these techniques to make sure your viewers keep watching.

Another way you can attract viewer interest is through interviews that use "real" people rather than celebrities. Give ordinary people "star" treatment. Find the best angle to shoot them and make sure the lighting is right. Seeing people your audience can relate to will help to get and hold their attention. You'll want to frame your shots for the small screen and use more close-ups, making sure the foreground is well lit. Some videographers even overexpose a bit for the Web to compensate for compression—just make sure you don't overdo it.

Storytelling is an essential part of covering an event for the Web. Each interview and all the footage you shoot will be combined to give viewers a "you are there" experience. Your event coverage needs a satisfying beginning, middle, and end that will often depart from the event's actual timeline.

Find the drama in the event you're covering to keep things interesting. If participants are passionate about what they're doing, show people standing and cheering to share the excitement. If there is a competition involved, show the audience what it means to win, not just the Oscar statue, but the admiring crowd and the press attention that follows. Small details help viewers to feel like they're part of the experience. Shoot details you might notice as an informed observer: the quality of a musician's fingering or an executive who bounds on stage before a talk. The response of individual audience members tells more than a wide shot of a clapping crowd. Seeing a performer recover from a mistake helps the audience to relate to them and can be endearing. A view of the next act waiting in the wings can provide the enticing experience of being behind the scenes.

One key component of visual storytelling is what filmmaker Alfred Hitchcock calls the McGuffin, an object or detail that has little meaning for viewers when first revealed but results in an a-ha moment as the plot thickens or the story comes to its conclusion. The detail might be red shoes on an otherwise timid looking woman or a wild tie on a conservatively dressed man. Your camera and microphone become the audience's eyes and ears and capture the details that make up a visual story. For the small screen you'll need to frame these details as close-ups to make them visible to the audience.

Sometimes you'll have to take chances to shake things up by shooting from an odd angle or recruiting a knowledgeable participant as a narrator and looking at the event through her eyes. You won't always know what's going to work. Create a margin of safety by making it a priority to shoot those parts of the event you must document. Add additional footage and interesting side stories as time permits.

Find a Creative Approach

Web audiences expect smart, irreverant, innovative approaches to event coverage, particularly if the event is also being covered by mainstream media. Most would rather sample an event rather than watch from start to finish. Assume your online viewers will have a short attention span. Providing a host to interpret the event or add running commentary is a common approach. I often use interviews with key participants to provide commentary I can edit in during post production. Another approach is to interview people in the audience, borrowing their reactions and perspectives for the Web viewers.

When I found myself at a Web video conference moderating a panel that included some of San Francisco's most interesting Web video makers, I was torn. I wanted to shoot it, not stand at the podium introducing speakers. The shooting conditions were horrendous: a crowded room with a partition that was doing a bad job of keeping out the sound from the next room. The room was also dark to make it easier for the audience to see the videos being projected onstage. I set my camera up on a tripod expecting to capture little but boring footage of a stage and a noisy soundtrack.

But just before I started the session, I had a moment of inspiration and handed my camera to a man in the front row. My instructions were brief: "Shoot."

One of the first speakers was Justin Kan (**www.justin.tv**), who Webcasts his life from a camera on his hat (**FIGURE 3.1**).

During the presentation, Justin logged onto his site and showed the audience from his point of view. I had another flash of inspiration and asked Justin to sit in the front row to capture his perspective of the event. Between speakers, the A.V. technician switched to Justin's live Webcast of the session (**FIGURE 3.2**).

FIGURE 3.1 Justin Kan speaking at Web Video Summit and Webcasting live.

FIGURE 3.2 The Justin.tv screen as seen during the session.

My accidental cameraman shooting handheld from the audience caught the spirit and flavor of the event on tape (**FIGURE 3.3**). In spite of the conditions, it turned out to be some of the most visually interesting footage of a conference I'd seen in a long time. That's when I began to understand how Web video makers work. They take chances. Sometimes the results are extraordinary.

FIGURE 3.3 Images from the San Francisco "Innovators" session of Web Video Summit show a fresh perspective captured by a "volunteer" video shooter.

The official conference camera team—a professional video crew that had full control over lighting and sound—sat idle during this session. They set up on a riser in the center of the conference's main room and covered the keynotes in a wide shot. Later, the conference used my footage on the web to publicize their next event.

Finding interesting ways to cover events is hard work. If you're a videographer who shoots news, corporate video, weddings, or college lectures, you may have to rethink your approach in order to cultivate a wider audience on the Web. Fresh approaches make an impact on the Web; they get passed around and go viral. Even if the quality of your video is good, if viewers have the feeling they've seen it before, they won't watch—and they won't pass it on to their friends.

Capturing live events on video and keeping them interesting enough for Web audiences is more like making a documentary than it is like shooting corporate video or news. It takes ingenuity and a strong point of view. Key participants become characters in the video as producers translate the experience of being there for viewers online.

Coordinate with the venue before the event and make sure you contact the event's organizers for permission to shoot. In addition to securing permissions, there are some things you'll need to keep in mind. Sometimes, the venue or the event will also be shooting and have its own audiovisual (AV) crew with priorities for lighting and sound that conflict with your needs, so you'll need to factor in time to negotiate compromises. Always show up early to give yourself time to meet the crew, to assess the situation, and to come up with creative solutions to any problems that may arise.

NOTE See "Working with a Venue" later in this chapter for more information.

Although there are always technical considerations to keep in mind, many of the things that make shooting events and interviews for the Web different have more to do with creating an approach that will work for Web audiences. I'll give you specifics on lighting and sound for events later in this chapter because you'll want to match the equipment with your plans for shooting the event.

There are many approaches to shooting events from a "set it and forget it," camera-in-the-back-of-the-room approach to multicamera shoots that include streaming the event live. Often Web video makers choose highly personal approaches specifically tailored to their audiences.

Tell a Story About the Event

Whether the event you're shooting is a competition at a comedy club, a concert, or a historic gathering of the people who shaped the Internet, you'll need to think about pacing and point of view to create a unique experience for your Web audience.

Many Web video producers tell me their work is much more like producing radio than it is like TV. Having spent many years producing radio, I agree. The challenge is to create an intimate bond with each viewer to make her feel like she's part of a group experience. Getting the best sound possible plays a key role in creating a powerful viewer experience. This is particularly important because Web video producers often don't have control over lighting when shooting events.

When I was asked to shoot a small conference in Washington, D.C., gratis, I asked for one thing: a pair of professional lights. But when I showed up, a conference manager who'd deemed the lights too disruptive had returned them to the rental house. So, I was stuck once again, shooting in the dark. I cranked up my video gain so far that the cork background behind the speakers' heads shone like a golden halo in an illuminated manuscript. I was forced to change exposure for on the fly, reverse angles of the audience members who had enough light during the Q&A session.

Although it's technically possible to present long events online in their entirety, event coverage of talks as short as 15 minutes are often broken up into Web-sized chunks to make them easier to index on search engines and easier for Web viewers to sample.

There are as many reasons for videotaping events for the Web as there are potential audiences. Professional organizations often document conferences and meetings for the Web to help colleagues keep up with current trends *and* the competition. Many professionals, including teachers, attorneys, and social workers, require continuing education as a condition of employment; to meet this need, experts in their fields provide Web-based "in-service" courses.

Not-for-profit organizations that depend on public and private funding sometimes put videotaped events on the Web to increase their audiences and spread the word about their work.

Bringing Conferences and Meetings to Life on the Web

When you're planning event coverage, be selective. Most Web viewers would rather see an edited highlight reel than the whole event. Sometimes, however, you'll want to make both available. Speeches on very specialized topics often generate large audiences of viewers who were unable to attend but really want to hear the whole talk. They'll log on and stay tuned in even when there's little to see.

Although many organizations take an uninspiring "camera at the back of the hall" approach to capturing events for the Web, a new breed of Web producers is using multiple perspectives of an event to create kaleidoscopic coverage, giving online viewers a never-before-possible viewing experience.

The annual National Association of Broadcasters (NAB) convention took this approach in 2006 when it gave video bloggers press credentials and invited a team of Web videomakers to cover the conference and upload their footage to an unofficial conference Web video site.

In 2007, the Computer Electronics Show (CES) followed suit. Organizers created a production suite for video bloggers and outfitted it with the resources of a pressroom, including high-speed connections to upload their work. As a result, many Web reporters covered the trade show more fully than they were able to in the past on their video blogs.

That same year, Jeff Pulver used the power of the Web to take his popular Voice on the Net conference live to a virtual world. In a surprise move during his keynote speech, he welcomed viewers participating in Second Life, a virtual online world, and took comments from them live.

Taking Talking Heads to a Whole New Level

Every event includes some talking heads. Many business conferences and organizational meetings consist mostly of people talking. There's some visual relief in conference floors where booths compete for participants' attention, each larger and more elaborate than the next. But when people come together to network, they talk in auditoriums to large audiences and in small groups. Although footage of people talking will seldom be the most interesting thing you shoot, it's a necessity, so it makes sense to take the opportunity to keep it visually interesting. Get an angle that offers a new perspective and even says something about the person talking by including something in the background. Use dramatic lighting, or include a graphic or a sign in the shot. Consider starting with a wide shot to show the size of the stage and shoot reaction shots of the audience.

Pay attention to what the speaker is saying, and try to find visuals in the shooting environment that underscore her points. You can incorporate these as cutaways in post-production. Sometimes you won't be able to do this during the speech itself (especially if you're shooting with a single camera), so make a note and shoot additional footage later. For example, you might shoot an executive speaking and cut to a shot of the technology she's describing in a booth on a showroom floor or add a graphic or chart from her original PowerPoint slides.

In general, it's more interesting to shoot a person talking in medium close-up or tight close-up. That way you can see the expression on her face. This can be a problem at business conferences because many of the speakers allay their discomfort by pacing up and down, which will take them in and out of a tight shot. If you think this might be an issue, start with a wider shot and zoom in selectively for emphasis. You'll find they often stop pacing briefly when making an important point.

Visuals Capture the Flavor of Events

Even if you've been hired to document an event, shooting everything from a fixed position will seldom make your video visually interesting and dynamic. You may not need to shoot everything. Instead, talk with the organizers in advance, and plan what you'll shoot. Find visually compelling moments that will tell the story of the event. Sometimes that will require going behind the scenes, such as in the dressing room of a fashion show. Usually, your most exciting footage won't be footage of someone talking.

Use video to convey the flavor of the event: how many people attended, the food or decor, interactions between guests and speakers, the location where it took place. Sometimes you'll end up using a speech to narrate an event with the speaker offscreen, so keep your ears open and shoot images that will help to tell the story when you assemble it in the editing room.

Develop visual curiosity about the events you shoot. We're always learning from what we see; capture that experience for your viewers on tape. Bring a sense of discovery and sharing to your work as a videographer. Shooting a few minutes of colorful footage or B-roll is a start, but it's no substitute for taking a perspective on the event and using your camera to share it with your audience.

Two Weddings, a Funeral, a Birthday Party, and an Animal Attack

Not every event is a conference or a meeting. When you shoot video, you'll often be asked to document events for family and friends. Don't hesitate. These informal occasions can provide opportunities for innovation and lots of interesting visuals.

Although I never aspired to wedding videography, I found myself shooting my father's wedding when he remarried at age 80, and I learned a lot in the process. Because the wedding was rescheduled, I opted to shoot it with a small handheld camera rather than lugging all my gear cross-country again (as I had for the original wedding date). Shooting handheld provided the flexibility to move quickly when I needed to, and I learned why most weddings are shot with more than one camera.

I shot all the standard shots—the vows, the kiss, the happy couple walking down the aisle—but it didn't get interesting until the reception when the couple broke out of church-wedding mode and jumped over the broom, an African-American tradition.

What happened when I got tired and handed the camera over to a friend is instructive. She interviewed well-wishers informally, asking for greetings and advice for the happy couple.

I used her straight-to-camera interview technique with great success when I was pressed into service to shoot another friend's wedding (**FIGURE 3.4**) and again to make the celebration of my aunt's 90th birthday party available to family in Barbados. The short interviews created a kind of video guestbook, just right for helping participants remember the event and for sharing it with those not present.

FIGURE 3.4 Details make a difference. Close up of wreath at a ceremony for fallen emergency service workers (left). Challah is an essential part of Jewish weddings (right).

Part of the excitement of user-generated Web video is this kind of accidental expertise that often happens when amateurs find a way to shoot what interests them rather than copying TV or other video they've seen. Viewers see something new and interesting.

Texan tourist David Budzinski was on safari in South Africa in 2004. When the bus stopped at an animal watering hole at the end of the day, he shot footage of the many species there with his consumer camera. When a pride of lions attacked a baby buffalo calf, Budzinski almost turned off his camera. He told a reporter, "I didn't want to see the bloody mess." But he kept his camera rolling as the lions attacked. Before the lions could kill the calf, they all fell into the pond where a 30-foot crocodile took hold of the prey. A tug of war ensued. Victorious, the lions returned to shore with their prey but were attacked by adult water buffalo, and the calf miraculously ran free. Budzinski kept his camera running and caught it all in eight minutes of videotape.

When Budzinski approached National Geographic and Animal Planet with what everyone agreed was extraordinary footage, they patiently explained that the quality from his amateur equipment did not meet their exacting standards. Undeterred, he put the footage on YouTube. The title "Battle at Kruger" refers to the wildlife park where the attack took place.

After 30 million viewers watched, National Geographic saw the error of its ways and produced an hour-long show around an enhanced version of the footage. The promo promised footage of the animal attack in the way 30 million viewers (YouTube viewers) never saw it.

National Geographic took Budzinski back to the scene, shot interviews with park officials and anyone else they could find, and then ran the footage again and again to fill up the hour-long time slot. The results were just awful. The one thing that saved the National Geographic program was an interview with a nature videographer that showed him holding a large, expensive-looking camera. He said it takes his crew two years to shoot a simple animal attack, and he'd never seen footage of anything like "Battle at Kruger." Perhaps, he suggested, professionals shooting nature footage should learn something from an amateur's success online.

In this case, the baby calf got away, but not all events that lend themselves to Web video have happy endings. Funerals are another kind of event you may be asked to shoot. When the deceased is a well-known personality, some of the mourners might be celebrities or other newsworthy types. Although you'll want to shoot the speeches, as I did when my documentary subject Jef Raskin died, often the best footage will come from informal remembrances. I set up and interviewed people in the lobby and at the reception that followed and got great stories about the man and his work.

When my cousin died in his 50s, my footage documented the service for two of his sisters who could not be there. I had to decide whether to shoot footage of him in his coffin. I did, and it provided closure for his siblings when they saw the tape online.

Most events will be joyous and full of color. Earth Day in Central Park, for example, is full of interesting faces, costumes, and other visuals that help to tell the story. But when you're stuck inside a hotel or a conference facility, you'll really have to get creative to keep a Web viewer's attention.

Working with a Venue

Before you show up to shoot an event, find out the rules of the venue. Some theaters and conference centers are union shops where only members can shoot. They may provide links directly into the sound system if you ask, but you'll need the right cables to connect and monitor your sound. There are often rules, and sometimes insurance requirements, that apply if you're setting up your own lighting.

You'll usually need permission from event organizers to shoot. If you don't get a backstage pass or badge identifying you as crew, it can help to have permission in writing. Show up before the event, and get to know the AV crew. You'll need to ask for certain things in advance, and there may be costs involved.

For example, you might need additional lighting, a riser to put your camera at eye level to performers on a stage, or a way to plug into the soundboard. Don't be afraid to ask for what you need. Knowing who to ask makes it more likely that your requests will be met.

Shooting for the organization sponsoring the event is no guarantee you'll get what you need. AV teams can be very territorial, and often they'll be shooting video as well for an entirely different purpose. Knowing who to ask, getting an introduction, and being specific about your needs in advance can help.

Keep Compression in Mind to Keep Video Quality High

When shooting for the Web, you'll always need to anticipate what compression will do to your video and sound. You'll need more light to shoot, and you'll need to take extra care to keep your sound quality high. Starting with the best-quality video and sound makes a good-quality encode possible, so take time to make your original video great.

NOTE Producer Shelly Palmer has an easy way to remember the impact of motion on video: Web video is not a motion picture, so you want less motion and less detail in each shot rather than more.

You'll make a dozen small decisions each day to make your work look better on the Web. Minimizing camera movement means you'll have to think twice before shooting a swish pan of the room as a transition for your video because during encoding for the Web, fast pans can break up in a visually disturbing sawtooth pattern.

When you make a decision about whether to use a wired or wireless mic, you'll also be keeping in mind that the quality of sound you record is strong enough to compensate for minor deficiencies in the quality of the compressed video. After compression, viewers may not be able to see someone's mouth clearly enough to sort out what's being said.

Framing your shots for the small screen may mean leaving out some of the action onstage. You'll have to decide when the close-up does a better job of telling the story online. All this becomes second nature with experience, but your life will be easier, and your work will be better if you always keep compression in mind when shooting for the Web.

Preparing for a Location Shoot

I prefer to travel light when I head out to shoot on location, but I've learned it's more painful not to have what I need on location than it is to lug it along. Organizing your equipment and doing regular maintenance help. An infrequent problem or glitch is a warning that your equipment might be getting ready to fail.

NOTE See the sidebar "Checklist for Shooting on Location" in Chapter 2 for more details.

If you're renting or borrowing equipment, check it out before you shoot anything. I test my camera and make sure the batteries are charged before each shoot; then I try to anticipate what I'll need for the job. My kit includes a heavy-duty extension cord, extra cables and adapters, a screwdriver, a flashlight, the AC adapter for my camera, and sometimes a portable light and stand.

If I'm working alone I generally carry the smallest rolling case I can get away with. A lot depends on how much time I'll have to get set up on location. If time is short, I'll use a larger case so I can carry my camera all set up and ready to go. Then all I have to do is put it on the tripod, white balance, plug into the soundboard, and shoot.

Even if you're traveling by car, you'll need to be able to carry everything once you're on-site. Many professionals carry a flat rolling cart in their trucks. I find it more convenient to strap as much as I can to a camera dolly that fits under my tripod, and roll in. As you get more experienced, you'll be able to make a mental checklist. But I've been shooting video for many years, and I still forget things if I don't make a list.

Getting Optimal Event Sound

If you're shooting someone talking, you'll want a direct feed from the microphone, not off a speaker. First ask the AV crew for a feed, and either run a cable to your camera or transmit wirelessly to it. If there is a podium, you may need to set up your own microphone in advance.

If you set your microphone up on a podium during a long event, you'll be tethered to your camera by your mic cable. If you do connect to a mic or sound source, you'll need to tape your cable to the floor with gaffer's tape to keep people from tripping. Gaffer's tape is black or silver tape that is very sticky and designed to hold well even if you use it around hot lights. Some venues have insurance rules against this, so check before you start taping. Carry an extra mic so that if you find yourself in this situation, you can unplug and roam free until you can reclaim your mic at the end of the event.

Wireless mics are one solution to this problem. They come in two parts: the transmitter and the receiver. Sennheiser makes a device (below top left) you can plug into a powered mic or a mult-box and transmit your sound to your camera (**FIGURE 3.5**).

FIGURE 3.5 Sennheiser wireless microphone includes a transmitter that the mic plugs into and a receiver that plugs into your camera. An additional transmitter (shown on the left) transmits signals wirelessly from a mult-box, handheld microphone, or mixing board.

This will free you up from taping yards of mic cable to the floor, but test ahead of time to make sure you chose a frequency without interference. Note: Each country has its own frequencies for wireless mics, so check in advance if you're traveling abroad.

From the Horse's Mouth

Good sound is not optional. Quality sound can save your project when the lighting isn't right. This is particularly true in Web video because many viewers watch while wearing headphones.

One way to tell prosumer gear from professional is the built-in mics. Professional cameras just don't have them. No matter how expensive the camera, built-in camera microphones aren't good enough to capture quality sound, especially at a distance. Sound is even more important for poetry and drama than for dance or fashion shows; with dance and fashion shows, you can always cut in the original music (if you have the rights to air it) during post.

Cultivate an ear for good sound. When I worked in radio, I learned to record high-quality sound and to use sound to help me tell the story. If you don't have a strong background in these areas, learn about microphones and sound recording, or work with someone who knows more.

Sound is one area where it pays to get the best equipment you can afford. Your microphones will be with you long after you've abandoned your camera for the latest model. But even the best microphones have to be placed properly to get good results.

I often see amateur video producers pointing an inexpensive handheld microphone toward a speaker at an event. Sometimes this is your only option, but keep in mind that this produces absolutely awful secondhand sound.

Plug In to Get Good Sound

If an event is newsworthy, the sound engineer will likely set up a mult-box, which is a device connected directly to the sound system that allows several people to connect directly. This allows several people to take sound directly from the source (**FIGURE 3.6**). Typically it will have several XLR male outputs and a few 1/4" outlets, so come prepared with the cables and adapters you need to plug in.

FIGURE 3.6 My work in radio taught me the importance of wearing headphones and using high quality microphones. A shotgun microphone is shown lower right, and the speaker is using a desk microphone.

When there's no mult-box, you'll have to plug in directly to the sound board. Some conference halls and theaters have sound patched into outlets along the wall or floor, but since there's no standard arrangement, you won't know how things work until you ask. Another reason to show up before the event.

Other venues require a wired or wireless connection directly to the sound board. This is easier when the board is located in the audience rather than in a distant booth. Sometimes you'll have to set up your own microphones, which is a lot easier when there's a podium.

When Tripods Give You an Extra Edge

A tall, sturdy tripod can put your camera literally head and shoulders above the crowd. It can be helpful to have more choices of angles to shoot from and, if the event is a long one, can save wear and tear on the camera operator.

Many events require flexibility. When you need mobility, a brace or monopod can help. But be careful using a monopod when you're zoomed in tight, which Web video producers often are in order to compose better for small screens.

There's always a little shake. The best tripods are tall, at least 6'6", are very sturdy, and they have fluid heads that make your camera movements smooth. Many documentary filmmakers choose to work without them. There are a few things you should know about this choice. First, the cameras they are using are often heavier—20 pounds or more, compared to 2 to 10 pounds for the average DV or HDV camcorder. This extra weight makes the camera more stable when balanced on the videographer's shoulder.

Also, faster broadband connections mean you won't pay as dearly for footage that uses the image stabilizer built into your camera. Stabilized images require more key frames during editing, result in larger files sizes because they can't be compressed as heavily without degrading image quality, and thus take longer to download to viewers' computers. They may also stutter or stall if connection speeds drop because the video bit rate is, by necessity, so high. But like automatic focus, sometimes image stabilization is quite useful. Like any other automatic feature on your camera, leaving it on routinely may have unwanted consequences.

A good rule of thumb is to shoot handheld when it helps to tell the story or when you are prohibited by law from setting up a tripod without a shooting permit. Many cities have this rule. Find out whether your location is one of them.

If you choose to shoot handheld, do your best to stabilize yourself while shooting by bending your knees slightly and holding your elbows close to your body. A constantly moving frame can make your viewers feel queasy or seasick. So, always use as little handheld footage as possible.

If you find yourself frequently shooting handheld, consider investing in a shoulder-mount camera, a mini Steadicam, or another brace or support system. But be warned: many of these support systems are heavy enough that you'll want to use them only for a few moments at a time (the relatively new Steadicam Merlin is one of the lightest), and some, like the Steadicam, take experience to use well and require additional monitors.

Cameras are set up this way because most amateurs don't want to be bothered with setting up lights. You can shoot without lights, but the results will be grainy and low in contrast, and your footage won't look as good as it would if you took the time to expose it well.

Light also affects focus. When you (or your camera's automatic functions) open up the lens to let in more light, the mechanics of the lens shorten the depth of field so the range of things in the shot that remain in focus is shorter.

All light has a measurable intensity (brightness) and color temperature. Most videographers don't use light meters, relying instead on what they see in their viewfinders or monitors. White balancing your camera adjusts for the color temperature of your light sources by allowing you to designate what "white" looks like (see Chapter 2, *Shooting for the Web*, for more detail).

Light has subtle color. Like a rainbow, it's redder in the lower spectrum and bluer in the higher spectrum, no matter how bright it is. In addition to brightness and color, light can be hard or soft. Hard light can be very unflattering for human subjects, especially as they get older. Many lighting techniques diffuse or soften light to make it more flattering (**FIGURE 3.9**).

Lights cast shadows, and many of the techniques that work with more than one light are designed to compensate for and eradicate shadows.

FIGURE 3.9 On the left is an image shot with hard, undiffused light; on the right, an image with the same light diffused.

Shooting Interviews

Any interview is only as good as the questions asked, but making the people interviewed comfortable goes a long way to relaxing them and getting a good interview on tape. It makes them look better too.

It's a good idea to keep interviews short when you're producing the Web. Asking the same question again in a different way will often result in a more concise answer.

Soft light will flatter your subjects and make them feel like stars. Good microphone technique will ensure that their message gets out clearly.

You also need to pay attention to what's in the background of your shot; everything that's in the frame will be viewable to your audience and, whenever possible, should be used to maximum effect (**FIGURE 3.10**).

FIGURE 3.10 This shot of Rocketboom creator Andrew Baron shows the door to the studio where this show is produced. See Chapter 4 for more about Rocketboom.

Whenever you can, set up interviews on location in the subject's living or working environment. This will provide visual context for your work. A bookshelf, tools, awards, artwork, plants, computer monitors, and other objects in the frame or in the background of your shot provide visual interest and say something about your subject.

Another technique is to use existing light patterns like shadows from venetian blinds or sheer curtains on the wall or to create them using lights and stencils called *cookies* that shape light into patterns. Even if you're grabbing a person for a quick sound bite, you can often create a more pleasing or less intrusive background by moving the subject a few feet.

Shooting interviews is one of the cornerstones of video production for the Web. Web viewers like seeing people onscreen. Information-oriented, news documentary, and how-to shows often require sound bites or short interviews and even longer conversations. It goes without saying that the key to getting great interviews is being prepared with great questions, but making your subjects comfortable and making them look and feel good are also part of the equation. It takes good mic technique, careful close-ups, and flattering lighting to make interviews (and interviewees) look good online.

Microphone Technique for Interviews

Careful sound recording is an essential part of shooting interviews. If you have good sound and something goes wrong with your picture, you'll still have several options. For quick shoots such as sound bites and man-on-the-street interviews, you'll often use a handheld microphone that appears in the shot rather than a lavalier, shotgun, or boom mic.

Decide in advance whether you'll be using the questions as part of your final video. If you plan to, make sure the interviewer has a mic, even if it's you interviewing from behind the camera.

TIP If you need to work with the built-in microphone on your camera for now and want to capture better sound, make sure the room is quiet, and keep your camera very close to the person speaking.

If you're close to your subject and the environment isn't too noisy, you might get away with using a shotgun mic (which, otherwise, is less than optimal). Or if you're a two-person team, a mic attached to a boom and held overhead is also an option.

If you don't get good-quality sound or if your sound is obscured by background noise, there's little you can do to correct it in post-production. Short clicks and pops and low, consistent hums can be eliminated with easy-to-use audio editing tools like Adobe Soundbooth or Apple Soundtrack Pro, but more intrusive noises are much more difficult to remove. You'll end up with useless, uninteresting footage of people talking.

Sound engineers talk about something called *signal-to-noise ratio*. Simply put, that means how clearly you can hear the important sound from your video in comparison to distracting background noise. This is the most important thing to consider when evaluating the quality of the audio that accompanies the video you produce for the Web.

I'm writing this in an apartment in New York City where the traffic noise from Central Park wafts through my windows along with cheerful bird sounds. I'm used to it and can shut most of it out with my double-pane windows, but often when I'm talking on the phone to someone in Colorado or Massachusetts, they'll comment on the noise, especially when a police car or fire engine goes by.

When I put on my headphones to shoot here, I'm reminded just how noisy it really is. One video blogger who works out of his home tells me he routinely unplugs his refrigerator while shooting to avoid the sound of the compressor. Air conditioners, fans, computers, telephones, cell phones, and people talking nearby are also distracting. Listen closely, and do whatever you have to in order to get rid of any extraneous noise. Sometimes it's not the loud sounds that will interrupt your sound but persistent irritating ones like the hum of a fan, the whish of an air conditioning vent, or the high-pitched whine of the starter on fluorescent lights.

In an on-the-go news situation, little of that matters, but when you set up for a quiet chat with an important interview subject, it does. Give yourself time to test your setup and to move, if necessary, to a quieter location.

I won't go into all the dynamics of sound that would just slow you down right now. Here are the most important things: the closer your microphone is to the source of your sound, the better the sound quality you'll get on your recording. But putting the mic too close to the source or trying to record something that's way too loud will result in *overmodulation*, a distortion that sounds noisy and cuts off part of the sound, leaving it muffled.

You won't get good sound using the mic built into your camera or a consumer microphone, and it's nearly impossible to get good sound if your camera doesn't have microphone inputs.

I used to work in radio, so I'm really sensitive to good sound. Cultivate your own sensitivity to good sound; it can really pay off. Often, when all else fails, your sound will work in voice over with B-roll, or over stills and graphics.

Using Handheld Microphones

Use a handheld mic when you need to record quick sound bites. Make sure you have a long enough cable to position your subject far enough away from the camera to frame the shot you want. Mic flags, that include a station or show logos, will help with branding your video, but they can also be visually distracting. You'll have to decide what works for you.

Handheld microphones pick up sound in a cardioid or heart-shaped pattern, as shown in **FIGURE 3.11**.

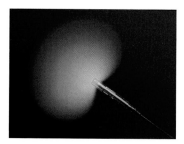

FIGURE 3.11 This illustration from Sennheiser shows a cardioid.

That means they're sensitive to how you hold the mic. Interviewees will often want to grab the mic from interviewers. If you are working solo, you won't have a choice, but it helps to have someone along to hold the mic and position it for optimal sound. This also controls the interview because people know they have to stop talking when you remove the mic or ask a follow-up question.

When people don't talk directly into a handheld, you don't get great sound. Hand-held mics are designed to reduce handling noise. In a pinch, you can handhold a short shotgun mic but keep movement minimal to avoid handling noise. Most mics have a battery inside and an off switch—another reason to monitor your sound with headphones is to make sure your mic is on and working.

If an interviewer is asking questions, she'll need to point the mic at herself during the question and at the interviewee during the answer (**FIGURE 3.12**).

Often you won't use the questions in the final edit, but having them on tape gives you more options during post-production.

FIGURE 3.12 When using a handheld microphone, point it toward yourself when speaking and toward your interviewee for a response.

Framing your subject in a medium close-up (MCU) from the waist up or a tighter, head-and-shoulder shot is the approach most commonly used for an interview. You may want to shoot a wide shot for context or zoom into the shot slowly from a wider one if you're at an event or have an interesting or informative backdrop.

For one short sound bite you may not change your framing or focal length at all, but sometimes it's interesting to zoom in if your interviewee makes an important point to mimic the way we look more closely as a conversation gets interesting.

If you change angles or focal lengths, be sure to pick up some B-roll to make editing easier. Street signs, reaction shots, visuals of the event where an interview is taking place, or close-ups of the feet, briefcase, or book all work.

Lavalier Microphones

Lavalier microphones have become tiny. Most come with a tie clip that can be positioned on a man's lapel or in the neckline of a woman's dress. Take care that the lavalier clears any collar sweater or other fabric, and listen before you shoot to make sure your subject isn't wearing any clanking earrings or other jewelry.

Let your subject position the cable under her clothing to keep it out of view. Lavaliers are highly directional, and being positioned close to the chest adds resonance to voices. Make sure your mic is positioned to pick up your subject, listen while adjusting your levels, and keep an eye on levels during shooting to make sure sound levels don't drop too low and to prevent overmodulation.

Lighting Interviews

Use available light whenever possible to shoot quick interviews. But consider investing in a battery-powered camera mounted light to give you a little extra fill. Professional news and documentary teams do this with great success.

Use light-colored walls and other reflective surfaces to bounce light when you need to fill in dark shadows.

NOTE Start with the old Brownie camera rule: keep the sun or any major light source at your back and shining on your subject to get the best light.

Identifying Source and Direction of Light

Use your hand to determine the direction of available light. Before you position your subject for the interview, test the light by holding up your palm. You'll see instantly which direction the light is coming from and be able to position your subject for the best lighting and contrast.

A backlit subject is shown in the image on the left in **FIGURE 3.13**. On the right, you see a subject getting soft fill from a window on a cloudy day.

FIGURE 3.13 Use your hand to determine the direction of the light. My hand (left) is backlit with light from the window. In the image on the right, using the same light but changing position, the hand is lit correctly.

The more light you have—even in an available-light situation—the better your subject will look. Light shuts down—or forces you to shut down—the camera's iris and makes thing look sharper. It also shapes your subject and separates her from the background.

Even though you can see your subjects just fine under moderately low-light conditions, your camera can't. Go the extra distance and light them to make them look better. After you've been shooting a while, you'll recognize when a scene is well lit and whether the light is harsh or flattering. You'll also be able to better anticipate what the scene you're shooting will look like in the editing room.

The Cost of Cheap Lights

You'll be tempted to buy inexpensive on-camera lights like small iLEDs that run on AA batteries, but be wary of these low-cost solutions; I have yet to find one that works. Take your time and test any light you plan to buy. Cheap lighting with bad color temperature, like some of the inexpensive LCD lights, can make your subjects look sick. Try to gel or diffuse them, and you lose most of the light. LCDs balanced for daylight or tungsten are a better choice.

There are also several small tungsten lights that run on batteries. Make sure any hard lights you buy are bright enough to withstand diffusion.

The other cost of cheap lighting is safety. Make sure your lights have heavy grounded cables and use sandbags on portable stands to keep them from tipping over. Use only fireproof gels and diffusion materials. Paper, cloth, and aluminum foil can catch on fire.

You'll read about a lot of makeshift lighting kits on the Internet. They use photo floods, cheap metal reflectors, and work lights from the hardware store. Although you can save money using these, if you have to take your lights with you into the field to shoot, it's safer to use commercially produced lights. You'll also find that lights designed for video have better color temperature and are easier to control.

Finally, a word of advice about the 3-to-10-watt lights manufacturers make for consumer cameras: most are about as powerful as lighting a match; they're not a substitute for shooting with adequate light.

Working with On-Camera Lights

On-camera lights are often used for quick interviews and news-style shooting. The best and the brightest are called *sun guns*. Calibrated to the color of sunlight to provide fill light for shooting outside and gelled with an orange transparent gel for shooting indoors under tungsten light, these lights can improve the quality of your video dramatically. Use diffusion to avoid blinding interview subjects with too much light or light that is too harsh, a real danger when the light source is so close to your interviewee. Other lights start with tungsten sources and achieve sunlight with a dichroic filter.

Soften Your Light with Gels, a Chimera, Umbrellas, and Other Lighting Accessories

Controlling light is an art form. But learning how to use some basic tools can make your video look better. Using diffusion to soften light will make your subjects look better. Some lights might have frosted or etched glass to scatter light and make it softer. Light can also be controlled using gels that come in different levels of transparency.

Your light may come with barn doors to control the direction of the light. Filter holders make it easy to position gels, but you can also tape them in front of your light. Just make sure you leave some breathing room so things don't heat up too much. Gels also come in colors to change the color temperature of the light. Get a starter pack with several colors and experiment. There are also digital filters and gels that you can use during post-production.

Another way to soften light is by using a chimera, a special housing for your light that adds reflection behind the light and a large translucent surface to soften it. Some lights have a chimera built in. I use Lowel's highly portable Rifa-lite, which comes in several sizes and sets up like an umbrella, as described earlier.

Reflectors can take the place of fill lights on location when you don't want to carry a lot of lights. You can shine light through a white umbrella or bounce light off it. Use a silver or gold reflector to make the most of the light you have and to act as a fill when you shoot with one light source, whether it's the sun or a light you've set up. Round reflectors with a spring on the edge fold up small and often come with a different color on each side. Silver or white is better for balancing daylight or daylight light sources; gold is often better for tungsten or to warm faces.

An on-camera light has to be very bright to be able to be gelled or diffused and still get any light on the subject. You won't be able to do this with a dim or cheap light that doesn't have a controlled color temperature, so don't waste your money on either of those.

On-camera lights can be powered by the camera's battery if you are using a large Anton/Bauer-type battery in your camera; you can also power them with a separate battery or battery belt. Batteries are heavy and don't last long, so use them sparingly and turn them off in between shots.

There are several kinds of on-camera lights: tungsten, LED, and—if you can afford them—HMI lights. Keep weight in mind when choosing an on-camera light. When you're shooting handheld, adding a light and battery can get heavy and affect the balance (or weight distribution) of your camera. Bright on-camera lights can also make your subjects squint or reflect in their glasses, so you may have to moderate it using a gel or bounce it off a wall or ceiling to soften it.

The best light for an interview is soft, warm, diffused light. When you can plug into A/C, one soft light with an umbrella or chimera makes a great choice (**FIGURE 3.14**).

My favorite is the Lowel Rifa—lite, which sets up like an umbrella and is light and easy to carry (**FIGURE 3.15**, left). I pair it with a stand that folds up very small to make a small kit (**FIGURE 3.15**, right).

FIGURE 3.14 This Lowel Pro-light with a Silverdome chimera creates soft light for interviews.

FIGURE 3.15 This Lowel Rifa-lite folds up like an umbrella, making it easy to carry. On the right is a special Lowel light stand, which folds up small as well.

Three-Point Lighting

The most common lighting configuration for interviews is called *three-point lighting*, and it's easy to create when you know how to do it.

Your main, or *key*, light sits off-center from your subject and behind the camera. This is the brightest source of light you'll use. Your other two lights provide fill and background. Your second light, weaker than the first and positioned at a 45-degrees angle to it, is your fill light. The background light, the weakest of the three, separates your subjects from the background, which gives them dimension. This light is sometimes called a *hair light* because it creates a kind of halo of light around your subject's head.

Even though this will make little sense to you until you try it, get a tungsten light kit and practice creating the configuration (visit **www.webvideobook.tv** for an example). You'll see results faster if you play with lighting using your kids, your cat, and even still lifes in your downtime.

LED lights are another cool light option. Avoid inexpensive ones; the color temperature is terrible, and many aren't bright enough. High-quality LEDs, such as Lightpanels' 1x1 light (**FIGURE 3.16**), come in both daylight and tungsten versions. They can get expensive but are lighter and easier to carry than fluorescents.

FIGURE 3.16 Litepanels' 1x1 LED lights need to be very close to your subject, or you'll need several to light a scene.

Make sure the LED lights you get have power sources built in if you're going to use them mostly in the field. Some LED lights include red green and blue diodes and can be adjusted to the color temperature you choose. At the high end, HMI lights offer powerful light in a compact size and run cool but are very expensive.

Lighting on Location

Any light you can carry comfortably is likely to have a short throw. This means your light will need to be close to your subject. For more extensive lighting, you'll need high-powered lights and a professional to show you how to use them.

However, there's a lot you can do with three lights and reflectors (**FIGURE 3.17**). A Lowel light kit, which includes stands, can get heavy, so plan on additional crew to carry and set up your lights. Three tungsten lights in a case with light stands, barn doors, and a reflector is a good starting point for many people who want inexpensive lighting.

Fluorescent lights are a more expensive option, but they have the advantage of running cooler than tungsten lights (**FIGURE 3.18**). HMI lights are very compact and deliver a lot of light for their size but cost as much as many cameras.

FIGURE 3.17 A good starting light kit: three Frenel lights, stands, gels for changing color temperature, and an umbrella for diffusion.

FIGURE 3.18 Kinoflo's florescent Diva Lite provides cool, soft light but are large, heavy to carry, and expensive.

Shoot an Event

Put all you've learned in this chapter to work shooting an event. Pick something simple, friendly, and manageable such as a meeting, a school play, or a frisbee toss.

> **FOR THIS PROJECT, YOU'LL NEED:**
> - Your camera
> - A microphone
> - An event
> - Permission to shoot the event

If you choose an outside event, you'll have fewer problems with lighting. Get permission to shoot in advance. Learn the rules of shooting in your chosen venue. Get as much information about what will take place and when.

Plan your project. Think about how long your finished video will be, and make a list of shots you want to get to tell the story of your event. If you're shooting a football game, you'll want to choose sides and shoot the starting lineup, cheerleaders, and halftime activities as well. But you'll need to decide whether your goal is to show the whole game (or meeting or play) or just highlights.

You may have to shoot the whole event to get the footage you need to create a good highlights reel; whatever you decide will shape the way you shoot.

If the event is time-sensitive or includes scenes, it's important to shoot for continuity, keeping the "imaginary line" (as discussed in Chapter 2) in mind to keep screen direction clear.

Take stock of your lighting and sound. Get sound from the source whenever possible, or use your microphones to record good sound.

If your event is outside, use a neutral-density filter to control the intensity of light. You'll also need to wear your headphones; outside events will have more interference from background noise.

Don't forget to shoot any signs or posters advertising the event and the outside of the venue, which may be decorated in an interesting way.

Show participants entering or leaving the event and cutaways of the audience.

After your shoot, log your footage using your camera's running time. Make a note of which shots you'll use when you're ready to edit.

PROJECT

Shoot a Quick Sound Bite

you can always cut a sound bite from a longer interview, but shooting man-on-the-street interviews is a great way to get short sound bites and to gain experience shooting interviews.

FOR THIS PROJECT, YOU'LL NEED:

- Your video camera
- A tripod
- A helpful assistant
- A handheld microphone with at least a 6' cable
- Headphones

For this project, you'll ask the same question to several people and videotape the answers. Do this at an indoor event where you have good light or outdoors in a park, a pedestrian mall, or another quiet location.

Your question should be brief and open-ended. That means a respondent can't limit her answer to "yes" or "no." For example, ask "How often do you watch Web video?" rather than "Do you watch Web video?" Sometimes it's interesting to ask respondents to say their name and some other identifier like where they live or their profession before they answer. While they're responding, check your sound levels.

Frame your shot as a medium close-up, and pay attention to what's in the background of your shot. If you hear something fascinating, zoom in slowly to a tighter shot.

Because the subjects will be standing, adjust your camera height to be at eye level. People generally look better on camera at eye level. Looking slightly up at them is fine. Looking down on a subject has different connotations.

If you have help, make sure she uses proper handheld mic technique, pointing the mic at herself when asking the question and at the subject during the answer. If you're working solo, you'll have to coax your subject into using the microphone correctly. Some people will put the mic too close or forget to talk directly into it. Remind them.

An odd thing happens when you show up with a camera and microphone. Some people have a story to tell and they don't care who they tell it to. If they have the mic, it's harder to stop them. Visibly stopping the camera and stepping slightly away from it may convince them to stop talking.

Sometimes subjects will give you a long answer to a short question. If you need a short answer, take advantage of the fact that people don't like to repeat themselves, and ask the same question again. They'll usually answer more quickly and concisely the second time. When you're shooting interviews, listen to what people are saying, even if there is a reporter or interviewer present and you're not the one doing the interviewing. You'll know very quickly whether the question isn't clear. Revise it and keep shooting.

Even though you're shooting for a short sound bite, some responses will need a follow-up question. Shoot it. Sometimes one long answer works with several short ones. If you have help, position your assistant with the camera looking over her right shoulder. That way, the respondent looking at her will appear to be looking at the camera, and you'll still be able to manipulate the camera's zoom and other controls, which are often on the right.

If you're working solo, ask the person to look at you and periodically take your eyes off the viewfinder and make eye contact to remind her. Few people can look directly into the camera without looking a little distracted.

PROJECT

Shoot a Two-Person Interview

Longer interviews are usually conducted seated. Use soft lighting to flatter your subject.

To shoot a two-person interview with one camera, position your interviewer and subject side-by-side and angled slightly toward one another at a shallow angle in a *V* formation.

Use the lighting instructions from this chapter to make sure each person has key light and fill. Using a third light adds depth and interest to the background and helps to make the people stand out from the background. It's also very flattering to light the hair, creating a little halo around your subject's head.

Spillover from the backlight also keeps the background from going black when you compress your footage for the Web.

Take an establishing shot that includes both participants and then zoom in to medium close-up for questions and answers. This kind of interview is easier to shoot using a tripod adjusted to your participants' sitting eye level. If they're not seated on a stage, platform, or riser, you may need to be seated too.

When you move from one subject to another, use a smooth panning movement. If the two participants are different heights, you'll also have to tilt to adjust height as you pan. This is when a fluid-head tripod comes in handy. It will keep your camera movements smooth. A high-quality tripod can also be adjusted to give you just the right amount of drag to keep your camera movements smooth.

Remind your interviewer in advance to pause between the question and answer to give you time to adjust and to ask the interviewee to answer in full sentences. This gives the editor more options when editing the interview.

If your camera has two mic inputs, put each person on a separate channel and check your levels carefully. If your camera has only one mic input, you'll need a portable field mixer or an adapter.

Use your headphones to check your sound levels before you start shooting, and keep them on during the interview. That way you'll know whether you have a dropout in your sound or a passing car or siren obliterates what your interviewee is saying.

Be sure to shoot some cutaways to make the editor's job easier. Reaction shots and close-ups of hands gesturing or feet will sometimes do the trick.

Mic placement is important with lavaliers. Putting them too close to the collar can result in the rustle of fabric against fabric. Placing them too low on the chest can give you too much resonance and a booming sound. After you position your mics, listen for noisy, clanking jewelry. You may have to ask your subjects to remove bangle bracelets or noisy, dangling earrings or just keep them still.

Just before the interview starts, ask for quiet so you can roll your camera and record sound with no one talking. Even studios aren't entirely silent. This room tone can help editors create breathing space in a conversation or interview during editing. And if you need to re-record a question after the fact, having room tone as a background audio track will be essential to creating a realistic overdub.

I suggest you turn off the red recording indicator light if your camera lets you. I also recommend that you don't turn off the camera right away when an interview is over. Often people don't really relax until they think the camera is off, and only then do they remember something they forgot to say. Many gems are spoken in the gap. Keep rolling, and you'll get all those last-minute quips.

Be matter of fact about telling an interview subject if her hair is out of place or if there is a problem with his makeup or grooming that shows up on camera. Keeping your subjects relaxed and comfortable results in better interviews.

CHAPTER 4

VIDEOBLOGS HOW-TO VIDEOS AND NEWS

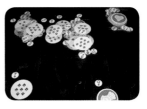

4 VIDEOBLOGS, HOW-TO VIDEOS, AND NEWS

Some of the best Web videos share information, instruction, and new perspectives with viewers. Commentary, news, and how-to video are drawing a lot of interest from viewers while commercial news operations such as CNN are launching programs that feature Web-only content online.

Rather than attempt to compete head-to-head with commercial news operations (that can defray costs by utilizing footage not used on TV), captivate your viewers by entertaining them while you inform. Include images to support your storytelling to keep viewers on board. If you're going to sit in front of a camera, make sure you look good, you know what you're talking about, and you don't appear to be lecturing your viewers—no matter how interesting your subject is—chances are you'll lose them as fast as they can click away to a show that adds personality to the mix.

Find ways to get your audience thinking about the information you want to share. Provocative presentations work on the Web where viewers tire quickly of the ordinary and favor the outrageous. Few people are good enough orators to hold an audience for more than a few minutes on the Web. Graphics and visuals help to tell a story but try to use them in new ways. Giving a PowerPoint lecture on camera or sticking a news-style graphic box over your shoulder as you lecture your audience will get old quick.

Moving pictures tell your story and help viewers draw their own conclusions about what you're saying. "Show, don't tell" is one of the key strategies journalists use to dispatch the news. Al Gore used this technique effectively in his acclaimed documentary *An Inconvenient Truth*. All those photos of melting glaciers made pretty convincing evidence for his predictions about global warming.

One of the best ways to understand how to share information visually and to bring personality, humor, and entertainment to your work is to study Web video producers who do just that. In this chapter, you'll hear from producers who create all kinds of information video for the Web, from a plea to become a more conscious consumer to a unique perspective on the war in Iraq. You'll also learn how to use continuity to craft effective how-to sequences and get tips about how to develop an online image for your personality-driven Web show.

Bringing Point of View to Your Web Video

Some of the most successful Web video producers build shows around uniquely personal worldviews. They're not afraid to let their personalities show and make an art of expressing their opinions. Even news video on the Web often includes a not-so-subtle point of view. Although traditional journalism relies on the legitimacy of the publication to alert readers to what's true, Web video producers take a different approach.

Viewers rely on the variety of information sources to sort out what's real, not on an individual source. They've become their own gatekeepers and have developed a sophisticated appreciation for producers who tell the truth as they see it.

I like to think of Ze Frank (**www.zefrank.com**) as the Rocky Marciano of video blogging. Producer Josea Jan Frank, better known as Ze Frank (**FIGURE 4.1**), started his popular video blog in 2006 and then quit one year later at the top of his game.

FIGURE 4.1 Ze Frank won a Vloggy award for his popular video blog.

Frank's rapid-fire philosophical commentary and wide-eyed, straight-to-the-camera presentation are the stuff of Web video legend. He also made sure there were enough visuals of stuff other than him talking to keep the audience interested.

Roxanne Darling, host of the popular Web program *Beach Walks with Rox*, says she created her show to give viewers an island of peace during their hectic days. Each show shares Darling's unique perspective on relationships. Winner of three Vloggies (video blog awards), Darling seems to deliver the kind of positive message her viewers are looking for consistently. You can read more about her experience in the interview in this chapter.

▶ Take Viewers on a Personal Journey

Roxanne Darling, Host and creator, Beach Walks with Rox

Beach Walks with Rox (www.beachwalks.tv) is a welcome relief from the loud, fast talking style that's become popular on the Web. "When people think of Web video, they think loud and fast cuts," says *Beach Walks with Rox* host and creator Roxanne Darling. The production style for *Beach Walks with Rox* evolved naturally out of her own experience. She starts each day at the beach and decided to share that experience with viewers in her show. Sometimes her dog, Lexi, comes along (**FIGURE 4.2**).

FIGURE 4.2 Roxanne Darling of *Beachwalks with Rox* on the beach with her dog, Lexi.

Like many Hollywood producers, Darling makes her Hawaii beach location a character in her work. Her "secret cameraman" Shane Robinson does a heroic job of handheld shooting, delivering enviable vistas of blue sea and shore while Darling walks and talks. "They want something that's visually beautiful," she says of her audience. "The ocean, the blue sky, and the sound of the waves are very much a tonic for people."

Roxanne Darling's Tips for Creating a Show That's Uniquely Your Own

Network with others to get started: "You don't have to know everything to get started, but connect with people who are already doing video." She recommends the video blogger list at Yahoo. com (http://tech.groups.yahoo.com/group/videoblogging) and video podcast Izzyvideo.com (www.izzyvideo.com), which features how-to video tutorials.

Fall in love with what you're doing. "I love going to the beach every day," she says. "I didn't know if I'd love bringing the camera along until I tried it."

Keep your work fresh by adding new techniques. "Do what you're going to do, but try something new. Look around and learn from others doing it. You don't learn it all at once," she says. "Over the course of six months you'll learn how to do a lot of different things."

Let your personality show. "Forget about being popular. It doesn't matter if nobody likes you. Be who you are. If that's a loud-mouthed jerk, then be that person. There's a lot of people who will love that personality."

Darling makes a point of keeping the show's message positive, sharing her views on things such as compromise among couples, accepting your oddness, and the power of acceptance. "What we didn't know when we started is that people are really looking for a chance to breathe, a few minutes during the day when they can de-stress," says Darling. She says viewers write in that they start the day or end it with *Beach Walks with Rox* or simply tune in when they're feeling stressed.

> *"You've got to have good visuals... but sound is twice as important."*

Each episode takes up to two hours to shoot. The episodes aren't scripted because Darling, who has a day job as a life coach, says she just doesn't have time.

Robinson created what he calls a "super-poor man's Steadicam" by adding a five-pound weight to a tripod. He walks backward while she walks slowly, keeping an eye out for obstructions on the beach. Sometimes onlookers end up in a shot. Mostly they just walk around. A wireless lavalier tucked inside Darling's swimsuit does the best possible job of blocking wind noise. When the wind is high, she sometimes dons more clothes to block it and keep herself audible. "You've got to have good visuals," Darling says, "but sound is twice as important."

There are more than 600 episodes of *Beach Walks with Rox*. Darling produced 400 episodes of the popular show without missing a day. These days she sometimes delivers audio podcasts when she's on the road and occasionally even posts reruns.

But she regularly takes time out to try new techniques she and Robinson glean from watching movies. And after taping each episode, they doff their gear and take a swim. You can't beat that for working conditions.

Use Visuals to Share Your Point of View

If all your viewers have to look at is you, they'll get bored very quickly—even if you're really good looking. So if you're going to get in front of a camera, look your best and give your audience something to see.

Give viewers evidence to substantiate what you're saying. Some things are hard to show, such as apathy and greed. But things that happen as a result of them may make for compelling video. Create visual metaphors to help viewers understand your ideas. Sometimes the juxtaposition of an image and an idea will be surprising or funny. That helps keep audiences awake. Plan to include a few images to support what you're saying in each production.

The Story of Stuff (www.storyofstuff.com), produced by the Tides Foundation, uses simple animation to illustrate Annie Leonard's treatise on consumer economics. Leonard (**FIGURE 4.3**), who appears on camera to narrate the video, is reduced to a small figure at the bottom of the screen.

While she talks, we focus on the animation. Because the script is clever and the animation is quirky enough to hold our attention, the message comes through painlessly while we're being entertained (**FIGURE 4.4**).

FIGURE 4.3 Annie Leonard.

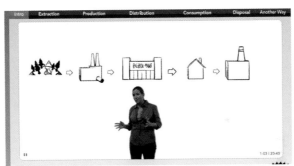

FIGURE 4.4 Annie Leonard, who wrote the script and appears in *The Story of Stuff*, keeps viewers' interest.

Redefining the News Online

While traditional news outlets supplement their broadcasts with additional footage and stories online, there are an increasing number of Web only news outlets (CNN's Pipeline, which crafts Web only stories, is a good example). If you want to be in the video news business don't try to compete with AP, the New York Times, and CNN. Instead, find a special niche. Draw in viewers with informative yet entertaining video. This section highlights some Web producers who manage to do both.

News and Views Online

Here are just a few of the many news style programs on the Web:

CNET.com (www.cnet.com)
Boing Boing TV (www.tv.boingboing.net)
Real News Network (www.therealnews.com/t)
Giga Om (www.gigaom.com and Newteevee.com)
Wallstrip (www.wallstrip.com)
The Smoking Gun (www.thesmokinggun.com/tsgtv)
Jerusalem Online (www.jerusalemonline.com)
Gawker (www.gawker.com)
CNN Pipeline Web only content (www.cnn.com/pipeline)
Associated Press online video network (www.ap.org/ovn/index.html)
ABC News Online (abcnews.go.com)
NBC nightly news (www.msnbc.msn.com/id/3032619)
MSNBC.com (www.msnbc.msn.com)

Rocketboom

Some Web video straddles the line between news and entertainment. Rocketboom (www.rocketboom.com/vlog/), one of the most watched video programs on the Web, is a well-scripted news program with an irreverent twist. Host Joanne Colan reads the news and discusses the issues of the day with a wink, giving the show the personality and style of a video blog backed up with solid reporting and a keen eye for issues.

The show is also visually engaging. What at first might seem to be merely sight gags are often skillfully delivered and well-produced visual information. On Earth Day, Colan greeted the audience by promising something special and then spent the next few minutes opening a succession of packaging that resembled a Russian nesting doll. Toward the end she showed the audience the contents, a single video-tape. After a moment off-camera, she returns and holds up a sign reading "LOOK at a product and THINK about how much of what you are PAYING for will end up in the TRASH" (FIGURE 4.5). The skit, which was scored with violin music reminiscent of a silent movie, got its point across far more effectively than a diatribe on ecology or a traditional news report ever could.

FIGURE 4.5 Rocketboom host Joanne Colan says few words in this Earth Day Webcast but makes her point eloquently.

Music often accompanies Rocketboom's Webcasts. Skillfully done, it makes you feel happy while watching, something the news tickers and triumphal trumpets that herald traditional news broadcasts never make me feel. The program uses stills, video footage, and reports from around the world. A recent show included footage from the Witness project, which documents human rights abuses around the world.

The Accidental Host

Rocketboom host Joanne Colan (**FIGURE 4.6**) says she became an anchor quite by accident while interning at a television show in the south of France. Producers of the show had assembled a cast of interns to "audition" for sponsors of a show hoping to make clear that their preselected candidate was the only clear choice.

FIGURE 4.6 Rocketboom host Joanne Colan.

The client chose intern Colan, and the job jump-started her career. When original host Amanda Congdon bailed out of the show for a solo career, Colan stepped in and won the Rocketboom audience over.

INTERVIEW ANDREW BARON

▶ Build a Great Team

Andrew Baron, Producer and creator, Rocketboom

Photo by Vu Bui

Andrew Baron is creator and producer of Rocketboom, one of the first and most successful original video programs for the Web. He also hosts the New York Videoblogging Meetup, where video bloggers critique each others' work and share techniques, shares a number of insights about the day-to-day challenges of producing a successful Web news program.

Baron is modest about the success of Rocketboom. If he hadn't created the show's simple but effective format, he says, someone else would have. But few would have been able to pull off the show, now in its eighth year, with as much style as Baron has brought to the project.

When Baron started, his goal was to create a show that presented "a critical overview of Internet culture, in a way that was fun, entertaining, and informative." Part of Rocketboom's appeal is its unique perspective on news and events. "It comes out of the need to present information very quickly in a way that's kind of entertaining and fun. It's also a way of relating to your audience," says Baron, who does much of the writing for Rocketboom himself.

Once your Web show gets popular, Baron says, it can become difficult to keep it going and deliver it on a regular schedule. Baron meets the challenge head-on with a tightly knit handpicked production team. He's full of praise for Elspeth Rountree, the first person he recruited; cinematographer Kenyatta Cheese, who's defined the show's look; and developer Jaimie Wilkinson. It's people, not technology, that make Rocketboom great, Baron says.

The show uses a very simple set (**FIGURE 4.7**) and basic equipment. Baron likens working with a simple video camera to learning to play music on a bad guitar or clarinet and says simple tools can inspire creativity. "When you have a poor-quality camera, you don't have a stabilizer, and your lights are minimal, you have to work a lot harder to figure out how can I make it look better and better."

116   VIDEOBLOGS, HOW-TO VIDEOS, AND NEWS

FIGURE 4.7 Rocketboom's set is a simple table. The background is a map of the world.

When developing the show, Baron asked himself and his crew, "How can we use tools in a way that's really interesting and compelling?" He explains, "We've always tried to push the tools as far as we could and tried to make the lighting as good as we can with what we've got."

The show's short format is designed to work for viewers sitting at a laptop or walking around with the media in their hand. They may be multitasking, says Baron, so it has to be short. The audience isn't shy about letting Baron and his team know what they like and what they don't. When viewers offer corrections on their own blogs or via social networking sites and the like, Baron invites them into the mix, sometimes linking to them to make the correction. He says, "The social networks allow people to follow your process and contribute their own ideas. This helps you to create a better show and helps you understand your audience better."

Rocketboom was recently named one of the fastest-growing video startups on the Internet by Compete, a prominent Web analytics firm. When I ask Baron for his own assessment of his audience's size, Baron says it's always changing. "Part of our method is to allow people to redistribute it so there might be people in China, for instance, taking it and adding a language to it, and we might not know for sure."

One of the reasons for the show's success is its large international audience. dot-SUB, an online translation tool, provides a wiki for viewers to translate Rocketboom into several languages. German and Japanese viewers top the list. "One of the things I'm inspired by is when we look into our stats, and I see someone coming from Turkey or Iran," says Baron. "It's just amazing that the world is coming together like that."

▶ ▶

Video helps to bridge language and cultural barriers, according to Baron, because it helps viewers understand the stories. "Part of our objective is always to make it as visually valuable as possible. Just having a talking head sit there and tell you information is not the best use of the medium; it's much better when you can see all kinds of graphics and you can see visually what's happening."

The growing number of viewers around the world has meant increased advertising dollars and sponsorships for Rocketboom, which started out managing ad sales in-house and is now exploring the option of working with an agency to keep the small team's focus on creating great programs.

Although he's received a number of offers to buy Rocketboom, Baron is not selling. But he has signed on with high-powered Creative Arts Agency (CAA) to get a clear idea of the show's net worth. He says the team has a lot of ideas on how to grow Rocketboom, but for now he's keeping costs down and keeping the production lean. "It's human power," Baron says of his team with a smile.

Andrew Baron's Tips

Hire a great team. Baron says his father told him, "Always try to find people who are better than you."

Understand your audience. "The best thing you can do is to understand the audience." By this he means the following:

- Decide who you want your audience to be.
- Go find them and play close attention to them.
- If they're on social networks or blogs, read what they're saying.
- See whether they're trading or buying things, their e-mail habits, using IM—study it all.
- Notice trends and become involved.

Andrew says the understanding you'll gain is the best thing you can do to help inform the creative process. It will also give you a better idea of the kind of response your ideas will meet with your target audience.

Geek Entertainment TV

Geek Entertainment TV (www.geekentertainment.tv) is one of the best interview blogs currently online. Host Irina Slutsky's delivery keeps things lively and the show gives a contemporary perspective on technology and its impact on daily life.

The interviews aren't boring. For example, Slutsky interviews undefeated video gamer Fatality in his bathrobe and then follows him through his day (**FIGURE 4.8**). We join her at a mass pillow fight in San Francisco. When there's video to tell the story, Irina stops talking, the producers overlay some music, and they let us see it for ourselves. The shooting and editing make Geek Entertainment TV fun to watch, and it delivers more information than many news channels.

FIGURE 4.8 Geek Entertainment TV's Irina Slutsky interviewing video gamer Fatality.

Video News "Web Style"

News on the Web is an unfiltered assortment of reports, opinions, and observations that somehow gets the scoop on commercial news media again and again. Its popularity astonishes commercial news operations that are used to filtering our news for viewers. Now a new breed of journalist is going straight to the Web with video. The result is news that is fresher and closer to the truth. Video provides the undisputable evidence to support online news reports. Sometimes a video clip travels "quick and dirty" via YouTube and virally from one Web host or site to another.

The strategy for delivering news on the Web is sometimes called "publish then filter." It puts the responsibility on readers to decide for themselves what's true. Astonishingly, it works. Like Wikipedia, the Web's open source encyclopedia, news on the Web is self-correcting.

Unlike traditional news media, Web news allows for a multitude of perspectives on the same story, and it doesn't round up the usual suspects when experts are needed for clarity or comment. In fact, news video on the Web helps keep traditional media honest by revealing what would have often been left on the cutting-room floor.

Networks can't compete with millions of eyes and ears reporting what they see and hear because they care about it. And it's not as if the two worlds never intersect; many reporters at traditional news organizations have moved to the Web or have presences on the Web in addition to their day jobs.

Traditional media outlets such as the *New York Times* extend their audiences by posting video on the Web. Television news operations rebroadcast on the Web and add features and footage that don't fit into their broadcasts. But it's renegade journalists like Josh Wolf (see his interview in this chapter) and *Alive in Baghdad*'s Brian Conley (www.aliveinbaghdad.org) who are using Web video to change the face of news.

Alive in Baghdad

Brian Conley created the Web-based weekly news program *Alive in Baghdad* (**FIGURE 4.9**) to counter what he calls the sound bite–driven "Live From" news model prevalent on CNN and other TV news outlets. He also wanted to give people in occupied Iraq a voice in the media and to show viewers around an unvarnished view of daily life in Iraq.

Initially, Conley worked with amateur videographers and volunteers in Baghdad to gather the footage for his show. But as the show caught on, professionals started coming on board. The show bridges the language gap with graphic footage that tells the story, along with subtitles and voice-overs.

This is first-rate journalism. A recent Webcast focused on the plight of the Kurdish minority in Iraq, nearly 10,000 of whom are missing. The show has sold footage to commercial news networks. But keeping the production afloat is a daily struggle; *Alive in Baghdad*'s Web site appeals for donations to sustain it. But funding isn't the only challenge the show's producers face. Because of the danger in Iraq, it's sometimes easier to send footage directly to the United States by DHL for translation than it is to ferry it across Baghdad.

Recently, Conley and partner Steve Wyshywaniuk started *Alive in Mexico*, which they call a sister show. Its mission is to cover everything from street battles in southern Mexico to Mexican culture and history.

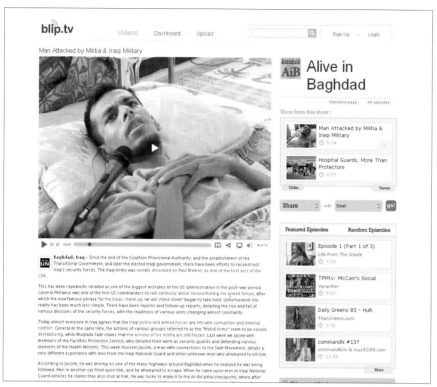

FIGURE 4.9 *Alive in Baghdad's* Web site, www.aliveinbaghdad.org. The show is hosted on Blip.tv.

Producing Informative Video

Pay careful attention to lighting, camera angles and your background when producing information video. Keeping your microphone on axis and in range will improve the sound of your on-camera presentation. Whether you're producing a personal video blog, how-to, or news show, high-quality production values will help to communicate your stories to viewers. Even if your camera and microphone are built into your laptop and your lighting is a desk lamp, you'll find it challenging to make your information-based video look and sound better.

When it becomes too difficult to concentrate on the quality of your production and gathering information for your shows, it's time to get help.

Creating a Strong Visual Presence on Camera

Video blogs, how-to videos, and news reports put you (or your talent) center stage. Take a little extra time to find the best camera angle and lighting when you're shooting talent (even if that talent is you). You may find you need a little translucent face powder to tone down a shiny forehead or nonreflective eyeglasses on camera. I'll let you decide about makeup, but test it on camera before the shoot—particularly if you're shooting in HD or HDV, which can be unforgiving.

This is no time to feign modesty; looking good is part of the job. Creating an interesting, flattering image takes the focus off the person talking and puts it back on what's being said. When your viewers don't have to wonder why your talent didn't comb her hair, your show will have their attention where you want it: on your story.

NOTE You don't have to be a model or an actress to look good on camera. Real people who know what they're talking about raise your work from entertaining to informative.

Many news and commentary shows feature young, pretty women behind the anchor desk; some are skilled actresses, others smart journalists. If you use actors (or anyone other than seasoned journalists or subject-matter experts) in front of the camera, however, they'll need good scripts to deliver effectively.

Real faces are interesting and add character and variety to your work, but few people look good on camera without a little extra attention to shooting them. Most people's faces aren't symmetrical. If you ask, they'll often tell you which side they think looks better. When you can, position your talent with his best face forward.

Developing an On-Camera Style

Some basic wisdom from television applies here. Simple necklines, jewelry, and hairstyles are less distracting for viewers than their more ornate counterparts. Avoid stripes and distracting patterns, which can strobe on camera—especially in the type of highly compressed video you'll deliver on the Web. White shirts can reflect too much light and take attention away from faces.

Men should make sure they have a close shave or neatly trimmed facial hair; it's hard to pull off "artfully grizzled" without looking disheveled. Don't be afraid to add a little tinted lip balm or even have your hair and makeup professionally done if it makes you look your best and feel more confident. If you routinely use your hands to gesture, consider getting a manicure. Make what your audience sees as interesting and appealing as possible.

Highlighting Your Talent

Marlene Dietrich never went anywhere without her lighting man, and she crafted an iconic image we still remember. Give your talent an extra boost and the sparkle of glamour by creating flattering lighting for him or her. That doesn't have to mean studio lighting. The magic hours just after sunrise and before sunlight give everything an attractive glow. You can also work with diffusers, reflectors, and battery-powered fill lights outside to give available sunlight an extra boost.

News teams routinely add fill light for stand-ups even when shooting outside. Television newsrooms use spectacular arrays of light to get the effect we've come to expect on TV. Keep your eyes open just before the commercial break on network news shows. They'll often pull the camera back to a wide shot, and you can get an idea how complex the lighting is and how many lights it takes to make your favorite new anchors look their best.

Your lighting can be one soft light or a stronger light bounced off a ceiling or wall plus reflectors, or it can be full three-point lighting. But don't make the mistake of blasting your talent (or yourself) with lights so bright they cause squinting or so harsh they're unflattering. The simple setup shown in **FIGURE 4.10** uses one soft light.

FIGURE 4.10 I used one light with a chimera for a how-to video about barbering techniques for a client.

You'll also need to turn off overhead lights, which cause unflattering shadows. Avoid lighting from beneath unless you're going for monster movie effects. Also, turn off fluorescent lights if you can. Not only do they cast green light, but they can interfere with your soundtrack. The best lighting makes subjects look lit from within or like the sun shines only on them, kind of like an old master's painting.

If you're showing a process or a product, make sure you have enough light and that the light you use doesn't cast harsh, distracting shadows that will confuse your audience or obstruct their view. Using a chimera or white umbrella to diffuse your light helps to keep it soft.

Controlling What Viewers See in the Background

Your background can be a simple roll of photographic background paper that comes in many colors and patterns, a (matte) painted wall, or a room that you've arranged carefully in the background. *Video Shooter* author Barry Braverman (see Chapter 2, *Shooting for the Web*, to read more about Braverman) warns that viewers are naturally cynical and suspicious and always looking at the background to see what they can find out. Although this may not be the best way to watch video, it's only natural. We're always trying to attach meaning to what we see, even if it's a series of unrelated images, and as a Web video producer, it's important to be attuned to what your audience is looking for. Visual storytelling often includes playing with viewer expectations and assumptions.

Less is more when it comes to backgrounds. I once dashed into a photo store on my way to shoot a series of interviews in Sweden and picked up a marbled cloth background. My boss joked that the interviews looked like they were shot in a cave. Having too much clutter in the background can be distracting (**FIGURE 4.11**).

FIGURE 4.11 This backdrop provided by a trade show was too shiny and called too much attention to itself.

Setting the Stage for Your Story

When it comes to backgrounds—and, for that matter, anything that might appear in the frame other than your subject—look at what appears on-screen and think about what it says to your audience. If you show viewers a scene of disarray, they will see creative chaos, conclude that you're a messy housekeeper, or simply think, "This person works in dismal surroundings." If any (or all) of those messages contradict the effect you're going for, clean up before you shoot. Make sure anything in the frame of your shot is there on purpose, looks good, and adds to the story you are telling, or at least doesn't get in the way.

When you're shooting on location, don't be afraid to change things a little to make them work for your shot. On one occasion, before I shot an interview with a college president for a documentary, I spent an hour arranging the contents of his cluttered desk in artful disarray.

Producers of the movie Brother From Another Planet used a friend's garage for a scene set outside a "funky Harlem garage." The location scout found what he thought was the perfect funky garage, but the set team spent half a day repainting the wall.

If you don't want to clean up your basement, office, or garage to create a set, invest in a half roll of photographer's background paper (about $20) and a small roll of gaffer's tape to attach it to the wall behind your talent, and keep her far enough away from the wall to prevent shadows. If you want to get fancy, you can buy a simple background stand that can be supported by two light stands. Use a conservative, light gray or blue paper instead of white. Most people look better against a neutral color than stark white.

Creating Interesting Compositions

I really hate the look of video blogs shot with Webcams. Almost nobody looks good looking down into a Webcam (**FIGURE 4.12**). Instead, frame your shot, here's why. Most Webcams have wide-angle lenses that distort anything close up and at the center of the frame. That can make your nose look, well...prominent, especially when you look down into the camera. You'll have more flexibility to define your shot if you use a simple video camera with a zoom lens on a tripod rather than a fixed-lens Webcam.

FIGURE 4.12 The overhead light in this shot is creating back light which tricks the camera into the wrong exposure for the blogger in the foreground.

It's also important to connect with the audience. Professional newscasters and talk-show hosts make talking into a camera and reading off a teleprompter look easy. It's not. Practice looking directly into the camera to connect to your audience, or you'll end up looking like you're talking to yourself. One way to practice is to have someone stand behind the camera and talk to her. Having another person in the room will keep your tone conversational and prevent you from declaiming as if you're taking part in a debate.

While they're standing there, you might as well have them shoot. If you frame the shot and control the lighting, even your roommate or significant other will often get a better shot than a stationary Webcam. But use a tripod, and don't let your recruit get carried away with zooming in and out. If no one is available, consider putting a picture of a smiling friend on the wall at eye level.

Scripting Information Video

Working with a script will help you to communicate information effectively on video. You'll need a teleprompter if you want to read a script without constantly looking down. Fortunately, teleprompters come in a range of shapes, sizes, and costs. Some from companies such as the Prompter People fit directly over your lens. Some blogging software programs, such as Adobe's Vlog It!, include an ersatz teleprompter (**FIGURE 4.13**). With these you read from your laptop screen and control with your mouse or a specialized device that controls the speed of scrolling text.

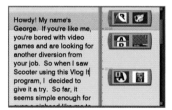

FIGURE 4.13 The built-in teleprompter in Adobe's Vlog It! software package.

Working with a teleprompter isn't easy. You'll need to control the speed of your text as it rolls by and look like you're not reading while doing it. You can control the speed of laptop-based teleprompters with a special mouse, or you can buy an inexpensive teleprompter and mount it in front of your camera. But if you're working solo or with a small crew, you probably have enough to deal with already.

Looking good while reading and controlling the speed of your text scrolling on the computer screen can really be difficult. Try cue cards written out large and taped to the wall instead. You can also print your script in a large font and perfect the art of looking down to read and then up at the camera to deliver your lines. Or you can make notes and then ad-lib for a more natural effect.

Either way, don't try to memorize. Trying to recall what you planned to say on camera looks awkward and won't give your video the conversational feel you want. Even if you have a real teleprompter that projects the text in front of the camera's lens so you appear to be looking into the camera, reading from it is a skill that takes practice.

Choosing a Flattering Camera Angle

Camera angle is an important part of any video. Using a tripod is the best way to adjust camera height but there are other ways to gain more control over the height and angle of your shot. If you must use a Webcam, balance it on a suitcase, or put your laptop on a stack of dictionaries to get just the right angle and improve your shot.

For most people, talking to another human makes a difference. You communicate differently than you do talking to an abstract audience. When I'm shooting interviews solo and see my subjects drifting off, I often wave from behind the tripod or point to my eyes or my heart to get their attention refocused.

You can vary your shots by moving the camera closer or farther away. Using a camera with a 12x zoom lens (as soon as you can afford one with a microphone input) makes things easier. A consumer camera with no mic input (that is, one that requires using your camera's built-in mic will work in a quiet room if the camera itself isn't too noisy, but it won't make you sound your best.

Developing a Visual Style

Add visual interest to your shots to give your viewers something to watch. Use expressions, thumbs up and down, graphics, props—whatever it takes. Once you develop a style, it's not hard to replicate. If your video blog includes footage you've shot in advance, make it the best quality you can with good lighting and good sound, even if no one is talking.

Create a signature style, a standard greeting, a way of dressing, or an approach to your work and adhere to it consistently. It will help your audience focus on your message rather than thinking, *"Now* what's she doing?" But don't be afraid to add some surprises.

INTERVIEW JOSH WOLF

 **Responsibilities of Online Journalists**

Josh Wolf, Independent journalist and documentary producer

Are video bloggers legitimate journalists? Ask independent journalist Josh Wolf, who was jailed by a federal district court in San Francisco after he refused to turn over footage of a protest he Webcast on a Bay Area independent media site (www.indybay.org). Wolf also sold the footage which included a police officer choking a protester and others threatening demonstrators with stun guns. The court questioned whether Wolf met the legal definition of a journalist and was entitled to First Amendment protection.

He spent 225 days in custody, longer than any journalist who's ever been jailed for protecting a source (**FIGURE 4.14**). In 2006, the Society of Professional Journalists named Wolf Journalist of the Year for upholding the principles of a free and independent press.

Photo by Dina Boyer

FIGURE 4.14 Josh was in custody longer than any journalist who's ever been jailed for protecting a source.

Wolf sees himself as a short-form documentary filmmaker focused on true events. He doesn't use the label "journalist" because, he says, "I feel an obligation to deliver information in a different way with a different paradigm."

Wolf believes that television, as a medium, is no more reliable than the Web. It's the source that matters. "All of us need more media sources and better media literacy to determine what's propaganda," says Wolf, who relies on traditional news organizations like the *New York Times* as well as CNN and Web sources. He subscribes to media RSS feeds and reads 50 or 60 blogs when he has time. He also stays in contact with about 100 people on Twitter.

Though he did work for a short time on a CNET blog, Wolf says he has no desire to be a professional video blogger. He'd prefer to work with a more traditional news operation that includes an editor.

You can follow Wolf's work at www.joshwolf.net.

Josh Wolf's Advice for News Video on the Web

Do it yourself. Register your domain name so you have the most control over what you write. If that's too much of an investment, start a Blogspot blog (http://blogspot.com).

Develop a reputation. Post information and stories you think are important on a regular basis.

Respond to your audience. And when you make a mistake, say so.

Getting the Sound Right

Many people are uncomfortable with the recorded sound of their voices. A good microphone will add warmth and resonance to your voice and give an authoritative air to whatever you have to say. Buy a lavalier (clip-on) microphone; even a cheap one with a mini-plug attached will give you a better sound than the microphone built into your camera or laptop.

Have someone else monitor your sound on headphones. If you're working alone, record a short take before you get started to make sure your levels are good and there are no distracting noises in the background. Traffic noise, people talking, air conditioners, fans, noisy radiators, bathrooms, elevators in close proximity, and even ice machines down the hall from hotel rooms can be distracting. Test your recording setup. If what you hear is great, proceed to record. If not, try again until you get it right.

I can't stress enough how important it is to get a good-quality microphone as soon as you can. When much of the information you have to share comes through the soundtrack, it's important that your viewers be able to hear clearly what's being said. If you're sitting at a desk as part of your commentary and you have a desk microphone, consider integrating it into your shot, but you'll have to remember to talk into the microphone. Sound is critical to informational video, and nothing sounds more amateur than sound that's recorded into the camera's mic. If you're using a desk or shotgun microphone, make sure it's pointed at the person speaking and remind her to talk into the mic.

Each information genre has its own special concerns and technical challenges. Start by learning the techniques that make your production easier and better (see Chapter 2, *Shooting for the Web*) and then borrow from other styles of shooting and presentation to create a distinctive style that will work for you and your audience.

Using Software for Video Blogging

One product designed specifically for video blogging is Adobe's Vlog It!, a software application that makes it easy to record a video with your Webcam, add titles and music, and get it up on the Web (**FIGURE 4.15**).

Some text-based blog-creation applications such as TypePad have plug-ins for video, but most video bloggers send their video to YouTube or a host more equipped to track viewers and get advertisers, such as Blip.tv; then they add links to their videos on their own Web sites.

Choose the option that's best for the way you work and your skill level. If you're comfortable creating your own Web page and adding links, work with the video host that can give you the most support.

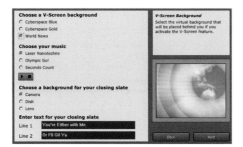

FIGURE 4.15 The Vlog It! interface includes a wizard that walks you through creating a video blog with titles.

If you need help with HTML, use blogging software or a program such as Adobe Dreamweaver to create your site and embed your video or add links to it from your video host.

If you need an RSS feed (Really Simple Syndication, which enables viewers to subscribe to your blog), choose a host which makes it easy by allowing you to set RSS as an option when you upload your video.

Producing How-to Video

Some of the most visually compelling video on the Web is educational. How-to video is a fast-growing genre that ranges from professionally produced exercise videos like Videojug.com's series on Pilates (**FIGURE 4.16**) to amateur efforts produced like home videos.

FIGURE 4.16 Pilates Class, one of a series on Videojug.com. The text instructions allow the lesson to work even with the sound turned off.

Videojug.com (www.videojug.com/tag/pilates) groups instruction into series. One on Pilates shows an instructor in a sunlit studio. Each video shows one exercise and how to do it. A running narration explains the benefits and gives tips, while a text overlay emphasizes important points and reinforces instruction. The quality of the voice-over sound is good, and a subtle music bed mixed under the voice creates a peaceful atmosphere.

At the other end of the spectrum, many how-to videos are user-generated (Web-speak for "produced by amateurs"). This genre was a lot more fun before advertisers perfected the trick of superimposing their messages over the earnest amateurs (and even worse, started creating fake user-generated videos to create the impression of populist support for their products), but it still works.

There's a kind of voyeur quality to these homemade videos. Most consist of people standing in front of the camera and declaiming what they want to share, often using comical spokesmodel-style gestures to point out something visual. More sophisticated producers build sequences that tell the story, while making sure there's enough light and that the sound is good. But it's what we see in the background that makes these simple videos work. We get a sneak peek into their homes and workshops, and we get to see real people showing what they do and sharing their expertise. Often, the most interesting parts of these videos are accidental.

I was fascinated by a series from Expert Village (www.expertvillage.com) that features Kevin Mouton, a carpenter from Austin, Texas. The videos intrigued me not because the production style was interesting (it wasn't) but because he seemed to have real information to share. I assumed he'd shot them himself.

It turns out a videographer contacted him and shot the series. Mouton, a carpenter who crafts custom wood furniture, demonstrates carpentry techniques and how to use the power tools of his trade. It doesn't hurt that he's really attractive and seems, well, humble (he's asked that I not publish his photo in the book). He shows, step-by-step, how to change the paper on a belt sander and other practical woodworking skills. The information is practical, and like a master craftsman training an apprentice, Mouton says he thought about how he learned when putting together the videos for Expert Village.

Mouton shows you what to do and how. He's not a TV-show fix-it guy. He's a real carpenter with real tools and the video is easy to find. Just search for *floor refinishing* or *belt sander*, so you can find it when you really need it.

Before you get started creating your own how-to video, let's take a look at some of the techniques that are specific to how-to video production.

Planning a How-to Video

Because how-to videos need to make sense, they depend heavily on continuity. The best start with carefully written scripts and storyboards. Many amateur efforts rely on memory or figuring it out as they go along, resulting in a more difficult shoot and a shopping-list structure that's guaranteed to bore the audience. The result is like listening to a story told with breathless repetition: he reached down, and then he opened the drawer, and then he removed the gun, and then he held up the gun, and then she saw it, and then she screamed. No drama, no buildup, no anticipation.

Even a simple script or shot list will help you keep track of all the shots you want to capture and their order in your finished video. The first step in creating a how-to video is breaking down the process you're describing into steps. Keep each short, and don't leave out important details. From these segments you can generate a storyboard for your video, or at least a simple shot list. Once you have your steps and their sequence, decide which ones need close-ups. Varying your shots creates a visual rhythm that gives your audience a chance to relax and take in what you're saying in between the most important steps.

When you're explaining how to do something, it's important to show the steps in sequence to avoid confusing your audience, but it's not always convenient to shoot them in sequence.

Using Voice-Overs and Narrations

Even if you're not planning to edit your footage, think about what can be shown and what must be explained verbally. Don't always show the host describing the process. Include voice-overs, while the footage onscreen shows something other than the host. You can record a narration after you finish shooting or while the camera focuses on the action. Record a little room tone—audio of the room with no one talking at the top of your shoot. It can come in handy if you need to mix sound recorded later with location sound. Just record 10 or 20 seconds of audio when nothing is happening that makes noise. Listen closely, and you'll realize even quiet rooms have a background sound. Editors like to have that to include in pauses, just as they like a little video footage before and after each shot. Sometimes you'll find it easier to strip the sound from a live-action sequence to use it as a narration during editing. Room tone helps editors mix sound that's shot at different times or in different locations together.

If you're producing for a site other than your own, think about that site's target audience. If they are older or less experienced than your usual viewers, go slower, show more intermediary steps, and take time to explain why you're doing things in case viewers need to make substitutions or changes.

Consider adding text and still photos to your Web page to support your video. Think about where the action is and use video to show it. Make sure you have lighting and camera angles that let viewers see details. You may also want to show your audience some common mistakes so they'll see what happens when they don't get it right and know how to fix it. If you're creating a series, adopt a consistent style of introduction and memorable opening and closing title sequences with music.

Creating a Simple Storyboard

Storyboarding, or making sketches of what the shots in your how-to video will look like, will help you plan and save time when you're shooting. Although off-the-shelf storyboarding software is available, unless you're doing films or complex corporate videos, you don't need it. You can map out your how-to videos just as well with two 8"x10" sheets of blank paper. Fold them once lengthwise and once along the width, and you'll get four rectangular blocks on each page. For a more complicated plan, add more sheets.

Drawing a storyboard also forces you to think about your shots before you look through the camera so you'll see your project in your mind's eye before you shoot.

To understand how storyboards work, take a look at a comic book or graphic novel. You'll see a story told in a series of images. The graphic novels in Neil Gaiman's *Sandman* series are among my favorites, and it's no accident that Gaiman, with his strongly developed sense of telling visual stories, has written several movies.

Another way to practice storyboarding is to go out with a still camera and shoot a few individual still shots to practice telling a story in pictures, as *Video Shooter* author Barry Braverman (see the Braverman interview in Chapter 2, *Shooting for the Web*) does with his students (**FIGURE 4.17**).

Doing exercises like these will help to train your eye and help you pay attention to the way people see things and process visual information. Once you understand how the eye works, you can mix up your images and create visual treats and surprises by deliberately breaking continuity.

Or you can do what many new to video do. Try something and see whether it works. If it makes sense to you, check with someone who's not so close to the project. Then learn from your mistakes. Unfortunately, so many amateurs are now learning how to produce video in public, on the Web, that sifting through the dross of poorly crafted video can be daunting.

You can often figure out a way to do something with a combination of observation, deductive reasoning, and trial and error, but it takes longer, and it's sometimes painful for viewers to watch. Bring your best work to viewers, or your audience may not come back when you have it all figured out.

FIGURE 4.17 These shots of a family visiting the cherry blossoms in Central Park suggest a story.

Maintaining Visual Continuity

Continuity might seem like a sweet, old-fashioned notion now that MTV-style jump cuts have become the norm. But it's important to shoot for continuity if your video includes sequences that must make sense to viewers. You can always disrupt continuity with jump cuts once you understand it. Altering time with flashbacks and flash forwards also requires continuity to make sense to viewers.

When you're creating a video, it's seldom shot in one long take. Master filmmaker Alfred Hitchcock once tried to create a whole movie with just a few very long, very complicated shots. Shooting the movie "Rope" was a difficult challenge that required meticulous storyboarding and military precision during shooting, lots of camera movement, and many assistants pulling focus. You'll more likely be stringing together several individual shots to create a sequence in the editing room.

To do that you'll need to plan your shots to get the footage you'll need to tell your story. Organizing your shots in a way that will make sense to your audience is called *shooting for visual continuity*. Understanding the basics will make your work easier to understand. It will also save you a lot of time and difficult fixes in the editing room—or worse, needing to reshoot or cobble together a video from footage that's missing key elements of your story.

Keeping Track of Screen Direction

What makes sense to viewers on video depends in part on the direction things move in across a video screen. The audience gets confused if direction changes arbitrarily. When they stop to think "Wasn't he just running to the left; now where's he going?" they'll stop paying attention to your story. To avoid this, video shooters use what they call the *imaginary line* to decide the direction they'll shoot from and to keep things straight for viewers (see Chapter 2, *Shooting for the Web*, for more about the imaginary line). It keeps things from changing direction onscreen without warning.

It works like this. Say you're shooting a parade coming down New York's Central Park West. As the numbered streets reach the 90s, participants turn a corner, and the parade ends. If you stay on one side of the action, they'll appear to keep moving naturally (**FIGURE 4.18**). Cross the street, and the direction goes haywire.

The imaginary line helps you keep track of where you need to shoot from to show your viewers what you want them to see without confusing them.

FIGURE 4.18 Stay on one side of the imaginary line to ensure visual continuity as shown in the shots of a parade.

Playing with Time

The imaginary line is just one part of visual continuity. The focal length of your shot, whether you shoot a wide shot, medium shot, or close-up, also helps tell the story.

Watching cooking and home-improvement TV shows is a good way to study visual continuity. But watch closely: all video plays with time, and often steps are left out of a sequence or represented for a disproportionately short time because they're boring or because there's little to say about them. Few how-to videos are presented in real time.

What you emphasize in your sequence and what you choose to show in detail shapes your production. For any how-to sequence, you'll want to pick a starting point. Often you'll start by showing viewers a finished product to clarify the goal of their efforts and inspire them.

Break down your process, and shoot the steps one at a time. Complicated subjects with many details require more steps. The number of steps and how fast you present them also depends on your audience. If they are experts or already know something about the subject, you can present the setups more quickly and with much less detail. If they're older or likely to be distracted—say, by having several other windows open on their computer while watching—your video will need to take it slower. The best cooking show hosts make observations and share related information while they work. Encourage your talent to prepare tips and observations to fill in the gaps.

Product Reviews

Product reviews are another type of informational video that's increasingly popular on the Web. If you're going to do them, make sure viewers can really see the product from different angles and perspectives, and put yourself in the user's shoes. Create a program that answers her questions or gives her an opportunity to ask them herself.

Don't be afraid to show your personal style. If you feel cynical about the product, say so and say why. Your audiences will trust you more if they believe you're telling the truth.

Showing a Process Step-by-Step

Showing a process effectively is the key to producing how-to videos. Sometimes you'll shoot a project that begs for a sequential approach: a makeover, a construction project, or instructions on how to change the oil in your car. Breaking down a process into steps makes it manageable, as shown in this sequence of a card game (**FIGURE 4.19**).

FIGURE 4.19 It takes several shots taken at different angles to show a process that takes place over time.

When showing each step in the process, it's helpful to ask yourself what each shot should communicate and whether it needs help from a graphic or an explanation in the soundtrack to make the point. Even if someone is narrating a process as it's being shot, it's helpful to record a clean version of the narration separately. This will allow you to play with time and make it easier to mix other visuals with the audio.

Many beginners doing how-to video on the Web focus the camera on themselves in a medium shot, losing much of the detail of what they're doing or talking about. Avoid this mistake by making a plan for when you'll use medium shots, close-ups, and wide shots and when you'll cut to other types of shots or graphics. Shoot and reshoot from different angles and focal lengths to illustrate different parts of a process.

Some editing programs such as Adobe Premiere Pro and Apple Final Cut Pro will let you zoom in on digital footage, but use this sparingly (especially if you plan to deliver in 640x480 or 720x480 from SD source footage, because it will cause pixelation); also, make sure the lighting is good enough to show the details your viewers will want to see (**FIGURE 4.20**).

FIGURE 4.20 Although it's possible to zoom in on this clip in Premiere Pro, because it's being edited in 720x480 SD, you can't zoom very far without causing pixelation and degrading the image (zoomed version on the right).

If you're compressing time while showing a process, decide how you will communicate this to your audience. Long dissolves traditionally indicate a lapse in time, but remember that they don't compress well and will increase the size of your final video if you budget the necessary bits to deliver them effectively on the Web—or they'll simply look bad.

It's always important to keep editing in mind when you shoot video and particularly important for instructional or how-to video. When you're producing a cooking or craft program you'll want to show viewers a finished product to inspire them. Remember to show your audience a list or visual overview of supplies and equipment needed before you begin the step-by-step

Educational Video

Not all educational video is how-to. Many colleges and universities videotape classes and lectures given by guest speakers and deliver them on the Web (or sometimes on an internal campus network). Although the video style is seldom inspired, the speakers often are.

Most universities shoot lectures and classes with one camera mounted on the ceiling or set up in the back of the classroom. Columbia Business School hires freelancers to shoot classes in classrooms not equipped with video cameras. The single-camera setup—often without any additional lighting—limits the quality of the production. Most of these lectures are shot in medium close-up and close-up shots. Professors are typically miked with wireless lavalier microphones.

A few classrooms are set up with multiple cameras wired into a central control room where a technician can control cameras by remote control and switch between them live as she tapes lectures. But these are the exception rather than the rule.

Guest lecturers often appear in theaters or larger lecture halls with lighting and AV crews to set up the sound. The sound is particularly important when video-taping these kinds of lectures because there's often little to see. Shooting or cutting in Microsoft PowerPoint slides can help but doesn't add much. Shooting in medium close-ups helps show the speaker's expressions, but beware of pacers who will walk in and out of your frame. Pull back or zoom out to keep them in frame, or settle on a wider shot.

It's helpful to have a second camera set up for a wide shot to provide cutaways for lectures. Shooting with multiple cameras adds interest.

K-12 classroom teachers now have their own forum to share video online; it's called Teachertube (www.teachertube.com).

instructions. When you do get started, think "baby steps" so people can really follow along.

Don't expect to shoot a sequence in real time or anything close to it. Reality TV is anything but. More often, it's highly produced and in documentary style to look like reality, with segments edited (to include cliff-hangers, and red herrings) carefully to build drama. Don't forget to anticipate any glitches or problems your viewer might encounter while trying to replicate the process. Include a "don't try this at home" disclaimer if any step in the process is dangerous or poses health hazards.

PROJECT

Plan and Shoot a How-to Video

Begin by creating a simple storyboard and shot list with at least four steps. Next, arrange your model and props so that you can stay on one side of the imaginary line and get all your shots.

Shoot each step of the sequence. If you use any pans to show action, make sure you start and end with a still shot. A better choice is to focus on including action within the frame.

FOR THIS PROJECT, YOU'LL NEED:
- Camera
- Microphone
- Headphones
- Paper for storyboard
- A model
- Props

NOTE Logging includes watching your footage and making notes about which shots work and what each shot includes. If you log before you capture footage to your computer you can capture much less.

Make sure you've included enough steps to show the process accurately. If there seem to be gaps, fill them in with additional steps.

Log your footage and transfer it to your computer for editing, which you'll do in the project in Chapter 6.

Record a Short Commentary

Begin by writing a script for a two-minute commentary about something you hate. It's sometimes easier and less cloying to generate passion for something that really bugs you. Read it and time yourself to get a better idea how long it should be.

The next step, believe it or not, is to throw your script away. To achieve the conversational tone you want your video to have, you'll be better off without it. Turn on your microphone.

Next, shoot a test for sound and listen to it. When you're satisfied with your sound setup, you're ready to start shooting. Ad-lib in front of your camera without referring to or trying to remember your script, now that you know what you want to say.

Now shoot at least one visual that shows what you're talking about.

Shoot your presentation all the way through from three different angles. When you're done, log all your footage and choose one angle for your edit, which you'll do in the project in Chapter 6.

During editing, you will create two cuts: one that uses only one angle and another that uses all three.

PROJECT

Shoot Visuals and Add Narration

N ote that an assistant will make this project easier and possibly eliminate the need for a tripod. If you're working solo, you'll need a tripod.

To begin, shoot footage that shows something happening in your community. A community garden under construction, a construction site, a protest, a parade, or a vacant lot where people have been dumping garbage make solid visual stories. Choose something that is clear without explanation. Your work will be easier if the topic you choose includes action. Look for someone doing something, or movement to help tell your story.

Next, shoot two interviews. You're looking for sound bites so you can cut each interview short when you have what you need. Log your footage.

Once you have your footage captured and logged, choose two 15-second sound bites and 60 seconds of footage to edit into a 90-second news-style package that explains the story to viewers. You'll edit this in the project in Chapter 6.

CHAPTER 5

TV TECHNIQUES FOR BETTER WEB VIDEO

5 TV TECHNIQUES FOR BETTER WEB VIDEO

Sometimes a quick setup on location just won't do. Working in a studio or using television production techniques to control light and sound on location will save time and improve the quality of your video. Even when you're working in the field with limited equipment, borrowing techniques from professional productions will improve your work.

Shooting with multiple cameras adds visual interest and cuts down setup times, but when you step up production, you'll face some real *gotchas*—things that, in the words of Kathleen Grace, producer of the popular Web series *The Burg*, will make you less nimble. You'll need more staff and more equipment, making advance planning and scheduling crucial.

Building a full production studio is beyond the budgets of most Web video producers. Broadcast studios are typically large soundproof spaces with specialized air conditioning and smooth, level floors. They also have lighting grids, control rooms, and reliable power supplies. But even in the absence of a state-of-the-art studio setup, you can do much to improve the way your video looks and sounds.

For some projects you will need to rent a studio. But for many, creating a background or set and then using more sophisticated lighting and camera techniques will reduce emphasis on the background and focus it on your talent or the action you want to capture, even if you are shooting in a conference room or a corner of your office.

Shooting a dramatic series for the Web requires a coordinated production. Once you get actors and additional crew involved, it's a lot harder to shift gears or recover from poor planning. A growing number of dramatic series on the Web are signaling a sea change in the way viewers watch original Web programming. *The Burg*, produced with some of the highest production values on the Web, quickly became a fan favorite. The show's clearly drawn characters, real-life locations in the trendy Williamsburg section of Brooklyn, and engaging plot helped to make it popular with viewers (**FIGURE 5.1**).

Now the producers have a new series that they're calling a scripted Web docu-comedy. *The All-for-Nots* follows a fictional band that plays real music on a cross-country tour in their quest for fame and fortune. Writer and coproducer Thom Woodley plays Paul, the band's keyboard player.

FIGURE 5.1 The cast of popular Web drama *The Burg*, which has been compared to *Friends*.

The High Price of Success

The highly acclaimed series *The Burg*, shot in Brooklyn's trendy Williamsburg neighborhood, followed the lives and loves of a trust-fund kid, an actress, an activist, a musician, and hipster roommate.

Originally the show was produced on a minimal budget with actors and technical talent receiving little or no pay. When a sponsor came along willing to pay for access to the show's growing audience, producers Thom Woodley and Kathleen Grace negotiated in good faith with the actors union to pay them fairly. Although they couldn't afford to pay actors scale (the normal rate for broadcast programs), the cost of producing the show skyrocketed from $400 an episode (which the producers had been paying out of pocket) to $1,000 a minute to cover insurance and pay the costume department, writers, and editors, as well as the actors.

Sponsor Motorola, which likely had its eye on the series for mobile distribution, pulled out at the end of its contract, leaving *The Burg* unable to meet its new higher payroll.

Woodley and Grace made a soft landing. With producer Melissa Schneider they're producing the *All-for-Nots* (www.theallfornots. com), a "scripted Web docu-comedy" about an indie music band. This time, former Disney CEO Michael Eisner is footing the bill.

▶ Shooting a Dramatic Series for the Web

Kathleen Grace, producer and director of The All-for-Nots *and* The Burg

This time around, *The Burg* producers Kathleen Grace and Thom Woodley aren't just shooting for the Web. *The All-for-Nots* appears on cable TV's HDNet, the Web, and mobile devices. The changes in production are vast. Shooting HD requires a larger crew and more equipment, and for the first time the team is recording stereo sound (**FIGURE 5.2**). Producer Kathleen Grace says shooting *The All-for-Nots* is a very different experience than working on *The Burg*.

When you get more equipment and a bigger crew, you're a lot less flexible. Did shooting in HD and recording stereo sound change your approach?

Definitely. It was slower. We shot a 22-minute episode of *The Burg* over a few days. We were really quick and light on our feet, which is what made *The Burg* possible. We were able to do it without going totally and insanely in debt. On *The Burg*, most of the time we were shooting outside; we were shooting guerilla on the streets and the sidewalks. I averaged around 20 to 25 (script) pages a day. We shot a 100-page script in three days.

Your average TV show gets four pages done a day. *The Burg* was shot very quickly, very minimal setup, very run-and-gun. *The All-for-Nots* is not as slow as TV because I'm a pretty speedy director, my crew is used to running, and the actors are used to my style of directing (**FIGURE 5.3**). There's a lot of discussion and thought, but there isn't a lot where we're doing tons and tons of takes. We get as many angles as we need and move on. We shoot 10 to 12 pages a day, which to me feels unbearably slow.

Are you shooting single-camera or multicamera?

We pretty much shoot with two cameras. Occasionally we'll pull in a third for little cutaways.

FIGURE 5.2 The *All-for-Nots* is recorded in stereo.

FIGURE 5.3 Shooting *The All-for-Nots* on location.

Then you're shooting double system sound as well. Talk to me about the lighting. It's just gorgeous. Tell me a little about what that takes. When you see a movie crew shooting on the street, there's a whole truck full of gaffer's gear and arc lights. Are you at that level?

We're somewhere in between. My production company owns a little four-light Arri Kit that you can buy for about $2,000. In the RV scenes, we use all these Kino Flos. We literally taped the Kino Flos to the ceiling—they're really tiny and light. And we had little on-camera lights that we used a lot.

It was really strategic; we used available light when we could. It was mostly that we took the time to set the cameras at the right settings. We have an HMI that you can power off batteries, which we used a lot for exterior stuff. It was the light we really consistently used on a regular basis. It was the workhorse for us. It was great.

We have good relationships with our vendors. They kind of think we're plucky, so they cut us deals.

Did you rent cameras or do you own your own cameras?

We got the cameras from HDNet [the all-HD television network]; they lent us two Panasonic GS400s, and we also own an HVX200. Then we got our lighting and camera support from Handheld (a New York equipment rental shop).

▶▶

The All-for Nots *includes several scenes that take place in an RV. Is there an RV set, or is it a real RV?*

It's actually an RV. Writer and producer Thom Woodley has a neighbor who has an old RV that we used. We literally set up craft services [meals for the crew] in his parents' house and shot in the RV for five days straight.

It was really tiny. You'd think it would be big because it's an RV, but when you get two cameramen in there, a sound guy, a boom op, five actors, your assistant director, and a monitor, you suddenly have very little room. We shot inside of it, and then we used it to get B-roll exterior shots of it.

Do you do any shooting in a studio?

It's all location. Later on in the series there's an episode that's shot in a TV studio, but it was specifically supposed to be a TV studio. We do all location shooting. We save so much time and money by shooting in actual locations because we don't have to art direct them. We leave them mostly as they are—like a bar is a bar (**FIGURE 5.4**); apartments in Williamsburg for *The Burg* look like apartments in Williamsburg. I don't want to take the time to buy crappy IKEA furniture when I can use my own in my apartment.

But on tape, a lot of stuff doesn't look like it looks in real life.

For us it was just a matter of doing it where we could do it. Even on *The All-for-Nots* it was about that. We did have financing, but we also were trying to accomplish a lot of material on that budget. We basically recorded (the equivalent of) two-and-a-half feature films by the time we were done, which is a lot of material on a Web series budget. They don't even know how to make money off them yet, really. There's product placement and sponsorships, so the budgets aren't super huge. [Grace is contractually prohibited from saying what the series' actual budget is.]

FIGURE 5.4 Production on *The All-for-Nots* included shooting in a bar.

We had a cast and crew of between 25 and 30 people. We recorded an album, and we did a lot of work for that. So, a six-figure budget for Web series is a lot, but not very much considering it was in HD. We squeezed every bit of content out of that money that we could.

You're calling The All-for-Nots *a scripted Web docu-comedy. What does that mean?*

It's a Web series. It's a comedy that is shot like a mockumentary, so it's like *The Office* or *Spinal Tap* or *A Mighty Wind*. But it's definitely scripted; the actors don't really improv other than when they do their performances as the band. They all play their own instruments and are real musicians, but there is this kind of level of fiction that's going on.

> *We save so much time and money by shooting in actual locations because we don't have to art direct them.*

Is the cast union?

It was a nonunion shoot. A lot of the crew was nonunion. For *The Burg* we actually had union actors, and we had negotiated a contract with SAG [Screen Actors Guild]. If we shoot *The Burg* again, we'll do the same thing.

Is The Burg *is coming back? You have a lot of fans out there.*

We'll see. We're trying to find a sponsor.

I noticed The All-for-Nots *has a large fan base on Bebo, and I'm wondering how your scripting encourages the audience involvement? Was that a conscious thing on your part when you were scripting* The All-for-Nots?

Definitely. Each show Thom and I do, we try to up the interactivity. On *The All-for-Nots*, the main point of interactivity was that people could come to see the band live, they could download the music, and they could interact with a fictional character in a real way you'd interact with a band.

For our next show we want to create a similar kind of interactivity or even take it further. In a perfect world we could be constantly shooting so that if the audience wanted the script to go one way, we could write an episode and post it or respond to people's comments. But it's not quite that nimble yet.

A lot of the Web series out there like *Rocketboom* or *Break a Leg* or some of these other scripted series like *Goodnight Burbank* are contained enough that they can be that nimble. The world of our shows tends to be a lot bigger; we have more characters and more locations. That sort of thing makes people more excited to

▶▶

watch the show, but it makes it more difficult for us to be super-nimble. If someone posts a comment [on the show's Web site suggesting a change or plot twist], we'd have to coordinate seven actors plus the camera guy and the sound guy to maintain that level of production value that we've come to be known for and want to deliver. We want to deliver, if not TV quality, then almost TV quality for the Web. Because there's definitely an audience out there for that. People aren't always going to be content to see grainy videos.

What are people telling you about the quality? What's the response been like?

A lot of people really like the quality. My sister, who's a layperson, said the video looked "crisp and awesome." For me it's been really great to be shooting [*The All-For-Nots*] on HD and have that kind of quality (**FIGURE 5.5**). It's such a big leap from *The Burg*. We really had a team of talented people working on the show. Beyond the quality of the show, we've gotten a lot of comments from people impressed with the quality of the music. They didn't expect the band to be as good as they are.

FIGURE 5.5 Checking out the equipment during a shoot.

We're really excited that people really like the band, and they can keep playing shows and eventually go on a "real tour" so the fans of the show can see them in their home town. The ideal situation would be that we would do that while filming season two. And fans of the show and the band would be extras in the show. I think people will be really into that.

How important was your background in the theater to being able to direct The Burg *or* The All-for-Nots?

It helps. Because I didn't go to film school, I didn't expect to have a gaffer and crafts service and a props person and all these people to help me make something. I was used to the world of theater where you make do and everyone has multiple jobs and you just do it (**FIGURE 5.6**). Often, when I go to see student films, their crew is twice the size of *The Burg* crew because they all went to film school and they know how many people you're "supposed to have" to make it work. Whereas I didn't know, and that made me a lot more open to doing things differently and a lot more hungry to do stuff.

FIGURE 5.6 Shooting in HD requires a different approach to makeup.

With the Web you have the same response as you do in theater. You get direct response from your audience. You post it on the Internet, you get 10 comments, and you know exactly what people are thinking about you, which, for me, is kind of like in the theater, where you have an experience with the audience when you watch a play. That's what I really like about the Web.

Are you still watching comments and how many views you get, or do you have somebody else do that?

I'm obsessed with that. I'm obsessed with our Bebo page and our MySpace profile, and I'll Google search about us and figure out what blogs are talking about us. It's really important to me to listen to the comments. You have to take them all with a grain of salt because everyone has something to say on the Internet and it's not always good, but it keeps you sharp.

Do you have any advice for people who want to produce their own dramatic show for the Web?

Don't let anyone tell you that you can't do it. Just do it. Make sure it's a good story that's worth telling. It should be a compelling story no matter what you're doing.

Planning a TV-Style Production

You'll find that multi-camera shoots and dramatic series shot on location require a lot of coordination. Studio rentals are costly, and you'll likely be paying camera operators, technical directors, talent, and the crew you'll need by the hour.

Planning helps keep projects on schedule and under budget. Even if your actors and support staff are volunteers, you'll be coordinating their schedules and will want to make the best use of their time.

Creating a Shooting Script

Creating a script will help you to manage your productions. Dramatic productions are always scripted. Variety shows and talk shows may script parts of the production and schedule others as segments with specific intros and defined time slots. You'll need to keep track of a number of things, ranging from locations and the permission to use them to props, costumes, and equipment. Fortunately, there are tools to help you keep everything organized, and some of them free.

Your script for a drama might be very simple, including only the actors' dialogue and screen directions, but more often it describes the location, suggests action, and provides details for the lighting director. Dramatic series also have what's called a *bible*, a document that describes the back story of the plot and some of the characters' histories.

Since you're working with other people, it's almost always best to use the standard format they know how to work with. Scriptwriting software speeds your formatting, keeps your work consistent, and makes it easy to make changes. Some programs include word processors. Others are add-ons to Microsoft Word.

Cinergy gives away its Script Editor (**FIGURE 5.7**) to encourage you to buy the company's complete production package, but there's no obligation to do so. It formats scripts with character names and identifies action, dialogue, and other elements while you write (www.mindstarprods.com/cinergy/scripteditor.html).

Celtx is a free, open source production package. The script writer included automatically formats dialogue, characters, and action. *Videomaker* magazine called Celtx (**FIGURE 5.8**) "perfect script-writing software for beginners and intermediate writers/producers."

A spirited community provides support through online forums and a wiki manual. The code is based on Firefox and runs on Windows, Mac, and Linux. After your script is completed it becomes the source material for producing a storyboard, breakdown, and production schedule. You'll find a free Celtx download as well as tutorials at www.celtx.com.

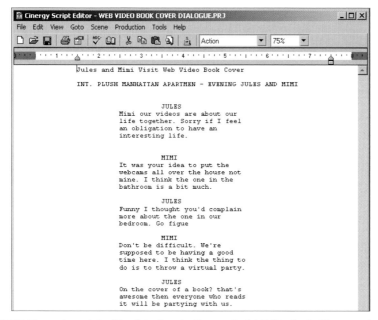

FIGURE 5.7 The main scriptwriting interface in Cinergy Script Editor looks like a word processor but includes features that make scriptwriting easier.

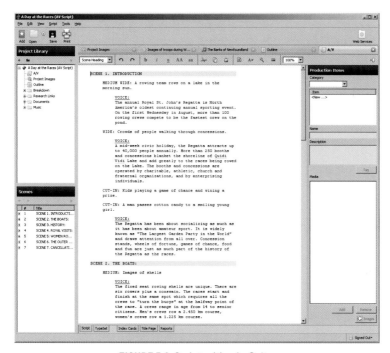

FIGURE 5.8 Scriptwriting in Celtx.

You don't always need a script. Interviews, for example, are typically unscripted. But the show they appear in might include scripted segments. Usually, a show will have a standard open and credit sequence that runs a set amount of time, and it may need to be formatted for billboard advertisements before and after the show.

Most interviewers prepare by researching guests and writing questions in advance, but interviews can be as informal as a list of topics to cover and others to avoid. Making your guest feel relaxed and comfortable helps to create a more interesting interview.

Dramatic productions require another kind of preparation. Scripts are the starting point for discussing the delivery you expect from actors and talking with them about their characters' motivation.

Typically on a large production, the heads of each department—lighting, sound, costume, and props—start with the script and anticipate equipment, staffing, and creative requirements. The director, for example, uses the script to set up shots and plan actor's movements. If a performer is going to make a dramatic entrance, you'll need to let your camera operators know if she'll enter from stage left or another location. If you're working with multiple cameras, you'll often want to plan what each operator should be doing.

For a music video, one camera may be responsible for a wide shot of the singer's entrance while the second camera stays on a close-up of the performer. If the next act is a group of dancers, you'll have different instructions about what each camera should be doing.

The lighting department will decide whether to light an exterior or supplement available light with reflectors or fill lights. When lighting is required outside, you'll need battery-powered lights or a generator to power it.

Developing a Storyboard

A *storyboard* is the visual plan for your production. It includes images that show framing and sometimes camera angles laid out on a grid. The drawings or photographs and related text help you visualize and plan the individual shots that will tell your story.

A simple storyboard like the one you created to identify the steps for in Chapter 4, *Videoblogs, How-to Videos, and News*, can be created with a few sketches using stick figures to illustrate the position of the actors.

As your project becomes more complex, you'll need to share your vision with others. A more developed storyboard that includes camera angles and details about your location can help you communicate with your team and make it easier to realize your vision for the project.

Complicated scenes often include several shots from different angles. A storyboard breaks down scenes and sequences into the individual elements you'll be shooting. Like a shopping list, it also reminds you of the shots you'll need to tell your story effectively when you get into the editing room. Celtx offers free storyboarding software that interfaces seamlessly with the company's free scripting software (**FIGURE 5.9**).

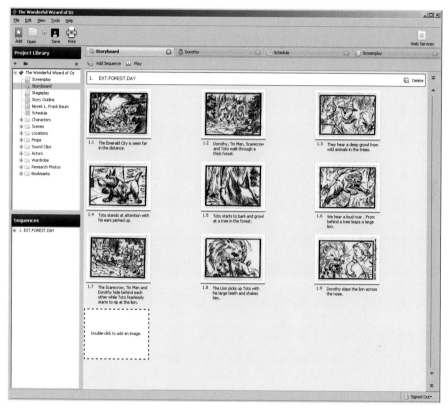

FIGURE 5.9 Celtx' storyboard tool integrates with its scriptwriting application and helps you organize your project.

Storyboard Pro (http://movies.atomiclearning.com/k12/storyboardpro), also free, is a simple-to-learn package originally created by Bill Bierden for use in schools. You can import existing video clips, still pictures, and sounds to better illustrate each shot. You can also add film and editing notes and print copies of your storyboard for use while filming or editing. A commercial package, Toon Boom Storyboard Pro, has a similar name but no connection to Bierden's free software (**FIGURE 5.10**).

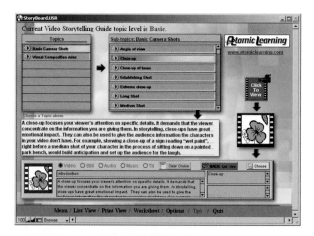

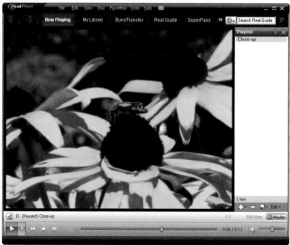

FIGURE 5.10 Storyboard Pro makes it easy to plan your production visually.

Although some high-end storyboarding packages carry four-figure price tags, some of the packages used for Hollywood productions sell for hundreds, not thousands. When the big bucks come in, you can use them to create a powerful presentation of your ideas rendered in 3D. But for now, save your time and money for your productions and go with the freeware options.

Scheduling Your Production

Once your production gets big or complicated, sticky notes won't be enough to keep everything organized. You'll need a production schedule and a list of everything needed and the related costs. A production budget breakdown lists everything needed for your shoot and tracks the costs. It helps you or your production manager keep a close eye on the budget.

This document is a producer's main tool for scheduling a production and keeping it on budget. It indicates which actors need to be on set and when. It also makes it easy to generate call lists. The detailed plan also includes what props, special lights, cameras, and equipment are needed, and it ties those needs to your schedule. That way you can make sure the actors, technicians, equipment, props, and costumes are available when they're needed. If you need permission to shoot, having a detailed plan will help a location manager to know in advance and arrange permission in time.

Experienced lighting, sound, makeup, and camera technicians use the script or project description to plan the equipment and supplies they'll need, which makes it even more important to have clearly written guidelines for them to work from. On large productions, a production manager goes through the script scene by scene to anticipate staffing and other production needs. On a smaller production, the producer or director may have much of this information in mind, but not on paper.

Writing down the details of production makes it easier to anticipate the needs of the project and to delegate responsibilities. This is another reason to use production software such as storyboarding and scripting tools. As you write, the format will remind you of what you need to include, such as the location of every scene. When you or someone else on your team makes plans in writing, the whole cast and crew end up on the same page. Celtx includes a module to help you prepare schedules budgets and call sheets (**FIGURE 5.11**).

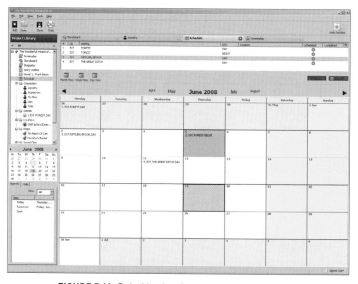

FIGURE 5.11 Celtx' budgeting and scheduling module.

Although e-mail and text messaging are convenient, make sure you print out schedules and call sheets as a backup. Also keep a hard copy of your crew and cast contact lists, and don't forget to get snail-mail addresses and landline numbers in addition to cell phone numbers and e-mail addresses.

Planning a Multicamera Shoot

Many dramatic series are shot with one camera. Single camera shooting is time consuming and can end up being more expensive. It requires repeating scenes and shooting them from several angles. Action movies and live events are shot with a different technique: one that requires several cameras, often saving time during production..

Shooting television studio style with multiple cameras allows you to vary your shots like a live-switched production, even if you're going to tape. The technique provides visual variety and helps keep the audience interested even if you're shooting something that has little movement or action, such as a lecture or interview.

In television studios and on large productions, cameras are synchronized, and operators are connected via intercom to a director in a control room who calls the shots and directs their work. A technical director switches the cameras live as the director chooses which shot best shows the event.

Simple Multicamera Production Without Switching

It's important to choose the right approach for the program you're creating. Most Web video projects don't require elaborate multicamera setups, but your work might benefit from using more than one camera to add visual interest and variety. When you're working with more than one camera, it's great if you can use two of the same model because that makes it easier to match the footage. Some professional cameras make this easier by allowing you to calibrate settings on a memory card so that they match on all cameras, but most prosumer cameras won't offer that option. If you're using different cameras for a multicamera shoot, make sure you white balance all of them.

A common multi-setup for a two-person interview uses three cameras: one on the host, one on the interviewee, and an additional camera on a tripod in a wide shot Instead of investing in studio cameras that must be synched and mixing your sound through a large board in a control room, designate one camera as the sound camera and use a clapboard or electronic slate to sync all your cameras during post production (**FIGURE 5.12**). It's also helpful to run sound on the camera's built-in mics as a reference track. Popular editing tools such as Adobe Premiere Pro and Apple Final Cut Pro have multicamera interfaces that make switching camera angles in the timeline as simple and straightforward as a switching live once you've synched your sources to a master audio track (**FIGURE 5.13**).

FIGURE 5.12 An electronic slate makes it easy to sync multicamera shoots during post-production but an inexpensive clapboard slate will work just fine.

FIGURE 5.13 Multicam editing interface in Premier Pro.

Orchestrating a multicamera shoot without a control room or intercom system requires more production planning up front and some creative hand signals on the part of your floor manager. But it will make it possible for you to produce high-quality video on a budget with a crew as small as two or three people either under controlled conditions on your set or in the field.

Helping Viewers Make Sense of Your Story

Visual continuity is both an art and a science. It's a strategy for shooting video in a way that makes it easier to combine shots in the editing room. Shooting for continuity makes a story flow visually and helps to tell your story. This is especially important on the Web, where attention spans are short and viewers bored by your video can click away quickly in search of something better.

NOTE You'll find references to books about continuity in the appendix at the end of this book.

Study movies and television shows to learn how shooting sequences and using camera movement enhance storytelling. The aim of shooting for visual continuity is to keep your viewers' attention on the content of your video rather than on the flashy pyrotechnics you use to deliver it.

When you break the rules of visual and cinematic continuity the result can be confusing or distract your audience. Always keep your viewers' experience in mind when you choose to ignore these strategies for traditional visual storytelling. The good news about shooting for visual continuity is that it can save you time because you won't have to shoot extra footage to cover yourself and make transitions work smoothly. These simple rules can do a lot to make your video better.

In Chapter 4, *Videoblogs, How-to Videos, and News*, you learned the basic rules for building a sequence, shooting a long shot to establish location, and mixing medium shots and close-ups, and you learned to shoot cutaways and cut-ins to enhance your interviews in Chapter 3, *Shooting Events and Interviews*. Now let's look at how continuity works in a little more detail. Here are some simple guidelines to apply to your shooting to make it better.

The Ten Commandments of Continuity

1. When you shoot a new scene, change your focal length (the size of your image) or angle to make it easy to edit. A good rule of thumb is to move 30 degrees between shots. *Dollying* (moving the camera forward or back physically) creates a different effect than zooming in or out. Try both, but avoid using your camera's digital zoom; you'll lose quality.

2. Use interesting angles while shooting to create a distinctive style. Shooting *flat*, or perpendicular to your subject, doesn't work. It's boring. High angles reduce your subject's height and make it appear to move more slowly; low angles increase height and speed things up. Side angles give depth and perspective. Angles can help to communicate emotion and point of view.

3. Pan to follow action. Panning smoothly handheld is hard. Use a tripod whenever possible. When panning handheld, keep your elbows in and pivot from the hips. Take it slow and smooth, and keep your pace constant. Left to right

feels more natural in the West, as does bottom to top when you tilt instead of pan. But pay attention to what works for your location and project. Always start and end your pan with a static shot to make editing easier. Sometimes letting action continue off screen after the camera stops moving can make an interesting transition.

4. Break down any action into its smallest components, and build a sequence of shots to show the action. Use one continuous shot only when it offers an element of surprise or discovery.

5. Use the imaginary line, sometimes called the *180-degree rule* (as described in Chapter 4, *Videoblogs, How-to Videos, and News*), to keep the direction of onscreen movement clear and keep your audience from getting confused.

6. Let action move into and out of your frame to add dynamic tension. Diagonal angles, such as birds flying from one corner of your screen to another or a train traveling at an angle, produce dramatic tension.

7. Keep lighting and background sound consistent from one shot to another.

8. Shoot overlapping action to cover your shots, and give editors movement within the frame to cut on. If a man raises his right hand in the wide shot, make sure he makes the same motion or a similar one in the medium shot to make your work easier to edit.

9. Pay attention to what's going on within your frame. Is a glass half empty or full? Is the main character wearing a hat or carrying an umbrella? Avoid confusing your audience with unexplained breaks in continuity.

10. Use your audience's natural instinct for distilling meaning from any series of shots to tell the story you want to tell.

The Whole World Is Watching

Just in case you think nobody is paying attention to mistakes in continuity, check out this Web site, which is dedicated to movie mistakes: **www.moviemistakes.com/best_continuity.php**. You'll find endless observations of continuity errors. One thread about *Blade Runner* on the Internet Movie Database (**www.imdb.com/title/tt0083658/goofs**) includes pages of comments that compare scenes and continuity over several releases of the movie.

The public's sense of betrayal is so strong when these mistakes happen, that one star publicly confessed the reason for a lapse in continuity. In an interview in *Playboy* magazine, Helena Bonham Carter revealed a lapse in continuity during the filming of *Sweeney Todd*, "Anyone who...pays attention to my breast size will see there's no continuity," says Carter. "The first half of filming I wasn't pregnant, and the second half I was, and because we didn't shoot it in order, I start off with huge breasts, and then I walk upstairs and suddenly I've got tangerines again. It's melons to tangerines."

A Glossary of Shooting Strategies for Visual Storytelling

Pan: A horizontal camera movement usually from left to right.

Tilt: A vertical camera movement from bottom to top or top down (both pan and tilt are facilitated by using a tripod).

Tracking: The camera travels in the direction of the action either using a dolly or on foot.

Long shot (LS): Sometimes called a *wide shot*, provides panoramic or big-picture view; it's seldom used on the Web because it creates images so small that few can see them with low-resolution or small-frame footage.

Medium shot (MS): A closer shot showing a person head to toe.

Medium close-up (MCU): A waist-up shot often used for interviews.

Close-up (CU): A tight shot, usually just head and shoulders.

Extreme close-up (ECU): Shows only the face, hands, or a small object full-screen; this is used for showing emotion and details.

Sequence: A classic sequence includes a long shot, a medium shot, and a close-up. But the order of shots may be varied to create suspense, drama, or tension.

Head-on and tail-away shots: When shooting for directional continuity, head-on or tail-away shots allow changes in screen direction without confusing the audience. Examples: A flat shot from in front of or behind moving object, a train moving directly toward the camera that appears to be standing still.

Establishing shot: A wide or medium shot used to establish a location or the people in a conversation.

Reestablishing shot: A return to location shot after action that might confuse the viewer.

Reverse shot: A strategy for capturing conversations in which the camera alternates to shoot the person talking from the listener's perspective.

Over-the-shoulder shot: Commonly used for interviews and conversations, this is a kind of reverse shot in which the listener's shoulder or hair or arm frames the shot of the speaker to establish both the speaker and the listener in the shot.

Creating a Set for Web Video Production

If you're producing a lot of video or working on a regular production, you may need to build a set or set up lighting for your project. Your studio can be very basic—a background and desk or two chairs for an interview in a corner of your living room or office. Or it can be as elaborate as a broadcast studio.

Either way, the essential production principles are the same. Controlling light, sound, backgrounds, and camera movement can dramatically improve the quality of your video.

Broadcast studios are soundproof. Don't bother trying to soundproof your shooting environment if the subway runs under your building or if your location is on a busy, noisy street unless you're ready to go to extraordinary expense. Broadcast studios also have specialized quiet air conditioning; smooth-level flooring; risers or stages; a grid of hanging pipes with power for lighting; backdrops, drapes, and sets; as well as storage for equipment. Most have control rooms in another location that communicate visually and aurally with the studio.

Instead of imitating commercial broadcasters, tailor your studio to the kind of projects you do most. If you're mainly producing commentary or two-person interviews, your studio can be quite small. But remember things can heat up fast if you're using tungsten lighting. You may need to turn off air conditioning temporarily to quiet your set while shooting, so make sure you have enough space for air circulation.

"New media concept" Web news outlet Good News Broadcast (www.goodnewsbroadcast.com) works and shoots in a Manhattan loft. Visitors find the wall behind producer Paul Slatikus's desk an odd color green, but it works as a green screen when they need one. Other walls are painted in different colors with subtle patterns to provide a variety of backgrounds.

Small touches can make shooting easier on the set you create. There are a number of things you can do to improve shooting conditions. For example, set up in a quiet place. If you plan to build a grid or hang lights overhead, you'll need high ceilings (at least 10–12 feet) and a reliable power supply—preferably a separate breaker box or fuse box if you have access to one. If you plan to store your equipment in the studio, you'll also need security or a locked closet large enough to store your cameras, mounted on their tripods, and other expensive gear.

Unless you're planning live multicamera Webcasts, you won't need a control room or mixer. But there are some portable, studio-in-a-box setups, such as NewTek's TriCaster Pro (www.newtek.com), that will give you the flexibility to switch live when you need to do so. If you have time to edit, you can use multicamera-editing features in many popular editing packages to make the same shot decisions you'd make live, during post-production.

Start with a basic setup for shooting video, and expand as your production needs grow. Also consider renting several small studios in your area before committing to building your own. You'll learn a lot about what you do and don't need.

Before you plan any construction, invest in any equipment or sign any contracts for studio design or labor; get a blueprint of the space and a schematic that shows electricity, lighting, air conditioning ducts, plumbing, and electrical wiring. You'll also want to find out the true height of your ceilings and whether you have access to beams or black iron. You'll need these to support rigging to hang heavy drapes and your lighting grid.

This step may change your mind or alter your plan substantially. You can still shoot video in a room that's not a real studio or requires substantial compromises, but it's better to know what you're getting into before you create your preliminary budget or plan. When professionals build studios, they bring in a consolidator who works with equipment manufacturers and comes up with the best plan for the project. If you have a large budget, hire a pro. Fair warning: their services cost in the tens of thousands.

You'll also need to think about staffing. Do you have the personnel to staff a studio, or will one additional static camera and two with operators do? Switching live requires an operator and a communications system. It's possible to limit staff by working with robotic cameras, but this approach requires an expensive setup.

Building a Small Studio

My experience building an inexpensive, highly flexible, functional setup for shooting Web video is instructive. I tranformed several small offices in a Long Island office building into a working studio—an experience I don't recommend. You'll find a video showing construction of the studio on the book's Web site (www. webvideobook.tv). I also offer some tips for smaller projects based on my experience. These include a green-screen backdrop and ideas for setting up an interview booth for shooting on location during a business conference.

I hope this guide will save you time and money. It takes a substantial investment to build even a simple studio. Before you do, ask why you're doing this. Perhaps after reading this chapter, you'll change your mind.

If you've worked in professional broadcasting, as I have, you know it takes a lot of people and a lot of equipment to make it work. If you haven't, go sit in on a taping of a live show the next time you're in New York or Los Angeles, or attend a football or baseball game that's being broadcast live to get a feel for what it takes.

To build a small studio, you'll take some of the techniques from the pros and accept some compromises with the goal of creating conditions that give you more control over the video you shoot.

Sound

Complete soundproofing is expensive. Basically, you would need to build a room within a room to completely control outside sounds. Instead, opt for relatively quiet. Start out with an interior room away from elevators, bathrooms, and air conditioning units. Add soundproofing to the walls and ceiling. If you have drop ceilings you can purchase special tiles to muffle sounds. Placing acoustic sound baffles or foam on the walls will also help to keep your studio quiet. If the room will be used for other purposes, get panels covered with fabric that look good (**FIGURE 5.14**). If not, egg-crate foam works fine.

Courtesy Auralex Acoustics

FIGURE 5.14 Auralex® SonoSuede Pro sound control panels (shown above in a studio control room) are easy to install and provide a cost-effective way to control sound in a studio environment. The panels, covered in a synthetic suede, are an attractive option when your studio must serve other purposes.

Microphones suspended overhead on booms are often used in studios. But using lavaliere microphones as newscasters do is a better option when your set is not soundproof or you have limited staff to set and monitor sound. For interviews with two people, plug both mics into your main camera. For more talent, feed mics through a mixer into the camera you designate as primary for sound, or into your video mixer.

Wireless microphones limit cable clutter but can pick up radio interference and noise; they're also very convenient for fieldwork, which makes them a good investment.

Mixing Sound and Video

A switcher is a key component in any studio. It can also be the most expensive, both in initial cost and in manpower to operate it. One good option for budget-conscious producers is a portable video and sound mixer sometimes called a *studio in a box*, such as Sony's Anycaster (**FIGURE 5.15**). Highly portable, the Anycaster has an HD plug-in but limited hard drive capacity.

FIGURE 5.15 Sony's Anycaster is essentially a studio in a box. It switches three cameras so you can record the video program or stream it live.

NewTek™ TriCaster (**FIGURE 5.16**), available in four configurations (TriCaster, TriCaster PRO, TriCaster Studio, and TriCaster BROADCAST), is less portable and doesn't do HD, but many professional operations (where you might find yourself working) use a TriCaster with its larger hard drive, built-in green screen, and titling capacity to deliver video to the Web.

Courtesy NewTek, Inc.

FIGURE 5.16 NewTek's TriCaster, sometimes described as a "studio in a box," is a portable solution for live multicamera switching. TriCaster BROADCAST is shown here.

Newspapers and radio stations that produce Web video programs often use the TriCaster because it gives them the ability to stream live programs and to record them to the unit's hard drive. The ability to switch multiple cameras with a small staff makes the TriCaster an attractive option for marketing departments and other communications professionals who want to improve the quality and look of their programs with a more professional multicamera look.

While traditional switchers require special cameras that can synchronize to them, TriCaster has "genlock" built in. Unlike the Sony Anycaster, you'll need a separate monitor, or monitors, to work with the TriCaster. An additional feature provided by NewTek is LiveSet™, a suite of virtual sets to use with the unit's green-screen option (**FIGURE 5.17**).

FIGURE 5.17 NewTek's LiveSet network-style live virtual sets work with the TriCaster video mixer's greenscreen keying capability. LiveSet Skybox virtual set is shown here.

You can use these devices on your set and in the field to switch several cameras live to tape or to hard drive. Both of these products can also send video live to the Web over a broadband connection.

Flooring

Flooring is another important component of your studio. You'll need smooth floors to make it easy for your camera dollies to maneuver and change shots during production. For Web video you won't need the most expensive studio flooring designed to withstand the weight of heavy broadcast cranes and dollies. Try dance flooring, which comes in wide rolls or large tiles and will probably work just fine. The floor does need to be level, smooth, and cushioned to reduce sound.

For very low-budget studios, low-pile industrial carpet with dense foam padding and dollies with large wheels will work. It's not optimal, but you can get away with it.

Preparing for a Live-to-Tape Production

Keep in mind that even with a simple-to-operate switcher, live switched video is one of the most challenging types of production to manage.

Live-to-tape or live-to-hard-drive production saves time in the editing room, but it takes planning and preparation to make it happen.

For any live production, you'll need to communicate with camera and boom operators to make changes in the moment. So even though studio-in-a-box switchers make things easier, you'll still need a large enough staff to dedicate one person to switching (**FIGURE 5.18**).

FIGURE 5.18 Headsets allow the director to communicate directly with camera operators during multicamera production.

Before you start your shoot, you'll need to prepare all the elements you'd need if you were working in a television studio.

Prepare any prerecorded tape you want to "roll in" to your program with a countdown leader to make it easier to cue up on your switcher (**FIGURE 5.19**).

FIGURE 5.19 Prepare your tape with a countdown leader.

Prepare all the graphics you'll need for the production, including the show's opening and closing credits. You'll also need to produce "lower third" identifiers for each person interviewed in the program (**FIGURE 5.20**). If you want rolling credits, you'll have to prepare them in advance and set them up in your switcher.

Once you start your production, switching live and adding footage and graphics on the fly takes nerves of steel and exquisite timing. Don't expect to master it on your first try. As with all equipment, learning the technology and how to use it is only step one. Using it in creative ways to enhance your productions is your goal.

FIGURE 5.20 Produce "lower third" identifiers for your interviewees.

Study live switched programs on television to get a sense of the kind of timing and the kind of shots that work, and practice recording live to tape and maintaining the footage from all three cameras to give you the option of making adjustments during editing, for editing adjustments, before you attempt live production with or without a studio.

The Set

There are many peculiarities to designing a set. One of the things you'll need to keep in mind is that reflective surfaces can cause hot spots. Colors may also read differently under studio lights so you'll need to test all the materials you plan to use on camera.

Drapes help to muffle sound and provide a neutral background for your set. Order black velvet drapes in standard lengths or from a broadcast or theater-supply company. Custom sizes are more expensive. Make sure they've been treated with flame retardant. Lights get hot, and you don't want to go up in smoke.

Building a stage or bringing in risers will put your cameras eye to eye with your talent sitting on stage, rather than forcing camera operators to bend down. You can purchase risers that can be bolted together and configured to meet your needs and are strong enough to hold a car (**FIGURE 5.21**). This will give you much more flexibility than building a stage. You can also rent similar equipment, but long-term rentals are more costly than buying outright.

FIGURE 5.21 A riser raises seated talent in relation to the camera, providing a better shooting angle and preventing the camera from looking down on the talent. This image shows the construction of a custom made plywood riser for PulverTV.

The carpenter who built the stage for PulverTV (http://pulvervblog.pulver.com/pulvertv.htm) was working on a network news set at the same time. The producers brought in and discarded hundreds of samples to test on camera before choosing the right Plexiglas panels.

When you're shopping for couches, chairs, and any other furniture that will appear on camera, photograph it with a still camera. If it still looks good after a few days, go back with a light and video camera to make sure it still works.

Not all chairs work; many couches are disasters. Make sure any seating is firm and discourages on-camera talent from slouching or sitting sloppily. Get help with the design of any set pieces you have built and test them on camera as they're built to make sure they're right.

Lighting

I suggest you use C-stands (**FIGURE 5.22**) to support your lights. They're heavy enough to stay upright, they're inexpensive, and they extend very high. The alternative is to build a lighting grid, or hang simple pipes for your main lighting. But that's not an option unless you're ready to do construction and have the ceiling height to handle a grid. Use sand bags to keep C-stands stable after you mount heavy lights on them, and consider getting at least one stand mounted on wheels to make adjusting lights easier.

Special fluorescent lighting designed for video keeps things cool, which is a big help. Unless you're planning to redo all your air conditioning, you may be forced to turn it off during shooting. C-stands with arm extensions and a few heavy-duty clamps that will hold lightweight Fresnels will give you flexible lighting options. Find a way to plug your light in that doesn't require draping cables over the floor, a real impediment to camera movement. I had an electrician mount outlets in the studio's drop ceiling so I could use lights with AC plugs that could also be carried into the field. Lights designed for lighting grids need to be wired in to your electrical system.

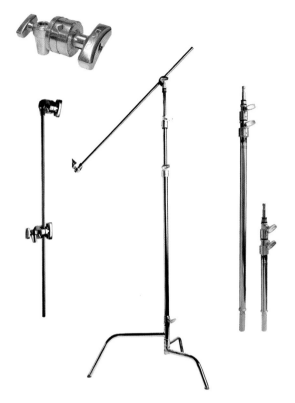

FIGURE 5.22 C-stands and attachments provide a sturdy support system for lights. Add sandbags to the base when using heavy lights.

Take advantage of existing light. Although most studios use entirely electric light, mine happened to have a wall of windows fitted with double-pane glass for quiet and blackout shades that could be raised so the windows functioned like they do in an artist's studio. For quick daytime interviews, I often supplemented daylight with daylight-balanced tungsten or fluorescent lights. This works only for short takes, however, because sunlight is a very unreliable source, as any cinematographer will tell you.

Studio lighting is an art form. If you need one setup that you'll use again and again, hire a pro to advise you. Good lighting can make you (or your talent) look like a Hollywood actor.

If you're lighting the set yourself, adjust your lights to make sure all the shadows fall on the floor. Each person you're lighting will need a key light and some fill. Sometimes, depending on your setup, the spillover from one person's key light can fill someone else on set.

The larger your light source, the softer your light will be. Soft light is flattering and casts fewer shadows (**FIGURE 5.23**).

For the PulverTV studio, I used a pair of four-tube fluorescents with diffusion as my main lights. I recommend fluorescents because they run cool and keep your talent comfortable and your studio bearable for your crew. You'll get fewer shadows and softer light.

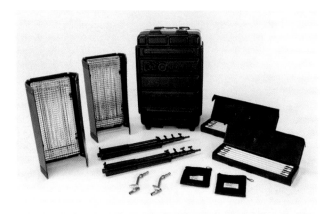

FIGURE 5.23 Broadcast studios use Kino-Flo fluorescents to provide flattering soft light. I used this kit both in the studio and on location.

You can also use Fresnel-style tunsgten lights, then add diffusion using gels scrims or umbrellas. They run hotter, but they're cheaper to buy. Barn doors will help you focus and direct your light. Barn doors made for Fresnels come in different shapes. Each controls light in its own way.

Gels provide subtle shifts in color or changes to the color temperature of light. It's common to use a pale orange gel on daylight lamps to match tungsten lights. Tungsten light gives people a warm, healthy glow (**FIGURE 5.24**). Daylight is bluer and colder-looking and matches sunlight.

The most common mistakes beginners make with light are flooding talent with too much light and using harsh, unflattering light. The best lighting directors paint with light using a number of tools to control it. These include flags and cutters to block light where it's not needed and specialized lights to add it where it is.

Cookies are another tool for shaping light and creating interesting light patterns. A recent public televison interview program created a silhouette of a large tree behind experts being interviewed. Cookies are placed in front of a light to create a shadow pattern.

FIGURE 5.24 Tungsten light gives people a warm, healthy glow.

Gobos are patterns that fit into a special light to project an image. A common pattern looks like the effect of sunlight shining through Venetian blinds on a wall (FIGURE 5.25). You'll recognize the effect from street advertising, where logos are often projected on the sidewalk. These can be specially designed with your logo or purchased in star patterns or a variety of designs.

FIGURE 5.25 Gobos are used to shape light. Often, custom-cut gobos project the title of a show on the background. Rosco Colorizer gobos are shown here, combined with steel gobos to provide shape and additional texture.

Create a Booth for Interviews at an Event

If you're shooting interviews at a conference or event, you'll need both the flexibility to go mobile and a location for interviews where you know the lighting and background are good and you can get good sound. Here is a list of some of the equipment I use at trade shows:

▶ I use two Kino Flo Diva lights, four bank fluorescents that come with their own rolling carrying case, and a Lowel Pro-Lite on a clamp for the backlight.

- If you can get C-stands from the event's AV department or from a rental house, it will save you from having to carry or ship heavy stands and sandbags. Weighting your lights down is important to make them safer in environments where there is a lot of traffic.

- A tripod and dolly with large wheels

- Tall stools with backs for guests let you remain standing. Director's chairs tend to invite bad posture, which looks bad on camera.

- Two lavalier microphones. Wired mics discourage talent from walking away with them.

- No matter how carefully you describe what you need, the venue or conference company will come up with shiny reflective signs and backdrops that don't work on camera. Bringing along a can of artist's spray wax can add a matte finish to shiny signs. Still, you're better off bringing your own background, which can be cloth stretched over a frame to get rid of all the wrinkles or a wide roll of photographic background paper.

- You'll also need a heavy-duty extension cord and a large roll of gaffer's tape to tape it down if you're not near an outlet.

- Reflectors, diffusion gel for your lights, and flags to block light from reflecting off glasses.

Decide how you're going to use your tape before you start shooting. If you know you'll be using only short takes to promote next year's event, ask short man-on-the-street-style questions and keep respondents standing. That way, they're less likely to give an extended answer. Keep a list of the people you interview and get business cards. This will help you to spell their names correctly and provide accurate titles for lower-third graphics.

TIP Once, a helpful marketing person insisted on setting up my interviews in a Plexiglass booth. It didn't block noise and was hot, claustrophobic, and quickly abandoned. Select an open space for your interviews.

Plan in advance what to do if asked for a copy of your tape. This will save you a lot of grief. Almost nobody wants raw footage. It will take you time to copy and output it as a DVD which is what they often want, and it's often a thankless job. Say no nicely or direct them to the appropriate department in your company so someone can decipher what they want and attach an appropriate charge. This discourages most requests. If you're an independent and want to make extra cash, come up with a price list for your services and give it to them on the spot to seal the deal.

Replacing a Background Using a Green Screen

Shooting green screen or chroma key is a special effect that lets you stage action in front of a specially designed background and then make the background transparent and replace it with another image. It can be a cost-effective option for producing a visually interesting program (**FIGURE 5.26**).

FIGURE 5.26 Balance the light on your subject with the light in the background image. Effective keying depends on good lighting.

Virtual sets don't look real, but they can be a lot of fun. You can also key in video textures or backgrounds from a graphics package, but it's not as easy as kits you can buy online make it seem.

Run tests with your software before shooting green-screen video that will be compressed for the Web, and be prepared to spend more time while formatting and compressing your footage for distribution to get it right. (There are some known problems with compositing HDV footage in some formats.)

NOTE Chroma key, also known as *green screen* or *compositing*, is a color replacement process that removes one color from your image and replaces it with another image.

There are two kinds of green screens. The first is traditional blue or green color replacement or chroma key. The second is a new kind of screen that appears gray to the eye but is embedded with tiny glass balls. Reflecmedia (**www.reflecmedia.com**) produces these specialized screens, called Chromatte, which are usually sold with an LED ring light that fits around your camera's lens. The package is more expensive than traditional green screens; it costs about $2,200 for the background, light ring, and adapters.

Traditional green screens require flat lighting and must always be lit very evenly. Look for one made of a stretchy fabric with a spring edge or that you can attach to light stands or a frame with clamps. Screens without a foam or stretch background often appear wrinkled, and sometimes this causes extra shadows that disturb the effect.

Green-Screen Shooting Tips

Once you get lighting and backdrops right, you do most of the work in post-production (**FIGURE 5.27**). There are a few things to keep in mind when you're shooting.

▶ Keep your talent at least 3 feet from the screen. This will help avoid *spill*, a green glow on your talent reflected from the screen.

▶ Don't plan to use blue backgrounds and blue color replacement keying with any talent who has blue eyes or is dressed in blue clothes.

▶ Use traditional methods of lighting your talent. Lighting is the most important consideration for shooting in front of a green screen. You'll need to light the green screen separately from your talent. Make sure you use a backlight to help separate your talent from the background.

▶ Keep stray hairs and shaggy fabrics to a minimum; they create difficult edges to work with in post-production. Your green-screen or editing software will do the heavy lifting with the time comes to replace the background of your shot and, if all goes well, provide you with a nice clean key.

FIGURE 5.27 When lighting for greenscreen, use 3-point lighting and add additional lighting for the background.

Shoot a Commentary Using a Green Screen Background

To begin, scan a horizontal postcard or snapshot and save the file as a TIFF or JPG using your image-editing software (such as Photoshop). For this project, you'll super-impose your talent using the postcard as a background. To work best, green screens need to be smooth. So, stretch yours, and tape it to a wall or clamp it to a background stand if you have one.

First you'll light your green screen. The lighting needs to be flat and even for the effect to work. Use large soft light sources like four-bank fluorescents or tungsten lights with softboxes or chimeras.

FOR THIS PROJECT, YOU'LL NEED:

- A green-screen background
- Lights both for the green screen and for your subject
- Camera on tripod
- Talent to act as a host
- Lavalier microphone
- A scanner and a photo or a digitized photograph
- A broadband connection and computer to download software

Position your talent at least three feet away from the green screen. The distance is important to create a realistic depth effect and to prevent the green light from reflecting onto your talent.

Light your talent separately from the green screen using three-point lighting and make sure he or she is not wearing green clothing or contact lenses. Anything green will disappear along with the background.

Mic your talent, and shoot a 90-second commentary. A good choice of topic is something that really bugs you and why. For example, "I really hate back-seat drivers because they distract me while I'm driving."

Frame your shot with your end background in mind. Decide whether your talent will sit or stand, and frame her for the best effect with your background. If she is sitting, consider draping green screen fabric over the chair to make it disappear when keyed. Look at the image you plan to use. If it is an outside scene, you may want to gel your lights for a daylight color temperature rather than tungsten for a better match.

Shoot your commentary. Change angle and focal length (zoom in or out), and shoot it again is when you review the footage in post-production, you'll see which is better.

Download a demo of green-screen software from the Web. Adobe's Visual Communicator Pro, developed by Serious Magic, is a good one. Final Cut and Premier also include "keying" effects as part of their effects palattes. In the next chapter, you'll compare the results you get using dedicated green-screen software to those you generate with the effects palette of your editing program.

Shoot a Talk Show–Style Interview with Three Cameras

Shoot a five-minute interview using three cameras. Not all the cameras have to be the same. If you have two similar cameras, use the third for an unmanned wide shot. Arrange the cameras as shown in **FIGURE 5.28.**

Make sure you white balance all three cameras after your lighting is set. Designate one camera as the primary one for your sound. Outfit the host and interviewee with lavaliere microphones. Feed both mics into one camera using a mixer or microphone adapter.

FOR THIS PROJECT, YOU'LL NEED:
- Three video cameras on tripods
- Headphone
- Two lavalier microphones
- Microphone adapter
- Three lights
- Background
- Slate

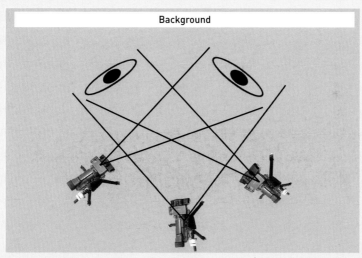

FIGURE 5.28 For your three-camera interview, arrange the cameras to cover the action on set fully.

Record sound on your remaining cameras as a reference track. Use a slate to identify a sync point for all three cameras. If you don't have a slate, have your host clap once loudly or clap two pieces of wood together within view of all three cameras after they are rolling.

Designate an angle for each of your two main cameras. Don't forget to record at least 30 seconds of silence before you cue your host with a countdown to start talking.

Record the interview. Instruct your camera operators to pay attention to what's being said and to zoom in slowly when things get interesting. Remind them to shoot cut-ins of hands, products, or other details while the person on their camera is listening.

Don't forget to label your tapes, identifying each camera and its subject in your notes; save them for editing in Chapter 6.

CHAPTER 6

EDITING & POST PRODUCTION

Attention is the most important commodity on the Web. If your video is boring, too long, or too confusing, viewers will click away. Editing makes your video more compelling to watch and more likely to command a viewer's interest for the duration of the clip. To get your audience's attention and keep it, you'll need to make hard decisions during editing about what footage to keep and what to discard. Make it easy for your viewers to get the most from your work by shortening it and breaking it into shorter segments. Before you put your work out for the world to see, get a second opinion, or rest and look at it through a fresh pair of eyes.

The mechanics of editing include arranging individual shots in a sequence; trimming or shortening your work; adding transitions, titles, and graphics; working with effects; and fixing mistakes. Working with sound is a big part of editing as well. Your projects may include voice-over soundtracks, music beds mixed with dialogue, or interviews and natural sound.

Editing shapes and focuses your video into a coherent message or story. Sometimes all that's required is fitting footage into a sequence or cutting out mistakes. But editing can be more complicated, shaping the meaning of your video, and creating dramatic tension. Unscripted projects, such as news packages and documentaries, take form during editing. To manage post production, you'll need to stay organized. What you do and when you do it, from capturing your footage to your computer for editing to outputting in a format for the Web and archiving your footage, is called *workflow*.

Organizing Your Project

When you're working on a short, simple project, it may not seem important to be organized, but as your projects get longer and more complicated, you'll discover that it saves time and stress. Labeling your tapes during shooting is the first step to managing your video. If you were in a rush or added confusing labels while on-site, then before you start editing, give your tapes a project name, a date, and a number. If you have notes about what's on each tape, make sure you add the new tape names to your notes. Use abbreviated but descriptive names like "scifair" for science fair or "firewks" for fireworks. Add a date and a tape number, such as "R-1_scifair_6_2_08" for "reel 1 science fair June 2, 2008." Remember not to use any special characters that will be rejected as file names by your computer.

Post Production Workflow

It takes several steps to get your video out of your camera, edit it, and prepare it for upload to the Web. If you have a large volume of video consider watching it and making notes about what you'll use before capture. Capturing only what you need will save time and hard drive space during editing.

1. Create a folder on your computer for your video project. Most editors store captured video footage on an external hard drive to make editing go more smoothly.

2. Capture the video from your camera to your computer's hard drive using your editing program's capture window. If you're using a hard drive camera, transfer your footage into the project folder on your hard drive.

3. Most editing programs capture footage directly into the project you've created and provide the option to log footage or add notes during capture.

4. If you haven't created descriptive file names during capture, consider renaming your files. Organize your footage and any stills, music, and graphics into bins in your project window.

5. Edit sequences.

6. Add transitions, graphics, and effects.

7. Mix sound.

8. Output in a Web-friendly format.

9. Archive the project for future. Most editors wait several weeks before deleting source footage from their hard drives. If you've been careful about identifying reel names during capture, professional editing software makes it easy to recapture only the footage used in your project for future revisions.

Before you start capturing video to your computer for editing you'll need to decide whether your finished video will use 4:3 frame dimensions or a 16:9 widescreen display. Typically you'll create a project in the format you've shot. Standard DV and HDV are popular for the Web. Many of the newer hard drive cameras shoot in MPEG. Most Web video producers edit full-resolution footage because many projects are short and simple and the storage requirements and system demands of working with the footage won't overwhelm their editing systems. If your projects are longer or more complicated, working "offline"—editing low-resolution copies of your video and then recapturing the final project for output at high resolution—saves time and hard drive space.

What You Need to Know About Editing

Larry Jordan, producer, editor and Apple Certified Trainer

Larry Jordan is more than an extraordinary Final Cut trainer; he's a producer and director with a unique perspective on Web video. Although many believe not much expertise is needed to produce for the Web, Jordan knows better. Video is a highly technical field, he says, where what you don't know will cost you time and money. Jordan also has an interesting take on what motivates people to learn. It's the project—the burning idea that a videomaker just has to get onto film (or tape)—that puts them in the receptive state for learning both the art and the craft of editing.

To edit efficiently, you'll need to learn to use editing software. Classes like those Jordan teaches online at lynda.com (www.lynda.com) are an easy, inexpensive way to learn about your editing software. Each title is broken down into several short QuickTime movies. Each demonstrates in depth how to handle a program's functions. But editing requires more than technical expertise; you'll need to develop your judgment. Take the time to get organized at the beginning of any project, Jordan suggests, by asking yourself a series of questions to help focus your approach:

▶ What do I want to create?
▶ Do I need to create any Photoshop files?
▶ Do I have to create any After Effects (a motion graphics program) work?
▶ Do I just need to shoot this?
▶ Do I need any titles?
▶ Do I have enough hard disk space?

"Decide what the heck are you doing," counsels Jordan. "If you spend just an hour thinking through how you are going to create your project," Jordan says, "things will go better." After you know what you want to create, he says, then you're ready to figure out what you need to know to be able to create it.

"Hollywood makes [production] look easy," Jordan says of production, but cautions that years of experience can make anything look easy. "Many beginners jump into editing for the first time and end up with files all over the place, resulting in frustration. You'll wonder why you got into this business in the first place."

Jordan's most practical advice for managing post production is to get organized. "Organize and plan," he says "that's the most important thing." He also cautions against overusing effects, a temptation for many beginners. "Ignore all effects," he says. Feature films use cuts almost exclusively. "If a feature never used a dissolve, nobody would know the difference," he explains, "and feature films never use wipes. Somehow, the film industry has become a multibillion dollar industry without ever using a single wipe."

It isn't the effects and it isn't the wipes and it isn't these fancy geegaws that get added onto software that will make your video successful; it's the story you're telling, and a story is always told best through cuts. "Get organized, plan what you want to do, capture to your software, cut it together, fade to black, and put it on the Web," he says—which isn't nearly as simple as it sounds.

Is there a rule of thumb for shooting ratios?

It used to be that film was expensive, and the more film you shot, the higher your budget was. So before you rolled your camera, you needed to plan your shots. Since tape is cheap, shooting ratios [minutes of video shot per minute of final edit] of 20, 50, or even 100 to 1 are not uncommon, but this means the director is incompetent. Any director who has to shoot more than 50 to 1 is someone who is not thinking through their shots ahead of time—someone who refuses to plan, who's trying to be "creative" on the set. You're not supposed to be creative on the set; you are supposed to execute. Do all of your pipe dreaming before you go onto the set because otherwise you're simply wasting somebody else's money. It all comes down to planning. Planning is the heavy lifting. Planning is hard; everybody wants to avoid planning because it forces you to think.

A lot of video on the Web includes a lot of talking heads. Should video makers focus on telling stories with pictures, or is the shift to people talking on camera a good thing?

I've found that editing falls into two camps: documentaries and news, which are driven by the story and the audio; and feature films and music video, driven by the visual. If we take a look at any kind of narrative film, it's always told visually, and the audio is there to accentuate the visual. But many documentaries are audio-driven as opposed to visually-driven; because you weren't at the event, you couldn't be at the sinking of the ship, or in that particular battle; you can only talk about it later. Some people are better at thinking visually, and some people are better at thinking aurally. There are stellar examples of both forms.

What's the best way to learn? Should a beginner use Final Cut Express or buy the pro software and learn a little at a time?

As long as you're willing to spend some time planning, I would say you should always learn software as you are trying to accomplish a task, because by needing to accomplish the task you're going to be focused on getting that task done and you're going to be willing to learn how to do what you need for the project. If you just learn because you want to learn it, the information is not going to stick.

Why are training classes important?

A training class gives you exposure to things you might not have thought about, better ways to organize, better ways to use the software. The more important value of training is that it allows you to get questions answered, whether it's face-to-face training or online training. A good trainer should be able to explain concepts to you in ways that are easy to grasp and stick with you. I try to teach through stories, through specific examples, because everyone grabs the information differently.

Your lynda.com training is geared to the beginner and intermediate. Tell me about your advanced courses.

I publish a newsletter in conjunction with Peachpit Press called Edit Well (www. peachpit.com/editwell). It is targeted toward the intermediate and advanced Final Cut editor. Then, twice a year, I do a seminar tour around North America: so I travel to 14 cities and do 4 seminars in each city, providing intermediate and advanced training on Final Cut so people can learn about how to get better organized, learn more about high-def, and learn about the applications.

A lot of people who shoot video say it makes their work better to have someone else edit it.

I think that's very true. There are very few people who are good at everything— good at producing, good at directing, good at editing. One of the benefits of working with a team is you can share creative ideas.

What does it mean to be a professional editor?

A professional is someone who cares about the quality of their work. Cheap dog tricks posted to YouTube may be funny and they may get 500,000 people to watch, but there's no attention to quality, no attention to the message you want to convey. Professional doesn't necessarily mean trained, but a professional is someone who cares about the quality of their work and their craft and cares enough to make it as good as they possibly can within the time they've got.

There are two parts to editing: making decisions and learning the tools that you use to execute the decisions. Which come first when people learn how to edit?

People won't take the time to learn to use a tool until they need it. The purpose of editing is [to answer the questions], how do I tell this story in the time I'm given? What's my story? How do I want to tell it? Start with a story, look at how you can tell it in as concise a way as possible, then polish it.

If all you're doing is a hobby, then the amount of technical information you need is significantly less than you need professionally. There is a certain fundamental level of technology that you need to know to do the job. This is a technological field. If you don't understand the technology you're just setting yourself up for failure.

I get these e-mails every day: "I bought a camera and I want to send my footage over to Discovery Channel or CBS, and they won't accept it." That's because you bought the camera without finding out what they'll accept. We're completely tied into a technical environment where what you don't know does cost you.

Yet there seems to be this idea on the Web that you don't have to know much.

If you look at my e-mails, I'd say there are a lot of people who are clueless and have no understanding of how Web stuff works. They're frustrated because they're trying to put stuff up on the Web, and they're distraught at how bad it looks or how big it is or if it's rejected. I get dozens of e-mails a day from people asking, "What do I have to do to improve the quality of my video?" They have to start at square one and think through the whole process.

Start with what's your final distribution—for example, YouTube. YouTube works on a 4:3 image size. That means you don't want to shoot 16:9 because you're not going to have a full YouTube image. It only deals with 100 MB, so you're not going to be able to upload a four-hour movie. Start with your distribution format; then ask yourself, "What do I need to edit?" Once you know what you need to edit, then you know what you need to shoot. What far too often happens is we get captivated by a sexy camera, buy it, and discover we can't do anything with it because the camera shoots a format that we can't do anything with. In standard-def, we'd pick the camera, and the workflow was well known. In high-def, we have to look at our distribution format, then back into it.

Video-Editing Software

Computer-based video-editing software, sometimes called *nonlinear editing* (NLE) software, represents your project as either a storyboard or a timeline. Each editing program gives you several ways to work. The simplest way is to arrange shots with drag-and-drop editing, much as you do when editing a text document in a word processor. This, however, is not the fastest or most efficient way to edit. Learning the *keystrokes*, or the combinations of keys on your computer's keyboard that access your editing programs' functions, is much faster once you learn them.

The "nonlinear" part of the name refers to the ability to manipulate the sequence of your clips without regard to the order they appeared on the source tape. Linear editing, used for analog video and film, requires a different approach to editing that is more difficult for beginners to learn.

In addition to editing software, you'll need a photo editor such as Photoshop or Photoshop Elements for your post-production work. Most of what you'll need to do on the audio side you can accomplish in your editing software, but you may find that the best bargain is to buy an integrated post-production bundle, such as Adobe Production Premium or Apple Final Cut Studio, that also includes sound editing, motion graphics, and DVD-authoring software.

Most editing software is fairly similar. Learn one program fully. It will speed your transition if you have to change to another later. Final Cut Pro, for example, allows beginners to use Premiere Pro keystrokes when they make the transition to make it easier to acclimate themselves to the Final Cut editing environment.

You can start with simple software and trade up as you need more features. Windows Movie Maker (**FIGURE 6.1**) ships with every Windows operating system. Every Macintosh ships with iMovie. There are also several freeware editing packages you can download from the Web. Most free editing software is very simple and has few features and more limitations. You'll probably outgrow it very quickly.

A cost effective option is to buy a consumer version of professional editing software. Adobe's Premiere Elements and Apple's Final Cut Express (**FIGURE 6.2**) will give you most of the tools you'll need for editing simple projects. In addition, you'll start learning about each product's interfaces and shortcuts. When you trade up, you'll be ready.

Premiere Pro CS3 is available in two configurations: bundled with a DVD/Blu-ray/Flash authoring tool called Encore, a compression tool called Media Encoder, and a direct-to-disk recording and monitoring tool called OnLocation; and in a package

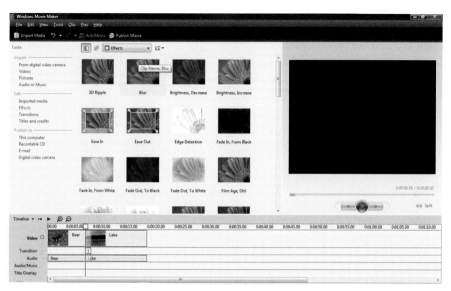

FIGURE 6.1 Windows Movie Maker is a simple video-editing tool that ships with every Windows operating system.

FIGURE 6.2 A consumer version of a pro tool like Apple Final Cut Express will give you much more functionality than a free tool like Movie Maker or iMovie, and when the time comes to move up to Final Cut Pro, you'll be ready.

called Production Premium that adds Photoshop, Soundbooth (audio editing and sound mixing), After Effects (motion graphics), Flash (interactive content), and Illustrator (vector graphics).

Final Cut Pro, formerly available as a stand-alone program, is now sold only as part of the Final Cut Studio bundle that includes Motion (motion graphics), Soundtrack Pro (audio editing and mixing), LiveType (titling), Color (color grading), Compressor (video compression), and DVD Studio Pro (DVD authoring).

If your aspirations include producing broadcast-quality video or selling your work to commercial media organizations, these packages may include tools you'll need. The packages can also streamline your work. Adobe Production Premium, for example, allows you to work on Premiere Pro projects in After Effects, and vice versa, without requiring you to render the file or leave either application; Final Cut Studio offers similar seamless "round-tripping" capabilities between Final Cut Pro and Live Type, Soundtrack Pro, and Motion.

Avid, a well-known provider of professional editing solutions scaling all the way up to broadcast news and feature films, recently stopped producing Avid Express, instead reducing the price of Avid Liquid, its low-end professional package. If your goal is to work in a large professional organization, consider learning Avid. It includes all the major features of Final Cut and Premiere, including multicamera editing. Some of Avid's features are less drag-and-drop user-friendly than popular consumer-oriented software, but it features a robust file management system. It is used by large operations such as television stations with many divisions and multiple offices because it scales well for use with servers, enabling teams to share work on projects seamlessly.

It takes time to learn all the features of your editing software. But once you learn the basics, you'll be able to start editing. Many projects require only simple cuts and transitions. I recommend you invest in a tutorial to learn the basics and regularly add new skills to your arsenal. There are many DVDs and books that teach you how to use these products. Lynda.com (www.lynda.com) features excellent online tutorials for many software packages. Monthly registration is quite reasonable. Highly skilled instructors explain how to use software from the basics to advanced skills by narrating as they navigate the software interfaces on your screen. You can view samples of the QuickTime movie tutorials free on the Web site. Learning this way is faster and much less painful than figuring it out on your own.

Steps for Editing Video

1. Make a plan for managing your media. Start by identifying hard drives where you will store captured files and choosing a naming convention for media files and source tapes.

2. Choose a format to edit in based on your source material and planned output format.

3. Create a project in your editing software. Identify project settings including a scratch disk where your captured files will be stored.

4. Log and capture or transfer the video to your computer.

5. Import it into your editing system.

6. Organize clips into folders, or *bins*.

7. Edit video into sequences to create a rough cut.

8. Fine-tune your edit.

9. Add transitions.

10. Insert titles and graphics.

11. Add voice-over and music beds.

12. Work with audio and video filters and effects including color correction and sound sweetening.

13. Mix sound.

14. Output in Web-friendly format(s).

15. Export a still frame to use as a thumbnail for your video.

16. Archive your project and original source tape for future use.

Building and Editing Sequences

The mechanics of editing and managing workflow are only a small part of an editor's work. Most of what an editor does each day is make decisions. She decides what shot to use, how long to let it run, and how to keep the audience's attention by building in suspense and surprises. Combining shots in an order that tells a story is called *building a sequence*. Even a short video might contain several sequences.

The editing room is where shooting for continuity really pays off. It's easy to shoot a lot of video, but it's not so easy to edit it for the Web without a plan. Many people find that they shoot much more than they can review and edit. A lot of video footage ends up in storage until it's deleted or discarded. You'll always shoot more than you edit. A common shooting ratio is 4:1, that is, four minutes of video shot for each minute used. It can be as high as 10:1 or more for documentaries and news. Shooting footage with the edit in mind helps make the process easier and gives you better and faster results.

Editors select shots and combine them into sequences to tell a story. It's always easier to cut on motion, which is one rule editors follow to combine shots into sequences. That motion might be a pan or another camera movement or motion within the frame. Shooting a variety of shots including cutaways, cut-ins, and transitional shots makes the editor's work easier. Handing an editor an interview shot in one long take with no variation limits her options to making rough assemblies or to stringing together sound bites with jump cuts—the crudest form of editing.

Knowing What to Cut

In its simplest form, editing video for the Web is taking out the bad parts, keeping the good, adding titles effects and transitions, and outputting it in a Web-friendly format. You can speed the shot selection process along by taking notes during shooting or during capture when you transfer video to you computer. Making notes before or during capture is called *logging* your footage. Most editing software includes options for making notes during capture, but you may find it easier to review your footage before capture and make notes of the timecode that identifies the selected sequences.

Typing timecodes into your software's capture window or formatting your list in advance and importing it makes batch capture (capturing multiple selected clips instead of the whole tape) possible. During batch capture, editing software captures the footage you select and imports it into your project. You specify a naming system to identify each shot when you set up the batch capture.

Editorial judgment and editing style develop with experience. If you give two seasoned editors the same footage, they'll likely cut it quite differently. Until you develop a distinctive style, discard anything that doesn't help you tell the story and put together footage in a way that keeps it interesting for viewers and doesn't confuse them. Start with the shape and format of a project in mind. Remember your editing creates an experience for viewers. Showing a whole event may not be the best strategy for your project. You'll often discover that even the people you're shooting for won't have time to review all the footage prior to editing. Selecting key events or footage to tell the story makes it not only shorter but more interesting.

Timecode Basics

If you're working with a digital video camera, the camera records timecode, which identifies each frame as you shoot. You can set your camera to drop-frame or non-drop-frame timecode. Drop-frame timecode is frame-accurate and is often used for broadcast projects. You won't need drop-frame for Web video. But your footage will appear in drop-frame if it was shot that way.

Frame-accurate describes the process by which the video runs at 29.97 frames per second for broadcast. Running at 30 frames per second, the video would lose 3.6 seconds each hour. To represent the footage accurately, the software drops frame numbers every 66 2/3 seconds.

When you look at your footage in your project window, footage shot in drop frame will be represented with semicolons between the hours, minutes, seconds, and frames, (HH;MM;SS;FF or 01;42;03;29). Non-drop frame footage is represented with colons in between, 01:42:03:29.

Most video shooters learn with experience that it improves their work to have someone else edit it. There's a phenomenon of falling in love with footage that was difficult to shoot or felt important while shooting. An editor will look at your work with cold clarity. When it works to tell the story, they'll use it; when it doesn't, it's history.

If you're cutting your own work, identifying clear goals for your project will focus it and help you decide what to keep and what to discard. If it's a long event or variety show, ask your client whether there are specific parts of the program important to documenting the event. You'll still want to look for really colorful visual or dramatic footage. Keep your eye out for happy accidents, a graceful recovery from a mistake, a good response from the audience, or a change in the program. Often producers make decisions about what to leave in and cut out, leaving editors to execute them.

As a young assistant film editor, one of my jobs was to keep track of each scrap of film by numbers printed on its edge. Organizing the edit required cataloging footage in large, loose-leaf volumes that included notes on continuity and often transcripts of dialogue or—when I was working on documentaries—interviews. Film was stored in boxes and in canvas bins. In a nod to traditional film terminology, the folders in your NLE are called *bins* because they store your video footage.

Compared to the physical process of cutting a film, editing on a computer and staying organized are easy. But you'll still need to put some effort into creating a system for identifying your footage on the hard drive where you capture and store it. You'll also need to create a system for backups and do version control if you reedit a piece for distribution in different formats.

Compressing Time

Compressing time to comic effect is a classic cinema trick that goes back to silent pictures. A new generation of videomakers is creating mashups using footage from video games and television shows. These entertaining compilations are designed for viewers' short attention spans.

7 Minute Sopranos is a popular example. Its creators edited HBO's 77-hour, multi-season *Sopranos* series down to seven minutes and posted it on the Web. When I wrote this book it had 80,000 views. Because HBO executives liked the video they chose not to sue editors Paul Guylas and Joe Sabia, two recent college grads, for unauthorized use of copyrighted footage.

Around the same time, Sony Corporation and Sony Pictures partnered to shorten episodes of their classic TV shows and post them on MySpace. The channel, called the Minisode Network (**www.myspace.com/minisodenetwork**), carries the tag line "The shows you love. Only shorter." Episodes run about five minutes; shows include: *Charlie's Angels, Fantasy Island, The Jeffersons, Ricky Lake,* and *T.J. Hooker.* Honda, the channel's first advertiser, truncated its advertising to eight seconds: a three-second preroll and a five-second ad.

Critics have suggested that the shows, which originally ran about 22 minutes in half-hour time slots with 8 minutes of ads, don't lose much in the editing. Yet the series still feels slow, and it's hard to watch for even 5 minutes. That's probably because simply compressing time isn't enough to keep things interesting. These shows lack the ironic edge of *7 Minute Sopranos*, which uses a music bed and humorous script in counterpoint with skillful editing. Producer Paul Gulyas reportedly wrote the script from memory after seeing each episode seven times. The *New York Times* reports it took Gulyas and Sabia 177 hours to edit the piece in Final Cut Pro before putting it up on YouTube.

The minisodes are a great example of what happens when a corporation imitates what works on the Web: they miss the point. Web viewers may have short attention spans, but that doesn't mean they'll watch anything just because it's short.

I recently shot a how-to video demonstrating barbering skills for a beauty supply company. The shoot took about an hour and resulted in about 40 minutes of tape. I needed to shorten it because the owners wanted to put it up on YouTube; and because nobody wants to look at someone getting shaved for a half hour. The resulting video, narrated by one of the shop's owners, runs a little more than two minutes. It's entertaining, and it's long enough. It wasn't difficult to figure out what to cut—any repeated actions, and anything that didn't move the story forward.

Cooking and home improvement shows often compress time so much participants seem like contestants on the classic television show *Beat the Clock*. Unless you're trying to create a comic effect, find ways to pace your edit that acknowledges the passage of time.

Before you sit down to edit for time, make a list of the key ideas and important footage you want to keep. It's easy to get overzealous while editing and cut out essential elements.

Advancing a Story with Editing

Compressing time is only one of the techniques editors use to tell stories. Video editing is like a language. The full arsenal of editing techniques helps give meaning to the completed video by arranging clips strategically. Depending on how you edit, you can create a tempo or visual rhythm in your video story. Juxtaposing one image against another with a straight cut can create contrast. For example, editing a shot of a mansion to footage of a modest home makes a statement; it might be a simple comparison or a more critical statement depending on context. Editing can also create a sense of excitement. Action sequences combine fast cuts and the movement within shots to create heart-thumping sense of excitement in viewers.

The most familiar form of action sequence is the chase scene. Like many other editing strategies, the chase scene depends heavily on footage shot for continuity. Chase scenes use directional continuity.

The editor's work also includes building another kind of sequence called the montage, which breaks an action into a series of small steps and reassembles it. One of the best-known montages is the shower scene in Alfred Hitchcock's 1960 thriller *Psycho*.

Keeping Video Short for the Web

Advertisers have made a science of understanding what viewers will and won't watch. They track how long viewers watch and even what they look at onscreen. Although there's no way to create a foolproof formula for what will engage viewers and what will bore them, keeping your work visual and lively during editing will help keep viewers watching.

If you're working on a show or a series, you'll start out knowing how long the finished video should be and how much time you'll need to leave for titles, credits, and advertising. When you're creating your own show, it's up to you to shape it to meet the needs of your project. Break longer or more complicated subjects into shorter, digestible chunks for delivery over the Web. Using a video player that cues up the next segment and plays it automatically will help maintain continuity for your viewers.

Most user-generated Web video runs between two and five minutes. Video hosts like YouTube limit either the length or the file size of your video. Because you'll want to keep your quality as high as possible and that requires bandwidth (which means larger file sizes), you'll need to keep your video for YouTube short. Each video host publishes guidelines and limits on file size. YouTube, for example, limits videos uploaded through its simple single-video upload to 10 minutes or 100 MB.

But it also offers another option that can give you a little more flexibility. Windows users can download and use the YouTube uploader (http://youtube.com/multifile_installer), which gives you the option of uploading multiple files at once. It also lets you post larger files. Each upload is limited to 10 minutes and 1 GB.

Techniques for Video Storytelling

A good edit creates a beginning, middle, and end for your video. It introduces and resolves conflict and shapes what is called the *story arc*. You don't have to create fancy montages or use loads of effects to shape a story; often using simple cuts that juxtapose one piece of footage against another will give your story shape and dramatic impact.

When the story is not a scripted drama (often called narrative film), you'll need to be clear about its message to edit effectively. Does your footage showing the floor of a trade show depict a fast-growing industry or one in decline? Is your interview with an aging actor marking his swan song, or does it signal the start of a new phase in his career? Is the intersection you're shooting dangerous or pedestrian-friendly?

Video always shows viewers something about your subject. It can be a point of view that's critical or adoring. It can focus on flaws or celebrate beauty. Each piece of footage tells a story. Editing can enhance that story or combine images is a way that conveys something entirely different. Most of the time your work will be to focus and clarify the message, rather than subvert it (**FIGURE 6.3**).

FIGURE 6.3 Adobe Premier Pro lets you organize your shots as a storyboard.

The main ways you'll achieve this is by introducing details, including reaction shots, that give viewers more information about your story. If your video is about a boy playing with his dog, you'll want to show the relationship between boy and dog. Does the dog obey commands or rebel? Is the relationship friendly or is the boy afraid of the dog? You'll show viewers the boy giving a command, then show the dog's action and the boy's reaction. If the dog snarls and barks we look to the boy's reaction to see if he's afraid or going along with a game. If the boy calls and the dog doesn't respond we know that the dog, not the boy, is in control of the situation. If there is another person with a dog nearby, the camera can compare the behavior of the two dogs.

Everything you want to communicate is shown or said in a series of very specific details. Combining selected images creatively to create a sequence that communicates your message clearly is the editor's job. Technology can make this process easier and faster, but the thinking behind each choice makes it better.

Continuity Shapes the Story

It's up to the editor to make sure the ideas or message of the video come through loud and clear. Establishing visual continuity will help you make sure viewers can follow along. During editing you'll organize and combine footage shot for continuity in a sequence. Many amateurs don't shoot with continuity in mind, then when they get into the editing room, they don't understand why the footage won't cut together into the sequence they have in mind.

The best way to ensure continuity during editing is to sketch out your sequence in the form of a storyboard before shooting, as described in Chapter 5. That way, when it's time to edit, you'll have what you need. Editors often complain that directors want them to edit a film they never actually shot. The technique used by editors working on big-budget Hollywood films is to watch the footage shot daily and remind directors if anything is missing. That way, the director can reshoot or fill in the gaps. Hollywood directors also have script supervisors on set whose sole job is to keep an eye on continuity. Most Web video shoots aren't that long or well-staffed, so planning ahead is your best strategy. If the footage you're working with wasn't shot with visual continuity in mind, your job will be more difficult in the editing room.

The Language of Editing

Any series of shots can be put together in many different ways. That's why it's important to vary camera angle and focal length while you're shooting to give your editor choices. An editor presented with an interview shot in one long take and shot from the same angle doesn't have many choices, except to keep it short or use as much of the interview as possible in voice-over if she can get stills or cover footage to add visual interest. If your cameraperson was shooting for continuity, you'll have long shots, medium shots, and close-ups to tell your story. You'll also have the cut-ins, cutaways, and transitional shots that you'll need as the editor to complete your story.

As a storytelling medium, video has its own language that, like written language, has its own syntax. When you combine shots to create a sequence, certain shots and combinations of shots have come to mean very specific things to viewers. The most overused of these become clichés and have lost the freshness and visual impact they once had. But there are many other more subtle conventions used in video storytelling that you don't even notice when they work well. They're transparent to the viewer because they carry the action along so effectively they don't jolt the eye into noticing them.

The opposite is true of jump cuts. They call attention to themselves because they jolt the eye. Watching classic film on video or DVD is a great way to study continuity. But because the editor's work often seems seamless, you'll learn best by identifying an interesting scene and watching it in slow motion. Train your eye to look for the cuts and see how they work. Then try some of the techniques you like.

The visual language of editing speaks to the part of our brains that understands images, not words. You can say a lot with images; for example, you can show what caused something to happen or make it appear as if one thing led to another. You can show relationships between people by showing small actions like the touch of a hand or a facial expression. Or you can use a sequence of shots to show details and give the audience information about a place or a time in what are called *establishing sequences*. One of the most interesting uses of images is to create visual metaphors. When we say a deadline is "looming large"—a phrase I've been using a lot lately—it's a play on words that describes how we see things. As things get closer, they seem larger. With images, we can show a clock seeming to slow down or speed up. Like any language, visual language and editing for continuity take time to learn, and there are a lot of clichés to watch out for. You'll know them because, like calendar pages falling away to simulate the passage of time, they'll make you want to groan.

Using Transitions

Use straight cuts whenever you can when editing for the Web. Video editors often use what they call *soft cuts* to smooth transitions. These are actually two- or three-frame dissolves. All dissolves smooth transitions, but they're harder to encode and require large file sizes to look good on the Web. This means it will take longer for your video to download and play, and on sites with file size limitations, it will limit the duration of the video you're allowed to upload.

Fancy wipes and transitions seldom add much to your video. Keep them to a minimum, and don't make the beginner's mistake of using every transition in your toolbox in one edited piece. Get the impulse out of your system by editing a joke reel for your kids, who will be delighted by all the shapes and movement, and then move on.

Transitions should always be motivated by some aspect of the story you're telling in your video. For example, a transition might signify the passage of time, a significant change in location, or a change in the pace of the action. In all other instances where there's not a specific reason for a transition, use a cut.

Two key transitions that are useful are fade-up from black and fade to black. Nothing says "that's all, folks" like a fade to black. There are also times when a fade to white works. It's a common metaphor for death in movies—"Go into the light, darling." Use it only if and when it works.

Designing Titles and Graphics

When it comes to titles and graphics that open and close your video or identify a new speaker, time, or location, choose a style and stick to it. You can use full-screen titles, overlays, lower-thirds, crawls, and rolls. Most editing software includes simple tools for creating titles (**FIGURE 6.4**) and templates you can customize. They'll also allow you to save titles you've created so you don't have to reinvent the wheel when you want to replicate a particular style.

FIGURE 6.4 Creating titles in your NLE's title window is almost as easy as word processing.

Your title window will include lines indicating the title-safe areas for broadcast or DVD projects. You can ignore it for the Web. You won't lose anything. Choose fonts for any text that appears onscreen carefully. Traditionally, lower thirds (the text appears on the lower third of the screen identifying a person being interviewed) and titles use sans serif fonts. Fonts such as Arial and Futura have fewer fine lines, or *serifs* (the tiny hooks on the end of characters), which makes them easier to read onscreen.

Opening sequences and title packages that come with your software may be over-used and too familiar to Web audiences. If you opt to use them, change them or adapt them in interesting ways to make your video distinctive.

Editing Sound

Sound is one of the key elements that distinguishes amateur video from profes-sional. Once you've recorded good-quality sound, you'll have many options for working with it during editing. Bad-quality sound limits your options. One of the biggest problems is sound recorded at too low a level. If you crank up the volume during post-production, you also increase the level of noise, which can be distract-ing to viewers. Although there are many filters and effects that can change sound, they will seldom fix a badly recorded original.

Sound editing can change viewers' perceptions about what is going on in a video. A scene of a man waking up with a track that includes traffic noise, for example, gives a very different impression than if the track contains birds chirping and the sound of a lawn mower.

Your soundtrack will appear synchronized to the video it was shot with by default in your editing program's timeline. But you can separate video from audio, or even remove a track for use as a narration in another part of your video, or you can replace the sound with effects or a mixed track that includes music. One common sound-editing trick is called an *L-cut*, where sound from one source is heard under an adjoining cut before or after the accompanying picture is seen (**FIGURE 6.5**).

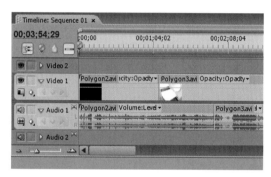

FIGURE 6.5 An L-cut in Premiere Pro. Notice how the audio clip extending into the next video clip makes an *L* in the timeline.

You'll also have the option to represent your sound as a waveform in some programs, which can be helpful during editing. When you represent your audio as a waveform, it's easier to see breaks in the sound and shifts in the audio levels (**FIGURE 6.6**).

FIGURE 6.6 An audio track represented as a waveform.

You'll use your NLE to edit sound much as you do picture by cutting out segments and creating transitions. Built-in effects include filters to remove noise from audio, transitions such as crossfades, and sound-equalizing tools.

Adding tracks to your sequence for sound effects or music tracks is easy. Editing programs include tools for editing the volume in a clip separately from the volume of the overall track. Adding key frames to track volume is one way to control it for output (**FIGURE 6.7**).

FIGURE 6.7 Key frames showing change in volume on the audio track.

Most Web video is delivered in mono, so it's a good idea to mix down your tracks after editing to a single track. First you'll want to make sure you've adjusted the volume of your clips and tracks to your satisfaction. When you output your video, you can have your NLE mix all your tracks down to one. To take more control over the process, use the mixer built in to your NLE (**FIGURE 6.8**). The mixer includes both manual and automated tools for mixing.

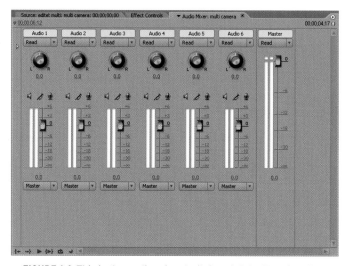

FIGURE 6.8 This is the audio mixer built into Adobe Premiere Pro.

You can also use Premiere Pro's mixer to record voice over tracks directly into your computer using your sound card's microphone input.

Some Premiere Pro production bundles include a separate audio-editing tool called Soundbooth that includes advanced features for editing sound, including audio filters and a visual interface for fixing common problems such as hisses, pops, and rumbling noises. Final Cut Pro ships with Soundtrack Pro 2, a suite of tools for audio post-production (**FIGURE 6.9**). Some of the advanced features in Soundtrack Pro include tools for matching double-system sound to picture tape–style scrubbing, allowing you use your cursor to locate specific points in your sound manually, and visual interfaces showing fades and transitions and 5.1 surround sound mixing.

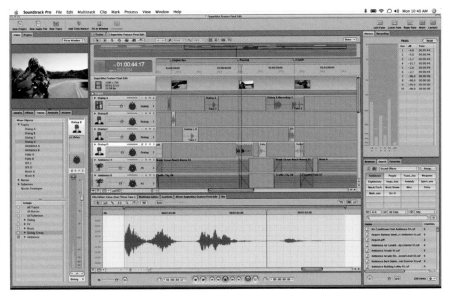

FIGURE 6.9 Apple Soundtrack Pro 2, the audio-editing application that ships with Final Cut Pro in the Final Cut Studio 2 suite.

You Can't Always Fix It in Post

Things on videotape don't always look the way they do in real life. With skill and planning, they can look better. Without effort, they often look worse. If your goal is to represent your subject as attractive, interesting, or desirable, you'll have to work at it during both production and post-production.

There is a common notion that everything from bad lighting to bad sound can be fixed during post-production. That just isn't true. There are some things you just can't fix with the filters and other corrective tools in your video editor or any sound-editing package or color-grading tool that comes with it. That said, these software tools can make a difference if you take the time to master them.

Color correction is an art form not easily learned. The most immediate challenge with color correction is that trusting your eyes (and your equipment) doesn't always work. Be careful about making corrections by eye if your monitor is not calibrated for video color. Macintosh computers and PCs interpret color differently, and you'll need to straddle the line. But color correction tools used properly can be quite effective. For example, minor changes can improve the look of video shot under office-grade fluorescents, or it can balance the color between two shots.

Fixing sound during editing is even harder. The more sophisticated your editing software is, the more options it will offer. Most of these options are copied or adapted from the analog tools. Taking a trial-and-error approach to working with audio filters is time-consuming, and the results can be disappointing. That's another reason to start out with the best picture and sound possible.

When you can, work around mistakes like a not-so-smooth pan by using a cut or a well-placed dissolve. This also works if there is an embarrassing problem during the event you are shooting. Just because there was a long wait for the live audience when a demo doesn't work smoothly doesn't mean you have to replicate it for your viewers, unless you're showing a glitch from the event to make a point.

Making people look good on video sometimes means using a medium close-up instead of an extreme close-up. If that doesn't solve the problem or if a medium shot isn't available, sometimes softening or blurring a shot slightly is more flattering. This is traditionally done in-camera using filters, but digital editing tools also provide these options. Keep the eyes in focus so your footage doesn't look like bad camera work. And don't overdo it.

NOTE Some video hosts like Brightcove provide tools for compressing your video and uploading it. Your video will look better online if you follow instructions and use the recommended settings.

Pay attention to the soundtrack, and keep your ears open for noise and dropouts in sound you capture on location. Sometimes in the process of editing you can fix a speaker's nervous tics like repeating "OK?" or "You know?" at the end of every sentence, but make sure this works for the overall edit. Also check your edits to make sure the continuity works and the speaker still makes sense. Whenever you finish applying an effect, save your project.

The final step of editing is to output in a format friendly to your video host. You'll need to understand a little about compression and format choices first, so be patient—I'll talk about that in the next chapter.

Edit a Simple Sequence

I n this project, you'll create a simple sequence with your editing software using straight cuts. Use at least one long shot, one medium shot, and one close-up. Choose the order that works for your video and that will make sense to a viewer. Use footage you shot for your how-to sequence in Chapter 4, *Videoblogs, How-to Videos, and News*, or any combination of shots that will give you a variety of focal lengths to work with.

FOR THE PROJECT, YOU'LL NEED:

- Computer
- Editing software
- Footage shot for one of the exercises in Chapter 4 or 5 that includes at least one long shot, one medium shot, and one close-up
- Notepad or other text-editing software or a pen and paper

Before you capture your video to your computer, write one sentence that describes what you will communicate with your sequence. It can be as simple as "Traffic moves fast on 42nd street," "Many people walk their dogs in the evening," or "It's spring in New York." When you're logging and capturing your footage, choose shots that will help make that statement without words.

After you capture your footage, arrange it on your timeline in the order you think tells the story best. Then try changing the order. Save the version that's most visually interesting and that makes your statement most effectively. After you edit your sequences, save your project.

Formatting for the Web takes several steps. We'll talk about formats and compression in Chapter 7.

PROJECT

Edit a Commentary Shot with Green Screen

When you shoot against a green screen and replace the background, you're actually creating a composite, or multi-layered, video. For this project, you will remove the green background, revealing a still photograph behind your talent. You can just as easily use a green-screen effect with a moving image in the background.

The easiest way to create composite video using footage shot against a green screen is to use the effects built into your editing software. In Premiere Pro, the Effects palette includes several "Key" effects: Blue Screen, Chroma Key, Color Replace, and Green Screen Key. For this project, use Premier. If you don't have a copy, download a trial copy from the Adobe Web site and install it on your computer.

Chroma key, also known as *green screen* and *compositing*, requires two steps: superimposing your green-screen footage on a background image and then removing the green background, leaving transparent areas where the background image shows through. Check whether your software has chroma key or key effects, sometimes also called *replace color* effects. Both Premiere Pro and Final Cut Pro will fit the bill. If your software does not include this feature, download a trial version of Adobe Premiere Pro (**www.adobe.com/products/premiere/?promoid=BONSM**), Adobe Visual Communicator (**www.adobe.com/products/visualcommunicator**), or another green screen program from the Web.

If you just downloaded your chroma key tool, install your software. Then, capture the footage you shot in front of a green screen in Chapter 5, *TV Techniques for Better Web Video*. Scan the image you selected for your green-screen exercise, and save it on your computer in 300 dpi. Import the image into your Premiere Pro project and follow these steps:

1. Drag the background image on to your timeline. Premiere Pro will assign a default length for still images. You can change this using the Edit > Preferences menu. For now, just grab the edge of the still image on your timeline, and drag it to the right to stretch it to three minutes.

2. Drag the green-screen footage to the second video track above your background image.

3. In the Effects palette, select the Video Effects tab, and choose chromakey.

In Premiere Pro, the path is Effects > Video Effects > Keying > Chroma Key, as shown in **FIGURE 6.10**.

FIGURE 6.10 In Premiere Pro, you'll find the Chroma Key function in Effects > Video Effects > Keying.

4. Drag and drop the effect onto your green-screen footage on the timeline.

5. If you're working in Premiere Pro, open the Effects Controls palette, and choose Effects Controls > Chroma Key (**FIGURE 6.11**).

FIGURE 6.11 Make adjustments to your chroma key effect.

6. The first thing you'll need to adjust is the key color for your composite. Click the eyedropper, and sample the green-screen background in your image to set the color. Then use the controls below Color to set Similarity, Blend, Threshold, Cutoff, and Smoothing by sight. You'll be able to see the changes in your program window. Each effect has parameters. Identify the window that shows the adjustments you can make on the effect.

7. Adjust the transparency while viewing the changes in your preview window. And then save your project (File > Save in Premiere Pro).

8. You'll need to render any effect before exporting the completed video. Choose Sequence > Render Work Area to render your effect (**FIGURE 6.12**).

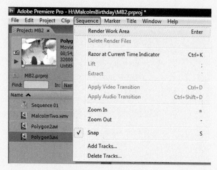

FIGURE 6.12 In Premiere Pro, you can choose Sequence > Render Work Area at any time to render an effect and see how it will look in your final video (before compression, anyway).

Try the same effect using Premiere Pro's Green Screen Key. You'll get a clean effect with less adjustment after you adjust Threshold and Cutoff. You can actually key using any color, but when you use colors other than chroma key green, you're more likely to have difficulty isolating the keying effect.

In Premiere Pro, a red line above any footage in the timeline indicates an effect that has not yet been rendered (**FIGURE 6.13**). Select Render from the Project menu. Render the work area and then save your work. The line above your footage in the timeline should now appear green. Save your project on your computer. You'll format it for upload in the next chapter.

FIGURE 6.13 This timeline shows unrendered footage indicated with a red line.

Edit a Multicamera Interview

Multicamera editing simulates live switching. To edit multicamera footage efficiently, you'll need software such as Adobe Premiere Pro or Final Cut Pro that allows you to import and align multiple video sources from the same shoot and view them in a quad-view display. Select clips from each camera to add to the timeline as if you were switching a live event. If you're using a simple editing package that doesn't have this feature, download a trial version of Adobe Premiere Pro for this exercise.

> **FOR THIS PROJECT, YOU'LL NEED:**
> - Footage shot with three cameras from different angles
> - Editing software with multi-camera edit capability

Follow these steps to edit a multicamera sequence:

1. Capture the first three minutes of your footage from each camera.

> **TIP** If you don't have footage shot multi-camera, you can synchronize any three clips.

2. Select the start point for each clip using the time code or clap from your slate. Make sure the footage you choose includes at least three opportunities for switching camera angles and is no more than five minutes long.

3. Add another video track to your timeline by choosing Sequence > Add Tracks. You should now have three video tracks.

4. Rename your sequence "multi-camera."

5. Select the start points for each clip using the monitor window.

6. Drag each clip onto a separate video track on your timeline, stacking them on top of one another (**FIGURE 6.14**).

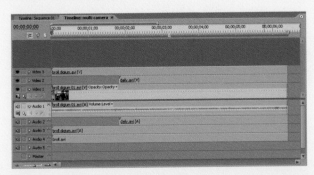

FIGURE 6.14 Arrange clips on separate tracks in the timeline window.

7. Synchronize your clips for editing. Premiere offers three options for synchronizing: at the top of the clip (Clip Start), by time code, and at the end of the clip. Use the Clip Start option for this example.

8. Choose Clip > Synchronize > Clip Start to link the clips together for editing. Save your project.

9. Create a new sequence for your edited video by selecting File > New Sequence. Name your new sequence "Edited Multi," and save your project.

10. Drag your multicamera sequence onto the timeline of your new sequence. It will appear as a clip on your timeline.

11. Select the clip with your cursor and then choose Clip > Multi camera > Enable.

12. Double-click the sequence in the timeline. You should now see all three camera views simultaneously in your monitor (**FIGURE 6.15**). Note your sequence must be selected in the timeline for this to display properly.

FIGURE 6.15 Premiere's Monitor window with clips for multicamera edit.

13. Select your Edited Multi sequence in the timeline.

14. Activate the Multiclip monitor by clicking the arrow next to your program monitor to open the menu. Select Multiclip Monitor (**FIGURE 6.16**).

15. Record your edited program (**FIGURE 6.17**). Activate the red Record button in the Multiclip Monitor, and play the video.

16. Use your mouse to select the clip you want to see at any given time, or use the 1, 2, or 3 key on your keyboard to select the clip you want during editing.

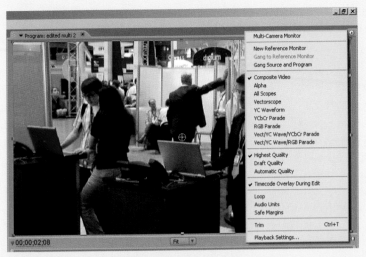

FIGURE 6.16 Open the Multiclip Monitor from Premiere's Program Monitor menu.

FIGURE 6.17 Start recording your multiclip edit before pressing Play.

17. Include audio from one of the clips by selecting "Audio follows video" from the Multiclip Monitor's menu.

18. Record your multiclip edit and play it back. You target sequence, Edited Multi, will be updated to show your edits. To refine your edits, open the Multiclip Monitor, click Record, and make different choices at selected points. Save your project.

If you haven't edited your projects from Chapters 3, 4, and 5, use them to practice editing and create a completed how-to sequence and a project with B-roll. Remember to edit for maximum initial impact by using a highly visual piece of footage or a provocative statement at the top of each video you edit. Be brutal during editing. Cut out anything that doesn't work or isn't interesting. Show your work to a friend, family member, or roommate and ask for honest feedback. Then let your work cool off for 24 hours and try looking at it again yourself as if you were a stranger. Is it still funny, provocative, or informative? If not, recut.

Some projects won't work out, but editing each project you shoot will provide much information that will aid you during future shoots. You'll learn how much you need to shoot, which angles work, and the kind of images that work for B-roll, as well as how to light and record sound more effectively. It's harder to learn from your footage immediately after you shoot it, because you're still excited about the experience. Look at it, log it, and make notes about what's on the tape, but—if at all possible—hold off on editing until you can do it with a cool, dispassionate eye.

We'll use your completed projects in the next chapter to compare the quality of options for displaying your video online.

CHAPTER 7

UPLOADING VIDEO TO THE WEB

7 UPLOADING VIDEO TO THE WEB

Making your video look great online starts with high-quality footage. But unless you understand encoding and work with a video host committed to delivering high-quality video to the public, your footage can end up looking terrible after it's uploaded to the Web. It's frustrating when your footage looks great in your camera and on your computer but somehow during encoding that quality disappears.

In this chapter you'll learn about choices you can make during encoding that will help to keep your video looking and sounding great online. Choosing a video host that delivers high-quality video to the Web is also important. You'll find guidelines for choosing a host and some questions to ask that will help you decide which is the best for your video.

I was reminded just how frustrating uploading to a new host can be when, after many years of success with professional hosts, a client asked me to upload a short video to YouTube. I faithfully followed the guidelines on the Web site, but my video looked and sounded awful on the Web.

TIP There's no one answer to what it takes to get great quality when you compress video for the Web. Each project requires careful consideration and sometimes different solutions for different audiences.

The video host you choose will determine what format you can upload and the quality viewers will see. Some popular hosts compress your video a lot. This not only makes it cheaper for them to send more video over the Web, but it also makes the video accessible to people who connect to the Internet at slower speeds. Delivering high-quality video to Web viewers is more challenging. Some hosts require viewers to download a special player to get the best quality.

NBC permits viewers to download network programs via a hybrid peer-to-peer (P2P) solution (see Chapter 8, *Getting Your Video Noticed*); ABC utilizes a downloadable player from Move Networks that delivers high-quality full-screen video. Advertisements that download in the background look so good you can't take your eyes away.

Compression Changes Everything

You can edit your video and save it for the Web without understanding anything about how compression works. Like the automatic settings on your camera, which work reasonably well in many situations, your video-editing program has default settings for any format you choose. But if you want your video to look really good, you'll need to make a few adjustments.

During compression, your software shrinks your video files so they can travel more easily and more quickly over the Internet. To do this, it throws away information from the files to make them smaller—sort of like jettisoning ballast if your boat or light plane gets into trouble.

Your editing software uses a mathematical equation called a *compression algorithm* to decide which pixels to keep and which to throw out. Stay with me—I'm not going to ask you to do any math here, and you really need to know this to make your video look good. The algorithm is called a *codec*, short for compression and decompression. There are many different codecs. Some have names such as On2's Flash codec or Sorenson's Spark and Squeeze; others are named for the formats they support such as WMV for Windows Media Video, H.264 (an MPEG-4 Part 10 codec), and many others.

Your editing program or encoding software (such as Apple's Compressor or Adobe Media Encoder) does the heavy lifting, compressing your video when you export it as a QuickTime .mov file, a Windows .avi or .wmv file, or a Flash Video .flv file, before you upload it to your video host. The choices you make during output will have a great impact on the way your video looks on the Web, so make them carefully. Often, in spite of all your hard work, your video host will re-recompress your video after you upload it to the Web. Each time your video is compressed, the quality goes down. The overall effect can be like tossing your footage into a blender.

Choosing a Video Host

There's no one video host that's right for every project. Your first concern should be quality. How the video on a host's Web site looks online is determined by decisions that host makes behind the scenes. Choose a host that delivers video in the quality you want your viewers to see. Your next concern should be the audience the host appeals to and reaches. You'll want to compare the host's existing audience with the one you want to reach. To do this, choose the best host for your video. You'll need to be clear about your goals, the audience you want to reach, and the services you expect your host to provide. Start by asking yourself a few questions about your video (**FIGURE 7.1**). Identify the genre or category your video best fits into. There may be more than one. Is it dramatic or documentary, how-to or entertainment, commentary or comedy?

FIGURE 7.1 **Make sure the decision you make about who hosts your video puts you in company with the pros.** *Smart Girls at the Party,* **(cast pictured above) produced by ON Networks® exemplifies the high quality production and distribution now possible on the Web.**

Now, think about your audience. Are they old or young, mainstream or ethnic, tech savvy or tech challenged, cutting edge or conservative? If you've received comments and feedback on your videos, you know something about who's watching. Who you *want* to watch may be a different audience altogether. Identify the target audience you're trying to reach.

If you think about it, there's a reason you make video. It might be to get famous, to get dates, or to share your point of view. But it could just as easily be to sell something or to bring someone around to your way of thinking or just to make them smile.

Now that you've identified a genre, a target audience, and a goal, you'll partner with a host to implement your strategy for achieving your goals. Picking the host or hosts that are right for you is a critical decision, particularly if your plan includes making money from your video. Your host will deliver your video to your audience, but it can provide additional services that will assist you in achieving your goals. Those services may include providing tracking information from your viewers, offering encoding assistance, providing sophisticated file management features (**FIGURE 7.2**), or paying you for videos that bring traffic to the site (**FIGURE 7.3**). That's why it's important to be clear about your needs and honest about your dreams and desires for your video.

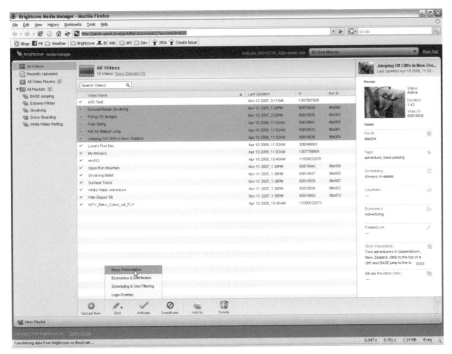

FIGURE 7.2 Brightcove's media manager helps producers with a large volume of content both to keep files organized and to upload video for Brightcove video players.

FIGURE 7.3 ExpoTV is a specialized video host that delivers only how-to videos that review products, and it pays its best producers a small fee.

NOTE You'll find more on choosing a video host and how your host can help you to promote and market your video in Chapter 8, *Getting Your Video Noticed.*

If you want to get famous, distributing your video widely is the right strategy, but if you want to profit, keeping a tight leash on video traffic might serve you better. Be realistic about your skill level when choosing a host. Can you create your own Web page, or do you need help? Would you like to limit who views your video to a select audience? Or perhaps you want to charge viewers to watch—not the best idea in today's Web video market (see Chapter 9, *Making It Pay*), but if that's your goal, you'll need an enterprise-level host to help you manage payments, user passwords, and histories.

Look for these features when choosing a video host:

▶ **Quality.** Your host determines the quality your viewers see as well as the size of the player your viewers can watch.

▶ **Bandwidth.** Viewers connecting at college will certainly have broadband connections; grandparents might need a low-bandwidth or download option.

▶ **Pay vs. free.** Paying a host gives you more control over quality, but if your video gets popular, it may become costly. Some high-quality hosts are willing to provide their service free to you in exchange for a share of advertising revenues.

▶ **The fine print.** Viewers typically don't read terms and conditions, but you should. Know your host's policies, and be clear on the terms stipulated by the contractual relationship you're entering into when you choose a host.

▶ **Strange bedfellows.** Being at the right portal or destination site can help drive traffic to your video. If a site has lots of content that appeals to your target audience, it's probably the right choice.

▶ **Features.** Does your host offer the features you need?

To better understand the kind of services a video host can provide, I'll use video host Magnify.net (**www.magnify.net**) as an example. Magnify.net offers three levels of hosting for delivering your video to the Web: Free, Pro, and Enterprise (**FIGURE 7.4**). CEO Steve Rosenbaum says producers can start with the free service and trade up to offerings that include the features they need as their audience develops. But he warns that if you're looking for advertisers or want to make money on your video, it's worth thinking about that in advance because it's hard to make money after your video is distributed widely.

It's smart to partner with a host that offers advanced features, such as a robust stats package and powerful codecs for formatting your video, according to Rosenbaum, because it allows you to focus on producing rather than keeping up with the Web's ever-changing technologies. Magnify.net offers an integrated package of services that includes a user-friendly uploader, video search, and content management.

FIGURE 7.4 Your video host can help you choose the best level of hosting for your video.

Strategies for Choosing a Video Host

Steve Rosenbaum, CEO of Magnify.net, offers these tips for choosing a video host:

Ask if there other videos hosted by this service that look or feel like yours. For example, Blip.tv is for long form shows; so if you're doing videos that have a "call to action," Blip.tv won't host them.

Ask how long the company has been around. Have they gotten good buzz in the blogs (but not just from folks who are investors in the company or paid endorsements)? Has their business model changed from free to paid, or from paid to more expensive?

Talk to their customers. Email a video maker or blogger and say "I'm thinking about putting my video on XYZ site. Do you like them? Are they reliable? Do they respond to tech questions?"

Read their forums or blogs. If they don't provide a space for their customers to complain, ask questions, or ask for new features, then run away. Web 2.0 companies always invite community input.

Recognize the features you need. If you've got a site, community tools, or a CMS (content management system), then all you need is dumb storage. For that, you can use Akamai, S3 (Amazon) or a few other competitors. If you need a player, then there are companies like Viddler who provide that. If you need a host that provides a full solution (upload, storage, player, community tools, and page design) then a host like us (Magnify.net), can fit the bill.

All video hosts are not the same. Look at the hosts other producers have chosen and see if you think your content would be at home with them. Size matters. Bigger companies are likely to stick around. Shifting your content out of a storage partner, for example, is no fun.

Trade-Offs to Consider When Putting Video Online

Putting your video on the Web requires a series of compromises. You have to figure out what's important for your work. Here are some key decisions to consider.

Quality of Video vs. Time It Takes to Download. A lower bit rate means your video downloads and starts playing faster. A higher bit rate will deliver improved picture and sound quality.

Free or Cheap Popular Distribution vs. Video Viewing Size and Quality. Keep this in mind when you upload to YouTube—it's going to compress your video heavily. The result is compromised video quality. You can look at YouTube video full-screen, but you won't like the results. However, because YouTube is available on many platforms that don't play Flash Video such as iPhones and PlayStations connected to television sets, many producers include YouTube as part of their distribution plans and provide additional URLs where viewers can view their videos at a higher quality.

Jerkiness vs. Smooth Motion. Lowering video frame rates reduces file size and speeds downloads but sacrifices smoothness of motion.

Your Time Working vs. Quality of the Results. Two-pass encoding takes longer but will almost always give you better results. During the first pass, an encoder examines your footage and makes a series of decisions about how to encode it. The actual encode happens on the second pass. Sometimes you'll need to re-encode video using different settings to improve its quality. That takes time.

Fast Motion vs. Visual Detail. Scenes with rapid motion read better against simple backgrounds. It's hard to see small details like a golf ball when there is a lot of fast motion. So, you may want to choose which is more important on a project-by-project basis.

Keeping Track of Your Viewers vs. Letting Go and Getting Your Video Out Widely. If you allow viewers to redistribute your video as Rocketboom does, you won't always know where it ends up. That can make it difficult to tally views for advertisers. But making your video successful isn't only about advertisers and page views. For some video producers, having their video viewed widely is more important than increased revenue.

The work you'll need to do to promote your video varies from host to host. Ask yourself the following questions: Do they have a program guide? Some do, some don't. Do they have Search Engine Optimization (SEO)? Do their channels seem to be taking off well? In any case the content creator needs to be building audience, using social media tools, and working the audience to create buzz, excitement, more views, and more links. Applications like Twitter and Facebook can be powerful marketing tools. Make sure you're blogging and getting the word out—it is essential that you tell your story to anyone who will listen.

Embrace your technology partner. The more you do, the more they're going to bend over backward for you. If you post on your blog that you LOVE working with your host, it's likely that your request for a new feature or some help with a wrinkle is going to get responded to super fast. Why? Because all sites need high-profile reference partners to keep the word out.

Track your stats. Stats on your site can come from Google Analytics (free). Off-site stats can come from TubeMogul. But the fact is that stats are hard to come by since more and more content is being widely distributed.

Consider your audience. Advertisers want a significant audience in a defined vertical audience segment. If you have a million unique visitors in a site about entertainment that's OK. But if you have 500,000 unique visitors in a site focused on adult car enthusiasts, that's really valuable. Focus on targeted visitors who have value and there's going to be an advertiser for you. Also, look at the ad networks. Many of them specialize in niche content representation. Sites like Blip.tv will even sell inventory for you.

Video on the Web will always include the funny, shocking, or sexy short item, like many of those that rise to the top at YouTube today. But an increasing number of people are connecting their computers to their television sets so they can sit back and watch something that takes longer to unfold. Look for patterns in your statistics and analyze what they mean about your audience and what kind of material is going to work for them. You can learn a lot more from the higher-quality statistics offered by some of the best hosting companies.

Understanding Encoding

Uncompressed video files are really big. So, unless you're working with a high-end SDI capture card to import raw video onto your computer, you're always working with video in compressed form. If you're shooting with a DV or HDV camera, the video is compressed when you use FireWire to import it from your camera into your computer. Your video will be compressed further during formatting before you publish it. Popular Web video formats include Flash Video (.flv), QuickTime (.mov), and MPEG (.mpg).

You and I Are Not Cameras

Your goal during encoding is to make your video look good to the human eye. Cameras record every little pixel. The human eye transforms everything it sees into patterns to communicate more efficiently with the brain. So, your eye doesn't see that 1/100th of an inch away the green is slightly more intense.

The result is that when you throw away some of these small differences, human beings watching won't notice. When we watch video on TV, our eyes see each frame for only 1/30th of a second (frame refresh rates vary a bit more on the Web). Our eyes pay most attention to motion and the edges of objects perhaps because that was the most effective way for our ancestors to see an animal they wanted to capture or run away from.

In addition, much of the picture doesn't change in 1/30th of a second, so you don't have to repeat the same information 10 times in half a second if the wall is still white and the camera isn't moving. That's why it sometimes makes sense to minimize unnecessary camera motion and even your subject's movement when shooting for the Web, as you learned in Chapter 2, *Shooting for the Web*. Encoding software does a better job of compressing scenes with minimal motion. Shots with a lot of motion like sports work better when encoded at higher bit rates (that is, with more bits of information allocated to each second of video to reduce the image degradation caused by compression).

Compression software removes information it sees as redundant. For example, if there is a blue wall behind a lecturer, the software checks in every few frames and communicates the equivalent of "yup, it's still blue" until something changes. Compression makes files substantially smaller with a minimal reduction in quality. Video devices use compression to save space on your hard drive once the video is captured and to make video easier and faster to transmit over the Web.

Under optimal conditions, any format you choose can deliver high-quality video if you make the right adjustments during encoding. You'll compress your video for one or several specific bandwidths (the number of bits allocated per second of video, expressed in kilobits per second (Kbps) or megabits per second (Mbps)). Some formats like Flash Video, work better with low-bandwidth/low-bit-rate video, while MPEG can deliver better quality when file size and bit rate are less of a concern and you'd like viewers to be able to watch full-screen. Learning how each codec and each format works will give you more control over the quality your viewers see.

When you get started, a simple solution is to choose a host by the quality of video it distributes. I started working with Streamhoster for small and low-budget clients and switched to Brightcove because I was impressed with the quality of its video output and because it offered content management features that made working with a large volume of video easier.

Choose one host and familiarize yourself with the formats and settings required to make your video look spectacular. This will give you a reliable "go-to" option. Then experimenting with other options won't be so risky. In general, you'll want to distribute your video using at least two hosts: one for widespread, reliable, low-bit-rate distribution across all platforms and devices and one that delivers stunning quality.

NOTE The formats your video host accepts and the bandwidth limitations it imposes define the quality viewers will see.

The format and bandwidth you use to compress your video will be determined in large part by your video host. If you use free services like YouTube, your choices will be very limited. Many pay hosts also publish strict guidelines to keep things simple, but often you can contract for additional services that meet your needs.

Enterprise-level hosts will allow you to serve high-quality video files. However, serving a large volume of high-quality video can get costly, and most viewers won't be able to accept video at speeds greater than 1.9 Mbps.

The Settings You Need to Keep Your Video Looking Great Online

There are many good formats for uploading video to the Web, but each video host will accept only one or two. The most popular formats for free hosts are QuickTime (.mov), Flash Video (.flv), Windows Media Video (.wmv), and MPEG-4 AVC/H.264 (.mp4). Check your host's guidelines for the formats it accepts and the limits imposed. You will probably be uploading to more than one host, so finding a common format saves time. The choices you'll need to make before you upload your video to your host include the format for your sound, how often to set key frames, the aspect ratio of your video (full-screen 4:3 or wide-screen 16:9), and other details usually found on the Advanced tab of your host's uploading interface. Each choice you make will affect the way your video looks to viewers.

Compression Tips

When you compress video, keep in mind the following recommendations:

Whenever possible, do not recompress video. Recompressing video reduces the quality of your video image and results in artifacts, which look like black dots, lines, and dropouts (or white spots) in your footage. Create a workflow that allows you to capture your video and export it without recompressing it.

Keep your video short. Trim the beginning and end of your video, and edit your video to remove any unnecessary content.

Adjust your compression settings. If you compress footage and it looks great, try changing your settings to reduce the file size until you find the best setting possible for the video you are compressing. Several attributes affect file size and the quality of compressed video. Some settings are simple to anticipate, and others require trial and error to find the best solution. When you find a setting that works well for a particular type of video, save it as a preset.

Limit effects and rapid movement if you are concerned about file size. Video that includes a lot of movement or complicated backgrounds results in larger file sizes when compressed. Handheld footage and zooms often cost more bandwidth than they are worth. Image stabilization also increases file size because it requires more key frames to keep up with a camera that's always seeking focus. Other effects such as blurs decrease the size of your compressed file.

Choose a frame size and aspect ratio that work for your audience. If your target audience includes mobile phone users or people on dial-up Internet connections, make the dimensions of your video smaller, such as 160x120 pixels. If your audience has broadband, you can make your dimensions larger (for example, 320x240 pixels). Most video players default to 4:3 aspect ratio; a few work with 16:9 footage.

Choose a frame rate that matches your footage. If you target users who typically have older computer processors, choose a lower frame rate, around 15 fps. Most video and broadcast TV in the United States run at about 30 fps (29.97), and movies run at 24 fps, but lower-frame rate video often looks fine on the Web. If your target audience includes viewers with newer computers, you can use a higher frame rate (30 fps is the standard for most video). Always choose a frame rate that is a multiple of your original frame rate. For example, if your original frame rate was 30 fps, compress to 15 fps or 7.5 fps.

Set key frames. Video key frames reproduce the entire image on a video frame when the video is compressed, so the more frequent your key frames are, the better quality the footage is. More key frames also mean a larger file size. If you choose 30, a video key frame draws every 30 frames. If you choose 15, the quality is higher because a key frame draws every 15 frames and the pixels in your footage are more accurate to the original.

Reduce noise. Noise (scattered pixels in your footage that look like snow) wastes bits that could be better allocated to improve video quality. Reduce noise using the noise reduction filter in your video editor. Using more solid colors in your video makes it possible to produce a good-looking video at a lower file size. If you're working with Adobe applications, you can use the Video Noise Reduction filter in the Adobe Media Encoder or a soft blur in After Effects to help reduce noise.

Choose optimal compression settings. Choosing compression settings is a balancing act. You'll need to consider the content of your video, the format you're encoding to, and your intended audience. Fewer key frames and more intermediate frames result in smaller file sizes but produce lower-quality images and can result in blurred motion. More key frames and fewer intermediate frames result in significantly larger file sizes but produce higher-quality images and clear motion. Often, you'll arrive at the optimal compression setting through trial and error.

Animation. If you're compressing low-motion animation, titles, or other graphics, or relatively still shots (talking heads or footage shot on a tripod), you can often get away with reducing your frame rate to 15 fps, significantly reducing the total video size. If you're compressing animated footage that includes large blocks of color or vector images such as *The Simpsons* or *South Park*, try an even lower rate like 8 fps—you might be pleasantly surprised with the results.

Sports and high-motion video. Sports are often shot at a higher frame rate, or higher resolution. A standard of 1 key frame per second is often suggested for footage that doesn't include fast motion; however, a higher rate such as 2 key frames per second is recommended for particularly high-motion footage. Some compression codecs and software select the key frame frequency for you based on standards or based on the number of frames per second and the data rate you've chosen.

The following sections highlight the settings required by a few popular hosts. You'll usually find information about settings on the host's "Frequently Asked Questions (FAQ)" or "Getting Started" page on the Web. Unfortunately, there's no standard that applies across the board. Not every host accepts every format, and two hosts that accept QuickTime files, for example, may vary in how they ask you to prepare them for uploading. Don't try to memorize these details. Familiarize yourself with the terms, and after you choose a host, return to these parameters for practical instructions or to find another host with similar requirements.

Google Video

Video formats: MPEG-1/2/4 (MPEG-4 preferred), H.264, H.263, Motion JPEG, AVI, ASF, QuickTime, and Windows Media. Note that Google does not accept Flash Video files.
Video bit rates: At least 260 Kbps (750 Kbps preferred)
Aspect ratio/frame size: 4:3 (640x480)
Frame rate: At least 12 fps; original preferred (usually 30 fps)
Audio codec: MP3 variable bit rate (VBR)
Audio bit rates: At least 70 Kbps (128 Kbps preferred)
File size limit: No limit on size or duration
Extras:
• NTSC video only
• Deinterlace during encoding

YouTube

Video formats: Windows Media, AVI, QuickTime, MPEG-1/2/4
Video bit rates: None specified
Aspect ratio: 4:3
Frame rate: None specified
Audio codec: MP3 preferred
Audio bit rates: None specified
File size limit: Single-file uploads are limited to 100 MB; 10-minute limit on all videos, most are less than 5 minutes
Extras:
• Downloading the free YouTube "uploader" makes it easy to upload several files at once; the limit is 1 GB.
• YouTube chooses automatic thumbnail from the center of your video, or you can use one uploaded image for all videos on one account.

Blip.tv

Video formats: QuickTime MOV
Video bit rates: 1500 Kbps
Aspect ratios/frame size: 16:9 (640x360), 4:3 (640x 480)
Audio codecs: AAC 48 kHz, at least 128 Kbps
File size limit: Recommended 100 MB but up to 1 GB
Extras:
• Key frames: Less than 24 or auto; lower is better
• Leave fast start on
• Frame rate: Current
• Frame controls: Off
• Multipass: On
• Frame reorder: On

Brightcove

Brightcove's console will guide you through uploading video files and creating players. Because it's an enterprise host, it offers settings for several different formats including one for high-quality WMV files that clients can offer for paid download.

Video formats: Flash 7 and Flash 8 Video, Windows Media
Video bit rates: 464 Kbps
Aspect ratio/frame size: 4:3 (480x360), 16:9 (480x270)
Audio codec: Not specified
Audio bit rate: 48 Kbps
Extras:
• Downloadable "Publishpod" uploader for posting multiple files and converting them to .flv files
• Creates thumbnail of your choice
• Compression recommendations: On2 VP6 codec for Flash 8, two-pass VBR, 30 fps, key frame every six seconds
• Additional settings for Flash 7: Maintain Aspect Ratio off, 24 and 25 fps footage should be encoded as "Same-as-source," key frame every two seconds

Brightcove Guidelines for Encoding Windows Media Video

Videos uploaded to Brightcove for purchase or rental must be encoded using the Windows Media Encoder (available free from Microsoft) and uploaded as WMV full-length video for use when you create a Pay Media Title for consumer download.

Video format: WMV 9
Video bit rate: 1300K bps

Aspect ratios: 4:3 (640x480), 16:9 (640x360), anamorphic 16:9 (720x480)
Audio codec: WMA Stereo
Audio bit rate: 96 Kbps, 44.1–48 kHz
Extras:
- WMV using Sorenson Squeeze, Anystream, Cleaner, or another popular encoding solution.
- **Total data rate:** 1.4 Mbps.
- **Total Bit Rate:** 1400 Kbps.
- **Audio:** Stereo two-pass VBR-supported resolutions.
- **Filters: Deinterlacing.** Video that is not shot and edited progressively (24p, 30p, or film with telecine removed) should be deinterlaced during the encoding process.

The kind of specific recommendations provided by Blip.tv and Brightcove.com help ensure consistent quality in the video hosted on these sites and can help tremendously when you're just getting started. Bandwidth and the settings provided are not the only considerations when you compress your video. Later in this chapter you'll learn about the options available in some of the most popular editing programs.

How MPEG Works

MPEG is similar to the JPEG format used for photographs and bit-map images in programs like Photoshop except it's for moving pictures. It is a lossy codec, which means it reduces file size by throwing away as many pixels as it can. Throwing away pixels always reduces quality, but the MPEG algorithm does a pretty good job of knocking file sizes down while maintaining the quality of images that include subtle shading and sophisticated color patterns such as drop shadows and gradients. MPEG stores the differences between frames, taking advantage of the fact that most things don't change 30 times a second.

H.264 is the current favorite for producing high-quality video files small enough to travel over the Internet. It uses the best of several methods in the codec to compress your video, making it very flexible. One method might work best if your video includes a lot of motion but has a limited color palette; another may serve best when there's little motion but a light is turned on and the colors change.

But there's one constant among all the different compression formats used in just about any project: encoding always drags on longer than you'd like. Why does it take so long to encode?

The MPEG standard has more than 20 different modes. The encoding software chooses the best mode for each scene. There are two categories of encoding: constant bit rate (CBR), which chooses one bit rate and encodes an entire clip at that rate; and variable bit rate (VBR), which aims to average a certain bit rate for compressed video but works within a preset range above and below that target rate, allocating more bits for harder-to-compress/higher-motion scenes and fewer bits for easier-to-compress/lower-motion scenes.

When you choose VBR encoding, you'll have a choice of either one-pass or two-pass. The two-pass method takes twice as long, but it gives you a much better chance of a successful, high-quality VBR encode. On the first pass, the software goes through a file, figures out the optimal encoding method by estimating the amount of motion in each section of a clip (among other factors), and uses what it learns to get the best result on the second pass. When you use a single-pass method, it looks ahead a few frames and makes its best guess which method to use, but as a practical matter, it can't do as precise a job.

Today, state-of-the-art encoders are used for live television, including programs shot and delivered in HD. What goes over the air is delayed a second or two to give the encoder time to work. This requires computers with powerful multiprocessors that can compress video footage much faster than your home or small office computer.

The compromise we make for computers we can afford is to give the encoder more time to encode than it takes to view the original video. If you're looking for the highest-quality encoding, it often takes 10 or 20 times your video's running time or length. If you have to encode more quickly—perhaps because your footage is newsworthy and you need to get it out right away—choose CBR and your encoding tool's fastest setting to get it done faster.

▶ Important Encoding Considerations

Ben Waggoner, Microsoft Technology Evangelist

Ben Waggoner, an expert in video compression technology and workflows, is currently a technology evangelist at Microsoft.

There are a few important things you need to keep in mind when compressing video for the Web. I asked encoding expert Ben Waggoner for his take on some of the key things you'll need to understand to make your video better.

BIT RATE

Most producers assume viewers have broadband connections that deliver between 300 Kbps and 2 Mbps, but many viewers' connections can't keep up. What's a practical target bit rate?

700 Kbps is pretty safe for most home users right now for streaming. If you're doing short clips via progressive download, you can always use a higher bit rate if the consumer is willing to put up with some buffering.

FORMAT

Producers are looking for the video format that gets their video to the most people in the highest quality. But it also has to be supported by video hosts. What's the best format: Flash Video, Windows Media, QuickTime, or others?

These days, it's really converging on MPEG-4 (used by Flash) or Windows Media (used by Silverlight) for Web video formats. QuickTime is mainly being used as an authoring API.

FRAME RATE

Does reducing your video's frame rate help make everything else, such as detail and color, look better?

With modern codecs, using a lower fps really doesn't pay off that much. As long as I can do at least 300 Kbps, I always encode at the same frame rate as the source, up to 30 fps. Since lowering the frame rate means there's more change between frames, cutting the frame rate in half lets you lower bit rate only by 20–30 percent at best.

KEY FRAMES

Adding key frames improves the quality of encodes but increases file size. Is there a logical limit to how many you need?

File size is really just data rate times duration. What using too many key frames does is lower the compression efficiency

> *700 Kbps is pretty safe for most home users right now for streaming.*

of the encode, meaning you need more bits to give higher quality. These days, for [clips encoded at] less than 2 Mbps, I use one key frame every 4–10 seconds.

SOUND

How much of your video file should be devoted to sound?

That really depends on the codec. If you're targeting Silverlight 2 and/or Windows Media Player 11, you can use WMA 10 Pro in low-bit-rate modes. It produces great quality at 48 Kbps in VBR and 64 Kbps in CBR; 32 Kbps is ample for FM radio quality.

DEINTERLACING

I often shoot 1080i (interlaced), but things look better on the Web using progressive scan. What's the best time to de-interlace, during capture or during output?

As early in the process as possible. Ideally, shoot progressive. My next favorite place is rendering out of the NLE so that titling and motion graphics are at least rendered as progressive.

ENCODERS

I've had a lot of trouble with encoding, including painful crashes that kept me up all night. Have encoders gotten more reliable?

Absolutely, thank goodness. I've been doing compression as the primary focus of my career for 13 years now, and back in the day I'd have to baby-sit a Premiere 4.0 encode all night, with maybe only a two-out-of-three chance that any given encode would actually make it all the way through. These days, with modern batch encoders, I don't even worry about a crash happening. The only errors I see come from between the chair and the keyboard.

I'd say 80 percent of the bad Web video out there is bad due to source or preprocessing issues, not codec issues.

BANDWIDTH

You were there at the beginning of encoding for the Web. What was it like?

One of my first Web video jobs was for golfer Peter Jacobsen. The bit rate was so low that the shaft of the club disappeared when it was moving on the diagonal, and the frame rate was so low that most times you could never even see the ball in flight. The combination of massively increased bandwidth (we use at least 10x what we had back then for even "low bandwidth" now) and big codec improvements as well (probably 2–3 times more efficient) has paid off hugely.

HARDWARE VS. SOFTWARE ENCODING

It takes so long to encode in software that many people have bought expensive add-in boards to do the encoding in hardware. Now that we have multi-core processors, is hardware encoding still that much faster?

The gap has shrunk, but products like the Tarari board from LSI still show a big performance advantage over pure software encoding, particularly for HD.

BUNDLED VS. STAND-ALONE ENCODING TOOLS

I do most of my work in Final Cut Pro, which includes Compressor, and Premiere Pro, which ships with Adobe Media Encoder, and these bundled encoding applications do most of what I need for the Web. But some of the best encoding tools for certain tasks may be available only as stand-alone tools. What other software would be helpful for Web video producers?

It all depends on workflow. I find that the output support is less important than how well the products can preprocess the video and manage jobs. So, stuff like scaling quality, ability of inverse telecine to handle cadence breaks, quality of deinterlacing, control over luma levels, flexibility in managing complex encoding jobs—those matter the most. It gets down to the best tool that can handle the source file format, process the video correctly, and do the right thing on encoding.

These days, my go-to tools are:

- Expression Encoder 2 for Silverlight authoring. Nothing else has the depth of special features.
- Rhozet Carbon Coder for batch encoding. It can handle almost anything on input and is the first high-volume encoder with VC-1 Encoder SDK support.
- Inlet Spinnaker for live broadcasting (using the live VC-1 Encoder SDK implementation).
- Telestream's Episode for Mac encoding.

The new Sorenson Squeeze 5 looks to be a big improvement, but it's just come out, and I haven't had a chance to do a lot of deep work with it. But Squeeze has long been my tool of choice to recommend to new and casual compressionists, due to its ease of use. No VC-1 Encoder SDK yet, though.

What advice to you have for people who want to get the best-quality compression for the Web?

Make sure your video looks great before it hits the encoder; no codec will ever give you back more information than you handed it. I'd say 80 percent of the bad Web video out there is bad due to source or preprocessing issues, not codec issues.

> *...there's really no excuse to have audio with distracting artifacts with modern codecs...*

Don't forget the audio. Bad audio is extremely fatiguing, and there's really no excuse to have audio with distracting artifacts with modern codecs, even at Web data rates.

Don't worry about the details of the technology until you've got a firm handle on the three questions: What is my content? Who is my audience? What are my communication goals? You can't start making the right technical choices until you understand your context.

The Best Settings for Web Video Formats

I've been asked again and again, "What settings should I use to make my video look better?" The only honest answer is, "It depends." It depends on what software you're using and what results you need. Are you more concerned about download speed or quality? Do you want your viewers to have the option of taking your video full-screen? Does your project need to be in a format friendly to advertising overlays?

There is no magic formula for how to set up your compression that will get you the best results every time. But there are guidelines that will help you sort through the options your editing software provides. Looking at the encoding options in your editing software can be a little like looking at controls in the cockpit of a plane. Unless you're a pilot, you'd have no idea what to do with the many switches in front of you. Setting up your project to work with the format of your footage is the first step to ensuring good quality. Make sure the project you create matches your footage. Final Cut Pro makes this easy by warning you when there's a mismatch. But you can get into trouble with other editing programs if you choose the wrong preset or don't pay attention to aspect ratio when you create a project and start capturing your video to it.

After you've edited your project and are ready to export it, you'll need to tell your software what format you'll need for the Web and what quality.

Guidelines for Encoding Web Video

Limiting your video's bandwidth has the greatest impact on what your viewers will see of any decision you make during encoding. Here are some general guidelines:

▶ Roughly 200–400 Kbps output on video with a lot of motion and demanding background yields low quality of the sort you typically see on YouTube.

▶ 500 Kbps to 1 Mbps isn't bad but is more like the quality of an old VHS tape than what we see on a good TV.

▶ At 1–2 Mbps you get the quality of a cable or satellite TV signal.

▶ At 4–8 Mbps you are getting a pretty good HD signal.

If you just have two people talking and the camera doesn't move, you can go much lower with good results. Bandwidth is the most important setting. Use the highest bit rate your host can support and all the viewers you want to reach can receive based on their connections. Basically, 70–80 percent of the world's broadband connections easily handle 1 Mbps; you could lose 50 percent of your audience at 2–3 Mbps and 80 percent at 6 Mbps.

When you send your video to YouTube and many other hosts, it is re-encoded and sometimes reformatted to Flash Video. YouTube reduces your video to the file size it wants to screen. If you send a gorgeous 2 Mbps video to YouTube, it knocks it down to one quarter of that bit rate, or whatever the YouTube standard is at the time you read this book. So, encoding for each host requires a dance between what you encode and what the host does to it.

In Japan, Paris, and Berlin, many people today have 15 and even 100 Mbps connections. Broadband speeds around the world will keep increasing. Faster Internet speeds and better compression codecs mean video quality on the Web will keep getting better.

Getting the best results when encoding your video with your editing software requires understanding how that tool works and knowing the best settings to use for each application. They vary based on the type of video you're encoding, your target audience, and the requirements set by your host. In the section below are some settings to use with QuickTime Pro, Windows Media Encoder, iMovie, Premiere, and Final Cut.

Keep in mind that audio takes up more space than most people realize. It's also very important to viewers. So consider bandwidth before you automatically choose the highest audio quality. Audio tracks formatted as MP3s at 192 Kbps take up nearly half your bandwidth if your target is 400 Kbps. Choosing a lower sampling rate if your content is mostly voice and mono instead of stereo can save bandwidth, and the changes are often so small they are imperceptible (**FIGURE 7.5**).

FIGURE 7.5 Choosing audio compression settings in Apple QuickTime.

Setting Parameters

Each host sets clear parameters for uploading to its site. These include limitations on video file size and bandwidth, as described earlier, expressed in kilobits per second or megabits per second. Some sites provide guidelines that prepare files for further processing. Others with more specific instructions—including formats for audio, key frames, and frame rates—depend on you to prepare video in the proper format for Web viewing on the site.

Windows Media Encoder

The default setting for Windows Media Encoder won't give you the best results. Instead use the Settings window to set the properties for your encode (**FIGURE 7.6**).

1. Instead of choosing from the presets in the New Sessions window, select View > Properties.
2. In the Session Properties dialog, choose Source in the pane on the left.
3. Click the File option, and browse for the file you want to convert.
4. Select both the Video: In File and Audio: In File check boxes. The type of file will show up onscreen.

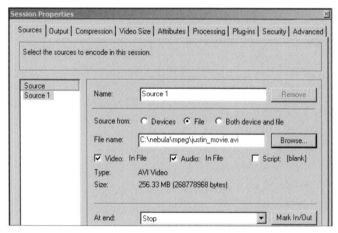

FIGURE 7.6 Windows Media Encoder settings window.

5. Choose Stop from the "At end" pop-up menu.
6. In the Output tab, select Encode to browse for your output folder and then name your file. Select the Limit by Files Size check box and type **100Mbps**; then click Apply.
7. In the Compression tab, choose "File download (computer playback)."
8. For video, select Video DVD quality (1 Mbps VBR).
9. For audio, select Audio CD quality (CBR).
10. In the Processing tab, select the Deinterlace option if your original footage is interlaced (that is, if you shot 1080i or 60i DV); then click Apply.

11. Click the green Start Encoding button. You can adjust the video display to show your encode. You won't be able to see the first pass (not supported). But you'll see the quality of your encode as it renders (**FIGURE 7.7**).

When the encode is done, you'll get the option to play your output file, and you'll get information about the bit rate and size of your file (**FIGURE 7.8**).

FIGURE 7.7 Windows Media Encoder converting footage.

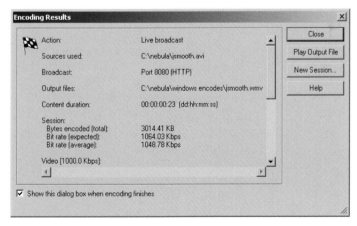

FIGURE 7.8 Windows Media Encoder encoding results.

iMovie

Apple's iMovie makes creating Web videos easy. When encoding video in iMovie, always use the Expert Settings from the "Compress movie for" dialog so you'll have control of the results (**FIGURE 7.9**).

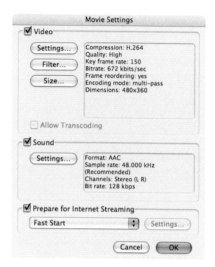

FIGURE 7.9 iMovie Expert Settings.

In iMovie's Expert Settings window, do the following:

1. With your edited movie in the timeline, choose File > Export.

2. In the QuickTime tab, choose Expert Settings from the "Compress Movie for" menu; then click Share.

3. In the "Save exported file as" window, choose the setting and file format (**FIGURE 7.10**).

   You'll be saving your movie in this example to an AVI file. You can also use iMovie to create movies for iPhone, Windows Media Video, QuickTime, and other formats.

4. Click the Options button, and select both the Video and Audio check boxes in the AVI Settings window. This window is context-sensitive, so you'll get different choices if you select another format for encoding (**FIGURE 7.11**).

5. For Compression type, choose DV/DVCPRO-NTSC (or PAL if you're reading this in Europe).

6. Select the frames per second that corresponds with your original video. My video is drop frame, so I'll choose 29.97 fps.

7. Choose Medium Quality for a small file, High or Best for a larger one.

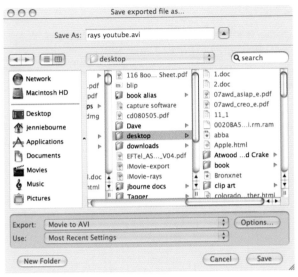

FIGURE 7.10 iMovie's "Save exported file as" window with Movie to AVI selected as the Export format.

FIGURE 7.11 iMovie's AVI Settings window.

8. For bit depth, choose millions of colors.

9. For Scan Mode, select Progressive.

10. Under the Sound setting, for Compressor, choose None. For Rate (audio sampling), 22.050 is fine for speech; use 41,000 for music. For Size, choose 16-bit, and finally select Mono.

11. Select the folder where you want to save your movie, and name it in the "Save exported file as" window, and click Save.

A dialog will show your movie compressing.

QuickTime Pro

QuickTime Pro exports to all the files QuickTime supports including MPEG-4, .mov, DV, and .avi files (**FIGURE 7.12**). To install it, start with the free QuickTime player and buy the upgrade to the Pro version on the Apple Web site. After you've installed the Pro upgrade, QuickTime Pro will run every time you open the QuickTime Player application. You can also use QuickTime Pro to do simple editing.

FIGURE 7.12 The export settings in QuickTime Pro.

To export and encode a file using QuickTime Pro, follow these steps:

1. Choose File > Export.
2. From the Export pop-up menu, choose Movie to QuickTime Movie.
3. Click Options to open the Movie Settings dialog (**FIGURE 7.13**). In the Video area, click Settings, and choose your settings. H.264 is recommended.
4. Click Settings in the Movie Settings window to access the Standard Video Compression Settings window. In the Data Rate section of that window, to let the compressor choose an appropriate data rate, select Automatic.
5. Choose your intended delivery method from the "Optimized for" pop-up menu. This setting tells the encoder how much the data rate can vary above and below the data rate you choose. This option is available only for compressors that can apply limits, such as H.264.

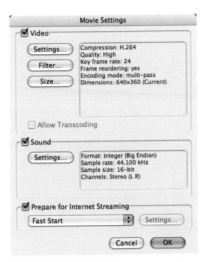

FIGURE 7.13 Choose your encoding parameters in the Movie Settings dialog.

6. For Frame Rate, select Current; if your video is standard (NTSC) video, it has a frame rate of 29.97 frames per second.

7. To let the compressor choose the key frame interval, select Automatic (**FIGURE 7.14**).

With QuickTime Pro, you can add special effects such as blur, emboss, and film noise to a movie before you export it. You add special effects by using filters.

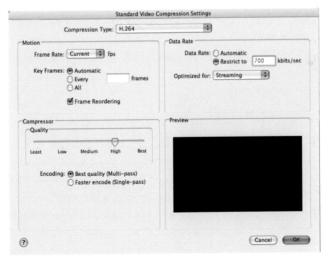

FIGURE 7.14 Set the key frames, data rate, compression quality, and more in the Standard Video Compression Settings dialog.

8. To set a filter for a movie, choose File > Export in QuickTime Player. Choose Movie to QuickTime Movie from the Export pop-up menu. Click Options to open the Movie Settings dialog; then click Filter, and select the filter and settings you want to use (**FIGURE 7.15**).

The selected filter is applied to the entire movie.

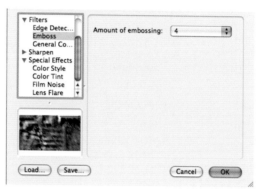

FIGURE 7.15 Apply filters in this window, accessed via the Movie Settings dialog.

9. To change the size of a movie's video frame to the size suggested by your host, choose File > Export.

10. Choose a file format from the Export pop-up menu. Then click Options. The Movie Settings dialog opens.

11. In the Video area, click Size, and then choose an option from the Dimensions pop-up menu. Using Current (the default) will create movies much too large for delivery on the Web.

12. Keep the height-to-width ratio the same as the source (so that objects don't appear distorted). In this window you can also choose to deinterlace the source video (**FIGURE 7.16**).

FIGURE 7.16 You can also choose to deinterlace the source video in this window.

13. To customize sound settings for export, choose File > Export and then choose Movie to QuickTime Movie from the Export pop-up menu. Click Options. In the Sound area of the Movie Settings dialog, click Settings, and then choose your options (**FIGURE 7.17**):

Format: Choose the compressor (codec) you want to use for compressing sound. For general use and Internet delivery of music, MPEG-4 Audio (AAC) is recommended.

Channels: Choose between Mono (1 channel) and Stereo (2 channels).

Rate: Digitized sound is made up of sound samples. The more samples per second, the better; use a sampling rate of 44.1 kHz.

Render Settings: Choose the quality of the signal processing that will be used; note that higher-quality settings take longer to process.

Other options: To see any additional options specific to your chosen codec, click the Options button.

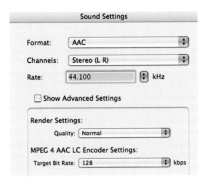

FIGURE 7.17 You can customize audio settings for export in the Sound area of the Movie Settings dialog.

14. Finally, with QuickTime Pro, you can set up a movie to start playing from a Web server before the movie has completely downloaded to the user's hard disk. This is called a Fast Start movie. Set the Fast Start setting in the Movie Settings dialog (see Figure 7.13) just before you distribute your movie.

Final Cut Pro

Final Cut Pro offers three options for exporting your video. Export using QuickTime creates files much too large for the Web. You can also export directly from the timeline to Compressor. For this demonstration, I'll show how to export using QuickTime Conversion, a flexible option for Web video.

NOTE Final Cut Express is similar to Final Cut Pro. It also offers export to QuickTime and export using QuickTime Conversion.

1. Name your file and the location where you want to save it in the Save window, choose your format (QuickTime movie), and use Broadband High settings. Start with the default H.264 settings for both Video and Sound. Make sure Prepare for Internet Streaming and Fast Start are selected (**FIGURE 7.18**).

2. Click OK in the Save window, and your movie will start encoding.

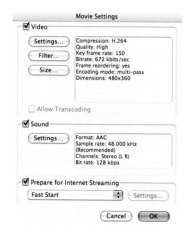

FIGURE 7.18 Final Cut Pro export using QuickTime Conversion.

Premiere Pro

Adobe Premiere Pro has two options for exporting video from the timeline. The first, Export > File, opens the Export Movie Settings dialog (**FIGURE 7.19**).

FIGURE 7.19 Premiere Pro's Export Movie Settings dialog creates files too big for the Web. The presets under File Type are for older streaming options.

The other option, which produces better results for Web video, is Export using Adobe Media Encoder. This opens a much broader palette of encoding options in its Export Settings window (**FIGURE 7.20**). I'll show how to use Adobe Media Encoder in this exercise because it offers more options and creates a better encode.

FIGURE 7.20 The Adobe Media Encoder application bundled with Premiere Pro lets you see the results of changes you make in the settings window.

1. In the Export Settings window, select the following parameters:

   Format: QuickTime

   Video Codec: H.264

   Basic Video Settings: Width: 480; Height: 360 (270 for 16:9 footage)

   Frame Rate: Custom 29.97 or your source footage rate

   Field Order: None (Progressive)

   Pixel Aspect Ratio: Same as Project

   Check Set Bit rate: 1.225.30

   You'll see your footage in the window, which will help you check aspect ratio and size.

2. Select the Output tab above the preview window, and select the Deinterlace check box (**FIGURE 7.21**). Click OK. The Save File dialog opens.

FIGURE 7.21 Don't forget to select the Deinterlace option, just because Adobe Media Encoder happens to put it in an out-of-the-way place.

3. Choose a filename and location, and make sure the file type is the one your selected QuickTime (.mov) file uses.

4. Click Save.

Premiere Elements

Premiere Elements is a limited version of Premiere Pro. We'll use it to export a Windows Media Video file for Web delivery.

1. Click Export on the Premiere Elements toolbar, and choose Windows Media from the menu that appears by selecting File > Export > Windows Media.

2. In the Export Windows Media window, choose Cable Modem/ DSL on the left. Click OK.

3. Choose a format.

4. In the Save File window, choose a location in which to save the file, type a filename for the movie file, and click Save. The Rendering dialog appears.

5. Save your project and your file.

Working with Large Volumes of Content

If you're working with larger volumes of content, you'll need timesaving strategies such as presets and multiple file upload options. You'll also need the highest-speed broadband connection you can afford and a host on the other end that accepts faster data rates to save you time during uploading. A robust file management system with clear naming conventions will help keep things organized.

If you're uploading short videos three or four times a week, the number of videos you upload can easily get out of hand. Include dates and topic slugs on both your source video labels and your digitized video files. If you add tape names during capture, you can comfortably discard digitized files after a short time and save only the project file. Later you'll be able to re-create your edited movie from source files.

A host like Brightcove, which has procedures based on its enterprise-level service, will get you in the habit of naming your files and keeping them organized by date on your host's server. That, as they say, is a good thing.

Format Your Video for the Web

To begin, set up accounts at two hosts, chosen from among the ones discussed in this chapter. Look up the guidelines for submitting video to both. Output a short video about three minutes long in two different formats. Use TubeMogul (www. tubemogul.com) to upload to both and compare results.

For the project file, output your sequence in the .avi or .mov format. To do this, you'll have to use the Export command found in the File menu of your editing or encoding software.

Your editing software will give you choices about the quality of file you want to output. Check the recommendations of the video host you plan to use to distribute your work. Most of the settings labeled "Web quality" or "streaming" are designed to create small files that will download fast.

Remember, you don't just want your video to download fast; you want it to look good. If your first efforts are disappointing, try again with different settings. When you're figuring out which settings work best, output only 30 seconds of your movie. Then, when you're satisfied with your results, output the complete file and save your project. Upload your files to your hosts and compare the results online. In **FIGURE 7.22** and **7.23** you'll see what happens when I take a high-quality video shot in HDV format and upload it to three hosts. In the bottom image in Figure 7.23, you can see the image quality that results when you upload using Brightcove's parameters and set the uploader to 2-pass encoding. Note that 2-pass encoding results in a higher-quality image because the encoder notes significant changes in the video on the first pass and adjusts for them during the second, rather than adjusting on the fly during a one-pass encode.

FOR THIS PROJECT, YOU'LL NEED:

- Editing software that outputs .flv, .mov, and .wmv files
- If you don't yet own an NLE package, download a trial version of Final Cut Express or Premiere Elements
- QuickTime Pro is an inexpensive addition you should also consider
- A short video less than three minutes long
- Accounts with three video hosts
- A broadband Internet connection

NOTE It's difficult to translate the quality of streamed video to the printed page but if you take the time to do this experiment yourself you'll learn much about the qualities of video streams served by different video hosts, and you'll quickly identify your favorites.

FIGURE 7.22 The image on top here is a still output from the original image. Below it is a high-quality video stream that resulted when I uploaded the video to Vimeo.com according to their directions for uploading HD footage. The quality is very similar to the original video.

FIGURE 7.23 To complete my experiment I uploaded the video to two additional hosts. At the top of this figure you see the result when the same footage was uploaded to YouTube, which streams at 300 kbps, a very low bit rate for video which results in a lower quality image. Note that the video which was originally in a 16:9 format has been cropped to fit a 4:3 screen, further reducing the image quality. I also uploaded the same video to Bright-cove, which translates uploaded video to Flash video (shown on bottom).

CHAPTER 8

GETTING YOUR VIDEO NOTICED

8 GETTING YOUR VIDEO NOTICED

D *iet Coke and Mentos* may be the world's best known viral video. It catapulted producers Stephen Voltz and Fritz Grobe (**FIGURE 8.1**) to video star status just a few days after it first appeared on the Web. The video features a magnificent fountain of choreographed "dancing waters" created using a chemical reaction that results when Mentos candy is inserted into bottles of Diet Coke.

Photo by Jaime Tardy. Courtesy of Eepybird.

FIGURE 8.1 Stephen Voltz (left) and Fritz Grobe (right) say no one recognizes them on the street without the lab coats and goggles they wear in their popular video.

Known collectively as EepyBird, Voltz and Grobe, who also star in the video studied the Web before making their video to find out what viewers watched. They found videos shot simply, often in one take, were among the most popular. They also found that viewers seemed to respond well when video showed a producer's passion for a subject. They discovered that passion, bordering on obsession, was one of the key things that made videos popular with viewers and pushed them into the most watched category. The dynamic duo spent six months creating and perfecting their video before sending it out to a friend to watch. They say it went viral instantly without any additional push, but their meticulous research into what works on the Web suggests otherwise. Nevertheless, hundreds of thousands viewed *Diet Coke and Mentos* during the first few days it appeared online.

Within three days, David Letterman called. They performed on the *Ellen DeGeneres Show* and the *Today Show*. Now *Diet Coke and Mentos* has become a full-time job, with the two former circus performers touring the world with a show based on their popular video (**FIGURE 8.2**).

FIGURE 8.2 Grobe and Voltz told two friends about the video, and within days millions were watching.

They've performed in Istanbul, Paris, and even Las Vegas, home of the Bellagio fountain that inspired their video. Because they prepared for success by putting their video on Revver, a revenue sharing site, they were also able to profit from the video's popularity. When I asked what was next, they would say only "It involves office products." They reminded me that the essence of their art is to do unexpected things with familiar materials, and they invited me to sign up for their newsletter so I'd be among the first to see the new video. I did, and what came back was a personalized e-mail from Fritz. Even though I know it was autogenerated, it made me feel that I was part of something wonderful, an object lesson in building an audience that feels like a community.

Eepybird's success is also a good example of what you have to do to get your video out there and get it noticed. Make a good video, and build a community around it. You'll hear more from EepyBird in Chapter 9, *Making It Pay*, because they also know a little something about getting paid. But first let's talk about what it takes to get your video out to millions.

The Truth About Viral Video

Dan Ackerman Greenberg rocked the Web when he revealed that many viral videos are the result of skillful clandestine marketing. Readers were incensed when Greenberg first published his exposé in the tech blog TechCrunch, which documented many questionable practices including paying bloggers to recommend videos. Many recognized that they had been manipulated, and they didn't like it.

As cofounder of viral video marketing company the Comotion Group, Greenberg promised clients that if they didn't get 100,000 views, they wouldn't have to pay. He studied how YouTube worked and used that information to generate hits in the millions.

Greenberg tells the story of a Hollywood client that created videos clips that looked like they were shot on a cell phone but were actually professionally produced. The studio's efforts managed to generate views only in the thousands. Working with Greenberg, they scored 6 million views on YouTube, 200 blog posts linking to the videos, and a "5 Most Viewed of the Day" status for all six clips. The two that really went viral with 1.5 million views each became the number-one and number-two most viewed on YouTube.

His forthright exposure of marketing practices raised awareness of the new, more commercial face of the Web in a way that violated Webizens' most dearly held notions about their community. He has since apologized and posted corrections, stating that his company did not engage in what he now calls "black hat" practices.

Greenberg's approach is instructive, but things move fast on the Web. Hosts catch on and change policies quickly, so you'll have to create your own tailored to your audience and your host if you want to increase your audience.

Greenberg's Tips for Taking Videos Viral

Keep it short. Keep your videos in the 15- to 30-minute range; break long stories down into bite-sized clips.

Design for remixing. Create a video that's simple enough to be remixed over and over again by others.

Don't make an obvious ad. If a video feels like an ad, viewers won't share it unless it's really amazing.

Make it shocking. Give a viewer no choice but to investigate further.

Use fake headlines. Make the viewer say, "Holy cow, did that actually happen?!"

Appeal to sex. If all else fails, hire the most attractive women available to be in the video.

The First 50,000 Views

It takes 50,000 views to get on YouTube's "Most Viewed" page, and getting his clients' work on that page was one of the keys to Greenberg's strategy. Once your video is there, it's easier for people to watch, and you'll get more views. To get the first 50,000, Greenberg and his team used multiple strategies, including joining conversations on forums, sending links out to e-mail lists, and embedding videos in the comments section of their MySpace pages.

Social networking plays a large part in making videos popular on the Web. Participating in an online community or building one around your work goes a long way toward getting your video noticed on the Web. Rather than looking at your viewers as an audience or a vehicle for your success, get to know them and what they want. You'll need to keep track of who's watching to know when it's time to look for advertisers. If you're spreadsheet-challenged, choosing a host who keeps track for you is a good start, but often you'll need to track views across several Web sites, because once your video becomes popular, it takes on a life of its own.

You'll want a home-court advantage for your video no matter how far it roams. Creating a video Web site—and using search engine strategies to help viewers find it—ensures your viewers will be able to see your video in the quality you intended and get more information about you and your other work. Once your work gets really popular or you've produced regular episodes of a show, you'll want to look into creating a channel or signing on with a host that will help you find advertisers in exchange for a share of the advertising revenue your video brings in.

Keep in mind that tens of thousands of videos are uploaded to the Web every day. The chances of anyone finding yours and passing it along are very low. Getting millions to watch is possible, but it won't happen unless you work at it.

The Name Game

Naming videos in a way that gets people to watch is a lot like writing tabloid headlines. What gets people's attention isn't always classy or subtle. An enterprising friend invited viewers to his live Webcam page with the come-on "Naked Chicks on the Internet." When viewers clicked through, they found themselves with a live view of his chicken coop.

Provocative video names are a great strategy for bringing viewers to your site, but it won't keep them there, and I recommend against doing anything that is obviously misleading. Headlines get hits, but they won't get viewers to come back for more once they figure out they've been hoodwinked.

Thumbnails Show Them What You've Got

Most video sites have thousands of thumbnails; yours needs to stand out. Even small thumbnails help a viewer to see what your video is all about; choose images that make people want to watch. YouTube harvests your thumbnail from the center of your video, so plant something there you want viewers to see. On sites where you have more control or can choose your thumbnail, create a visual come-on (FIGURE 8.3).

FIGURE 8.3 Attractive thumbnails invite viewers to watch your video.

Thumbnails that include images of people seem to be more effective. It doesn't hurt if the person is a scantily clad woman, but put time into thinking about what will interest your audience enough to click through. Think of your thumbnail as a tiny billboard that advertise your video to viewers. If you want viewers to click through and watch your video, give them a sneak peek in the form of an image that tells them something about its content.

Marketing Web Style

Dina Kaplan of Blip.tv (www.blip.tv) says effective marketing helps expand your audience, an important first step toward monetizing your video. For new producers and those who have shows just emerging, she says, using the Web to market your work is the most important thing you can do before you look for sponsors.

She suggests starting with your show's content and finding viewers with similar interests. "If you're doing a show about food or organic cooking, go to the Google group on organic cooking. Macrobiotic diets—go to the group on that; find communities on Facebook or on Ning that are relevant to what your show is about and be really active on them."

It's a mistake, according to Kaplan, to market aggressively to potential viewers. Sending out press releases and multiple postings or e-mails saying "watch my show" just doesn't work. Instead, become an active member of communities that share your interests. She says, "Listen to the thought leaders, pay attention to what they're saying, comment on their video blogs, and immerse yourself in that community."

She also suggests going to conferences on your topic to better understand what will appeal to your audience. After you've developed a large audience, she says, is the time to think about sponsorship, not before that. We'll hear more from Kaplan in Chapter 9, *Making It Pay*, where she outlines the specifics of getting advertisers and sponsors.

Promoting Your Video on Social Networks

Research blogs and interest groups related to your content. Get to know your target audience's interests. Be an active listener, and pay attention to what they want and need.

- **Blogs.** Reach out to individuals who run relevant blogs.
- **Forums.** Start new threads and discussions.
- **MySpace.** Plenty of users allow you to embed YouTube videos right in the comments section of their MySpace pages. Take advantage of this.
- **Facebook.** Use sites like Facebook to spread the word about your video efficiently.
- **E-mail lists.** Send a link to your video to an appropriate e-mail list.
- **Friends.** Make sure everyone you know watches the video and passes it along to friends.

Working with the Press

The news media can make your video very popular. To get your video noticed by the press, you'll need to think like a reporter. Like the best Web video makers, reporters are very keenly aware of their audiences. They also know a good story when they see it.

Make sure you have a clearly defined story. It's almost always a mistake to send out hundreds of announcements. Working reporters are inundated with press releases and discard most. Instead, when you have a real story, identify the reporters and publications most likely to be interested, and target your efforts toward them. Write each a personal note explaining why they their audiences might be interested and provide all the pertinent details. You'll have more success if you also do some of the legwork for them and provide the experts and contact information for the independent sources they'll need to verify and comment on your story. Local print media and cable TV shows are often interested in stories national media wouldn't touch. Like social networking on the Web, local media and small publications depend on affiliation.

If you're a member of a profession, are a member of an ethnic group, or are interested in ecology or politics, you might find support from related publications. When I edited *The Denver Weekly News*, I made a point of interviewing African American celebrities and political figures when they came to town, and I covered all the news of local churches and businesses in the Black community. When I traveled to Haiti as a reporter, New York's *Amsterdam News* ran my story on page 1 because there were many Haitian expatriates among its readers.

When Your Video Becomes News

Sometimes the media will find you. If your video is on a topic in the middle of a breaking news story, you'll often hear from the press. I had this experience when Jef Raskin, the original inventor of the Macintosh, died of cancer after I recorded a series of interviews with him for a documentary. Reporters found the Web site where I had posted video from the project (www.jefthemovie.com) and got in touch. Hits on the site exploded, and there were inquiries from television stations wanting to purchase footage.

If your video becomes popular enough to garner media attention, it's important to be prepared for the limelight. Make sure your Web site has a section for the press. Post a cell phone number and respond quickly; most reporters are on tight deadlines. When you post an e-mail address for press contacts, spell out the @ sign to foil spammers' spiders. Provide high-resolution photos for press to download from your site to assist print reporters, and post basic information about yourself and your video to make it easy for them to get accurate information for their reports.

When one large media outlet gets interested, more often follow. When David Letterman invited EepyBird's Stephen Voltz and Fritz Grobe to appear on the *Late Show with David Letterman*, their *Diet Coke and Mentos* video had been online for just three days. They subsequently appeared on the *Today Show*, the *Ellen DeGeneres Show*, and MTV's *Total Request Live*. Articles in the *Wall Street Journal*, *Rolling Stone*, the *New York Times*, and *GQ* followed. High visibility in traditional media brought millions to the Web to view their video.

When you do get media coverage, keep track of it for your records and share your success with your viewers by posting it on your Web site. Follow up by sending reporters a personal note and add them to your press list. If you come across a story you think they'll like, send them a note. They'll remember your kindness and that you kept the focus on their needs; it's always good to have a few friends in the media.

Internet Famous

Students at New York's Parsons School of Design are learning how to draw attention to their work on the Web in a class called "Internet Famous" (http:// internetfamo.us). Jamie Wilkinson, who is also development director for Rocketboom, one of the most popular Web video shows, says the rules for the class are simple: anything goes (**FIGURE 8.4**).

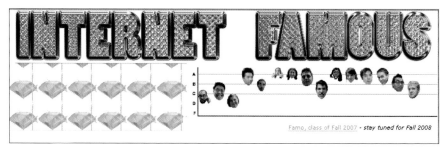

FIGURE 8.4 The Web site for a Parsons School of Design class on Internet fame.

Internet Famous's teachers know a little bit about getting famous off the Web too. A *Time* magazine article about the course described the class as "an effort to quantify Internet fame." The special software used by the class measures the number of views a producer's work is getting, the caliber of her social networking, and a variety of other factors.

Wilkinson (**FIGURE 8.5**) built the software used for the class. It measures just how popular students are with a combination of strategies that includes checking their MySpace pages and other social networking sites like Digg and del.icio.us. He calls the class the first to be graded by an algorithm. Wilkinson says the software replicates one of the key strategies for getting famous: paying attention to what's going on online.

Photo by Vu Bui

FIGURE 8.5 Jamie Wilkinson wrote software that evaluates and grades students on Web popularity for a class called "Internet Famous."

Be Prolific

Some of Wilkinson's tips for getting noticed on the Web are surprising. Many students spend two years creating a thesis project, he says, when it's often more important to be prolific than it is to be good. The class's tongue-in-cheek motto is "Release early, often, and with rap music." Joking aside, Wilkinson is serious about the volume of work you need when you're trying to get popular online.

"When I interview someone for a job," Wilkinson says, "I look at what they've done. If it's just one piece, I might not like it. But if they have 10 pieces online, the chances are better that one will catch my attention."

To take advantage of the viral video possibilities that social networking sites offer by playing an active role in online communities, create accounts at a number of online community sites including YouTube, Digg, and del.icio.us. Make your Web site easy to find and easy to use. Use tools and techniques to monitor and increase your site's popularity. Stay current with what's happening on the Web. Each site has its own personality, and what's popular or considered good on the Web can change from day to day. You have to stay on top of things. Put time into tracking your video. Pay attention to where it's going and how viewers respond.

Sites Recommended by "Internet Famous"

Try tracking your Internet fame on these social networking sites recommended by "Internet Famous":

Digg. http://digg.com

del.icio.us. http://del.icio.us

YouTube. http://youtube.com

Flickr. http://flickr.com

Technorati. http://technorati.com

Alexa. http://alexa.com

Compete. http://compete.com

Quantcast. http://quantcast.com

Reddit. http://reddit.com

Yahoo. http://yahoo.com

Google. http://google.com

Wikipedia. http://wikipedia.com

Instructables. http://instructables.com

Twitter. http://twitter.com

MySpace. http://myspace.com

Facebook. http://facebook.com

Icerocket. http://icerocket.com

DeviantArt. http://deviantart.com

Your Video Web Site

Your Web page can play a key role in developing your audience. While your work competes for attention on large sites with lots of video, on your site it can shine. Blip.tv hosts Web video shows. People come to the site to watch their favorite Web series.

Blip.tv's clean, simple design (**FIGURE 8.6**) is a welcome relief from sites like You-Tube, where thousands of videos compete for your attention and thumbnails are about the size their name suggests.

FIGURE 8.6 Blip.tv has a clean interface that keeps the focus on the videos.

One feature of the site is a window that promotes the latest shows with a short clip. Once you're on the site to watch one show, you learn about others effortlessly. Key to this equation is that the window is large enough to see the show and decide whether you like it.

BrightCove is a top destination for Web video. In spite of the sheer volume of video on the site, it works (**FIGURE 8.7**).

Scenes of Provincial Life (**www.somedancersandmusicians.com/vlog/ ScenesOfProvincialLife.cgi**) is an artist's Web site with beautiful images and a calm interface with lots of white space. It opens with an artistic list of several intriguing images as large and small snapshots (**FIGURE 8.8**). (For more on this site and its founder, Michael Szpakowski, see Chapter 9, *Making It Pay.*)

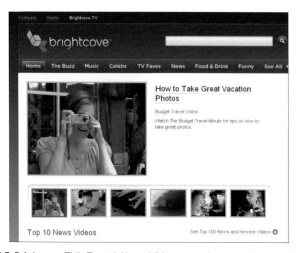

FIGURE 8.7 Brightcove.TV's Top 10 News Videos stands out at the top of the page.

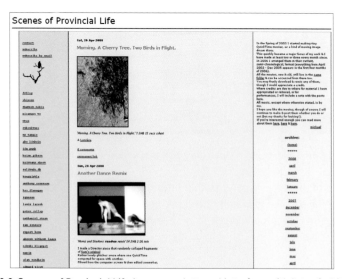

FIGURE 8.8 Scenes of Provincial Life has an uncluttered interface with lots of white space.

When you click a Scenes of Provincial Life video to play it, it's delivered to a pristine white page, which means you can turn your full attention to it (**FIGURE 8.9**).

Although not technically a Web site, the Miro player, a utility that connects to the Web and downloads selected Web video for you to watch when you want, is an excellent illustration of how much you can fit into an interface without it losing function. Videos from RSS feeds you subscribe to download automatically, but you can stop a download anytime you like (**FIGURE 8.10**). A built in video search engine also works as a recommendation engine to help you find videos you want to watch.

FIGURE 8.9 When you click a video in Scenes of Provincial Life, it pops up on a white background, keeping the focus on the video.

FIGURE 8.10 Miro's video player includes a search box at the bottom of the page and spinning arrows to show you when video is downloading from Miro's RSS feeds.

NOTE Like many manufacturers, Prada is working
with real artists to produce
videos that include product
placement but are also fun to
watch. Check it out for yourself at www.prada.com.

My favorite video Web site of all time is the lost, lamented site
designed for the launch for the Prada Parfums. Prada is still doing
interesting things with video on the Web (www.prada.com) including spectacular animation and an archive of past videos including
the one produced by Ridley Scott and his daughter Jordan for
Prada Parfums. Still, I miss the old site, which opened with a col-
lage that invited exploration and included several animated elements. That's what a well-done Web site can do—enhance your video. When I look
at Scott and Jordan's video now without the wonderful Web interface framing it, it
lacks something.

Tips for Creating Your Video Web Page

Many of you will opt to post your video on a video blog or video upload site such
as YouTube, Blip, or Brightcove. But don't miss the opportunity to create your own
Web page. Most video upload sites provide a URL you can link to. On your video
page you can control all of the elements that appear on the page with your video.
Create large attractive thumbnails to show viewers what they'll see, include additional information about your video or its topic, and provide subscriber links to your
RSS feed. Once you have your own page you can also sell advertising or include
ads from Google Adsense.

Even if you don't initially get enough traffic to attract large advertisers, there are
things you can do to take advantage of your video's popularity on the Web.

Making money off Web video isn't easy. But if you plan to keep making video for
the Web, you'll want to think about it. I'm not suggesting you spend the big bucks to
build a custom Web site, but at least consider tweaking the standard templates that
come free as part of your blogging software, and choose the player that will show
your video at its best.

It you do create a separate site for your video, here are some things to think about.
Once you have an audience, they'll come looking for more video produced with
your unique point of view. Tell them something about yourself. Your "About" page
provides an opportunity for shameless self-promotion. Use key words to make it
one of the places people see when they Google your name on the Web.

In addition to promoting yourself and your work, provide loads of information. If
your video is topic-oriented, that's another opportunity to place Google AdWords
on the page. Also register with Amazon.com and iTunes so that when those interested in the topic click through, you'll make a few pennies. Dave (my coauthor) just
got a check for more than $300 from Amazon. It's not a living, but it keeps the cost
of hosting a Web page down.

If your video goes viral, resulting in loads of traffic, you'll thank yourself for thinking about this in advance. Alternately, video may be just one part of a larger business for you, which is even more reason to make sure your Web site does its job. I say this because after many years of producing Web sites, I'm still amazed at how naïve many people are about the process. They somehow expect the Web site to make money for them. Heads up: Web sites *don't* make money. But they can be a tool for making money if you plan carefully.

My preference is for clean, well-organized Web sites with lots of white space and a few, carefully selected design elements. However, your style and your audience may dictate something different. This is your opportunity to be creative. While many video Web sites present a ubiquitous grid, you have plenty of chances to change that. Make your page a standout with an innovative design and clear communication of your mission. Your page title and tag lines are key to letting the viewers know who you are and what they'll find here. Go one step further and chunk your video if it's longer than one to three minutes. This will give viewers access to what they want to see. They'll probably still watch it all, but people are generally happier when they have choices.

Drive Traffic to Your Site

What you don't see on Web sites is as important as what you do. I'm talking about your site's visibility to search engines.

Tim Tuttle is the CEO and cofounder of Truveo, a video search engine. He says the most important thing you can do to develop your audience and get the word out about your video is effective tagging. Naming your video descriptively and adding descriptions to your video player will make it easier for video search engines to find your work online. This in turn will help viewers find and watch your video.

Once you've built a site for your video, you'll want to submit it to search engines. To make it easier for them to index your video, Google's site map tool, for example, automatically uploads the site to Google for spiders to index it.

Another strategy is to transcribe any interviews that appear in your videos and place the text on the page with the video. Identify key words, and make sure they're part of the text describing and introducing the video as well.

Facial recognition and voice recognition are fascinating ideas, and several of the video search sites are using them. These techniques tend to be expensive and are not totally reliable as yet. Mary Hodder, CEO of Dabble and a pioneer of the video search field, confirms that good tagging remains the best way to get noticed by video search engines.

Video Search Engines

One key to attracting viewers to your site is increasing its visibility to search engines. The following are some popular video search sites, some of which are also behind the scenes providing video search for many other sites.

There are two kinds of search engines: those that deliver results from sites universally, and those like Google, AOL, Yahoo, and YouTube that weight results and give preference to video on their own sites.

Google Video Search (http://video.google.com). You can conduct video searches in 10 languages and regions. This site has millions of videos indexed and available for viewing. Google indexes videos people have added using Google's services (YouTube and Google Video) as well as videos from other third-party sites.

Truveo (http://truveo.com). Among the largest of the video search engines, Truveo reaches an audience of more than 40 million users every month. Truveo's interface includes thumbnails and a tag cloud. Its search engine powers many of popular Web video destinations, including search for AOL, Microsoft Corporation, CNET's Search.com, Brightcove, Qwest, Excite, and hundreds of others.

Blinkx (http://blinkx.com). Providing more 18 million hours of video search with previews, Blinkx uses a combination of its patented search technology, speech recognition, and video analysis software to find online video.

Dabble (http://dabble.com). This is a favorite among independents that indexes Blip.tv, Atom Films, Dailymotion, and more than 600 other sites. Like other search engines, it uses metadata to index video sites. A community of Dabble members adds details and notes and corrects mistakes to ensure its accuracy. Dabble also offers playlists organized by members.

ClipBlast (http://clipblast.com). ClipBlast's stated mission is to simplify access to the "video Web." It helps viewers search and watch videos and works with video content providers, advertisers, and marketers to monetize their investments.

AltaVista (http://altavista.com). Providing global, multilingual video search that includes a "family filter," AltaVista was among the first to search video on the Internet.

Yahoo Search for Video (http://searchforvideo.com). This site lists more than a dozen video publishers it indexes on its home page, including HBO, Revver, Lonely Planet, AP, Forbes, and Newsweek.

Everyzing (http://everyzing.com). Formerly Podzinger, Everyzing provides a service connecting video content to major Web search engines. It uses speech-to-text technology to wrap video with metadata, including a full-text output of the spoken word track.

If your video includes closed-captioning, the captions can also provide the information necessary to index a video for video search. MPEG-4 and Windows Media are two popular Web video codecs that include specifications for closed captioning.

10 Tips for Optimizing Your Web Page for Search Engines

1. Use text instead of images for your page head and tag line.

2. Write a descriptive title and detailed description of your video that includes key words and concepts, participants' names, and locations, as well as your topic.

3. Study your competition. Look at other sites that cover your topic, and check out the key words they are using.

4. Consider sharing links with others to drive traffic to your site. Investigate communities online where you can post links.

5. Add as much useful content to your site as you can find. Resource information—such as a glossary of terms or explanations, how-to information, and reviews—ranks high among the popular sites on the Web.

6. Study search engines and keep up-to-date with what works.

7. Break your videos and the information on your site into small bites that are easily accessible to readers.

8. Make it clear what your site is about. Put the site's mission or your philosophy high on the page.

9. Clearly post some kind of contact information.

10. Even if your site is database-driven, make sure page titles include descriptive names, not just file names and numbers.

Keep the User Experience in Mind on Your Video Web Page

Aza Raskin, Head of User Experience for Mozilla

Interface designer Aza Raskin (www.humanized.com) says most people don't pay enough attention to user experience on the Web. "What people don't realize is that it's user experience that keeps people coming back to their site," he says. Instead of flashing as much information as possible, he suggests you figure out what you want viewers to focus on and make that prominent. He created Songza www.songza.com (**FIGURE 8.11**), a simple yet effective site for finding, listening to, and sharing music on the Web.

Most video Web pages are designed on a grid crowded with thumbnails because that's a format viewers are familiar with. Raskin suggests giving viewers visual clues instead of a lot of instruction. "The reason why tagging took off," he says, "is that del.icio.us and Flickr gave you examples of tags." Viewers seeing the tags people assigned to photos learned what to do when the time came to tag their own.

"Ads are cluttering up our interfaces," says Raskin, "giving us information overload, detracting from our pleasure, and driving us away."

One solution is to make sure any ads that you accept are contextually relevant to your viewer. In presentations he often points to Google's home page as an example of simple effective design. Raskin is working on new interfaces for the mobile Web at Mozilla. But for now he says Web video is at a kind of impasse. Raskin is working on new interfaces that serve users better. "Right now, the video platform is closed," he says. "There's Silverlight, and there's Flash. That means there's a limited number of things you can do with it because it's controlled by Microsoft or Adobe." As the Web moves toward open standards for video, he says we'll see better integration of video and a more integrated user experience. "The innovation that comes with an open platform will be the next step forward in video on the Web."

FIGURE 8.11 Songza.com's simple interface shows users only what they need to see but provides visual clues about how to use it.

Aza's Tips for Your Video Web Site

Talk about who is behind your work. The most popular sites and the ones people trust most talk about the site's creator.

Always have some kind of call to action. Your users have seen this video, what now? Invite them to participate in a community, whether it's leaving comments or posting responses or something else like telling a friend or coming back to view the next episode.

Keep it simple. The less interaction you require from your viewers, the more of your content they'll see. Take inspiration from print designs and limit interaction. You'll increase your viewers.

Using Statistics to Make Your Video Better

Statistics collected by your video host track how you're doing with viewers and provide information for advertisers if you decide you want sponsors or advertising. In their simplest form, the statistics provided by video hosts show how many viewers have watched your video, but they don't tell you how long they watched or who they are. More sophisticated analysis, sometimes asking viewers to register before viewing video, provides additional demographic information.

If you're collecting stats for advertisers, go along with the system they use. Today, each of the television networks has its own way of measuring. The one used by CBS is not compatible with that used by NBC; DoubleClick (www.doubleclick.com), a major Web advertising provider, does not work the same way as Microsoft's service. Everybody in the industry would like to see a standard. Companies like Nielsen are jumping into Web video to try to create a standard.

Follow the rules set down by your host or advertising partner, and remember why it's so important to do things right. Advertising is becoming more sophisticated. It can tell you who's watching, when they watch, and when they click off. If you do a good job providing information to advertisers, they're more likely to buy ads.

Tracking How You're Doing with Viewers

You discover remarkable things looking at the patterns of how people view your video. The Web is a very fast place. Do they leave your video after 15 seconds or 90 seconds, or do they watch all the way through? An amazing percentage of people click away very quickly after 15–45 seconds and just go on to something else. If you see that pattern, you know you're going to need to make your introduction more dramatic.

Most of those who don't turn away quickly will keep watching for a while, but if there's a particular point in your show where many turn away, say when you go to a guest or Q&A, you know you have a problem you need to deal with. You can also learn from the time of day your visitors watch. The most traffic for YouTube in the United States is not at prime TV time in the evening; instead, it's at a little after noon, and again around 5 p.m., as people take a break before leaving the office.

National Internet service providers get a consistent peak at these times, which roll across the nation as New York, Chicago, Denver, and Los Angeles hit noon and then later hit 5 p.m. If you see a pattern like this, you can guess a lot about your audience. They're at work, so they're not interested in anything that's too long. They're taking a break, so they're more likely to respond to something short, with attitude and some humor—as we've seen with Rocketboom—than to hard news. If your peak traffic is coming in the evening, you know that many of your viewers will spend more time with your video if they find something appealing.

Both your Web host and independent services such as the three listed below can provide statistical data about your video.

Services provided by your video host can be a big help in making your video popular. Nearly every host has a way to feature interesting or popular videos, such as posting viewer counts or including video in a "favorite" or "most watched" category.

▶ Google Analytics

▶ TubeMogul

▶ VidMetrix

VidMetrix also tracks video through social media sites and blogs. It includes comments and individual ratings on each individual video and draws graphs useful for tracking the viral spread of a video across the Internet.

While statistics tracking your video are in part attached to your video host's server, some services will aggregate information from several hosts to give you the big picture. These include Videoegg (www.videoegg.com), whose main business is tracking views to sell advertising; and Gigya (www.gigya.com), which offers widgets that you can attach to your video site to help track it through social networking sites. While sites like YouTube make popularity visible to viewers, some sites track viewer stats but keep them private. Some won't even share them with producers.

Marketing Help from Your Video Host

As we saw earlier, a studio's efforts to generate views for one video only reached into the thousands. When working with Dan Greenberg, the video's producers scored 6 million views on YouTube, 200 blog posts linking to the videos, and a "5 Most Viewed of the Day" status for all six clips.

If you want the largest possible audience, the first place to host your video is YouTube (http://youtube.com) and its peers around the world like Daily Motion in France and Tudoh in China. Except for a few special deals, nobody makes much money directly. The advantage of these sites is that they are ubiquitous and cost you absolutely nothing.

Most social networking sites, such as MySpace and Flickr, are working toward similar services, but YouTube is by far the most popular. It's a good idea to have your video on several networks because they have different audiences. What may be very popular on one network may bomb or get minimal views on another.

Look for These Helpful Features From Your Video Host

Social networking tools. Does your host provide for viewer comments or chat or make it easy to recommend your video to members of social networking sites?

RSS feeds. Does your host make it easy for viewers to subscribe to a feed of your video?

Content management. If you have (or expect to have) a large volume of video, you'll need a host that makes it easy to manage content.

Promotion opportunities. Some hosts highlight or feature your work in a "new" or "most-watched" category that helps build your audience by promoting it to new viewers.

Recommendation engine. Some hosts suggest your video to viewers watching related content.

Blip.tv (www.blip.tv) is the small video maker's favorite host. The site is smart, attractive, well promoted, and willing to go the extra mile, and CEO Dina Kaplan often answers questions directly on mailing lists. The Blip.tv crew makes a point of being helpful to users. They take only regularly produced shows, and if your show is successful, they'll happily work with you to find sponsors or advertisers.

Most producers won't want the responsibility of managing their video on a server. Instead, you'll contract with a company like the free service at Blip.tv or Brightcove (http://brightcove.com), which will pay the fee for the bandwidth it takes to serve your video in exchange for being able to place ads on their site.

Brightcove is a professional service used by some of the biggest names on the Web including the *New York Times*. It provides an interface that makes it easy for clients to manage their video libraries and offers a variety of players that include ways for users to embed video and RSS feeds. The interface also does an excellent job of adding metadata to video files. Because Brightcove also provides a free service for independents and small businesses, it's an effective bridge service for businesses that expect to grow.

Community sites like Motionbox (www.motionbox.com) make it easy to share your video, but you'll want to set your own standards for where you upload. You may want to post on YouTube for the millions who watch regularly as well as iPhone users desperate for something free to watch, but you should always start with the best-quality video you can produce so it won't look too bad on YouTube. If you really care about quality, make sure that's not the only place you post it. Think of YouTube as your "low bandwidth" and cell phone option.

If you care at all how people see your video, post it on a site that shows better quality as well. There are two options for doing this in a cost-effective manner. One is progressive download, which caches video to your hard drive as you watch it (you have to wait for the caching to get a head start on the playback, but as long as the playback doesn't catch up with the caching, after that the user experience resembles streaming). People will wait for something they know they want. The other option is hybrid, peer-to-peer (P2P) streaming technologies. These technologies can substantially reduce the cost of streaming your video live.

 TIP You'll have to do your own homework.
The times they are always a-changing on the Web. So, any rankings published today are likely to have shifted by the time you read this book. There is also some sleight of hand at play in the term *video-sharing site*. NBC, Hulu, and other commercial sites share loads of video and are likely, with their excellent-quality streaming, to jump to the top of many lists because they make commercial offerings easy to watch.

Top U.S. Video Web Sites, Ranked by Market Share

If you want to get your video out to the most people, consider these sites from Compete.com's top 10 list, rated by number of sessions.

1. YouTube (43 percent video sites market share)

2. MySpace (16 percent video sites market share)

3. Google Video (11 percent video sites market share)

4. AOL Video (7 percent video sites market share)

5. MSN Video (4 percent video sites market share)

6. StupidVideos (3 percent video sites market share)

7. Yahoo Video (3 percent video sites market share)

8. Break (2 percent video sites market share)

9. eBaum's World (2 percent video sites market share)

10. Daily Motion (1 percent video sites market share)

▶ Take Charge of Distribution

Yaron Samid, cofounder of Pando Networks

yaron Samid, one of the founders of Pando Networks, says he created Pando to address an important problem: "The Internet (HTTP protocol) was never designed to transmit video." Pando Networks (**www.pando.com**) developed a hybrid peer-to-peer (P2P) site and uses it successfully with clients like NBC, which delivers all of its on-air content for download using Pando's network.

P2P is an Internet protocol like HTTP, but instead of delivering Web pages, it's designed to transport video and audio over an intelligent network. Unlike traditional hosting, where the more video you send out, the more you pay, with P2P the cost goes down when more people view your video.

> *Exclusivity is very Web 1.0...put your video on as many hosts as possible.*

Hybrid P2P doesn't work well until you have a lot of people hosting your show, but if you have a popular show with a lot of viewers, it can pay off. For popular shows, hybrid P2P brings costs down 70 to 90 percent, which is why more networks have been using it to send out high-quality streams. Pando offers very friendly pricing for small producers as part of their strategy to get their player on as many computers as possible. This, he hopes, will allow more content producers to get into the business of Web video.

"There is a dramatic shift with your ability to get on a level playing field with the biggest content producers [who have] the deepest pockets," says Samid. "You don't need any money to put your content online and get potentially billions of viewers."

Samid is also the organizer of Video 2.0; with 1,700 members and growing, it's one of New York's largest Meetup networking groups. He says hosts such as YouTube, Motionbox, and Metacafe focus on user-generated content, while others such as Blip.tv, the Feedroom, and Vignette feature more produced content. Most of these sites are happy to pay your bandwidth bill, he says, in exchange for the opportunity to monetize your video. Because they aggregate a large volume of video on their sites, they have access to advertisers that individuals don't. The cost of bandwidth has come down so much over the past two years that it's practical for these companies to offer hosting services free—a dramatic shift from the previous business model for streaming video that has been around for about 10 years.

Exclusivity is very Web 1.0, according to Samid, who advises putting your video on as many hosts as possible. "You'll have to do the legwork," he says, to make your video stand out for users. One important step is networking—not just online, but in person.

Video 2.0 members meet monthly for presentations from Web video companies and discussions about issues. There's always time for announcements from people with jobs to fill and from others looking for work. It's a real community, according to Samid, who facilitates the growing group and discourages presenters from delivering sales pitches. "If you try to be a networker, a guy that schmoozes," he says, you won't get far. He suggests becoming an active part of a community instead of just trying to manipulate it.

You don't need any money to put your content online and get potentially billions of viewers.

Samid says networking is a key part of marketing your work and a step toward for monetizing it. Samid's tips for creating a content creation business that will support you full-time include making your video a valuable experience for viewers, considering product placement, and getting creative about creating opportunities for advertisers to support your work. Quality counts, he says, when you go after the real marketing dollars. So keep production values high.

You'll also have to decide whether you want ads on the pages showing your videos. When you first start out, they aren't likely to put much revenue in your pocket, and they are likely to irritate viewers enough to notice—especially if the ads come in a pre-roll (before), during, and/or after your video (post-roll).

If you do go with a site that tacks advertising onto your video, know what you're getting into. Some sites show the same ads over and over each time you select a video, prompting this writer to click away in frustration. Others populate the page with giant flashing banners and skyscraper ads.

Some of the best advertising is on the commercial sites that deliver television shows. Because ads appear to cache while you're watching shows on Move Networks (**www.movenetworks.com**), for example, the quality is mesmerizing. You're watching before you know it. Even though, like television, you have the option to walk away or avert your eyes during the ad, there's no such thing as TiVo for Web video, so you can't simply scroll through.

Whatever option you select, read the terms carefully. Make sure you can pull out at any time and that you retain the rights to your video. While we're on the topic, try to make sure your video is not used to someone else's financial advantage without your getting a cut.

Free or Pay Video Hosting—Which Is Right for You?

Why would you pay for video hosting when there are so many sites that will host your video free? The most important reason is to control the quality of experience your viewers have when they see your video on the Web. Another reason is to track viewers more effectively and to customize the tools you use to build that community through comments and other interactive features.

Some high-quality video being delivered on the Internet today uses the MPEG-4 AVC/H.264 codec. H.264 supports true HD quality video, although most of the video called "HD" on the Web is less than half the ideal HD bandwidth.

The technology behind the high-quality video on ABC.com is provided by Move Networks, which offers a package that includes the streaming server and players. Move keeps the quality of its full-screen video high by encoding at several bit rates and sending to viewers the highest-quality video they can watch, based on the bandwidth the viewers' Internet connections support. With the best connections, ABC/Move provides a 1.9 megabit stream with quality close to a DVD. If you can't handle more than 600K, Move will send a 600K stream to you. Each program is encoded to a dozen or so different bit rates, so they can find the best for each viewer. Their proprietary player smoothly switches if your connection speed varies.

Few other sites offer more than two or three speeds, so it is harder for them to match your actual speed.

When someone tunes in to a show at a customer like ABC, Move immediately sends a low- or medium-quality file that starts on the viewer's computer almost instantly. Within a few seconds, a buffer builds up and a high-bandwidth file kicks in. This happens so quickly the viewer often doesn't notice.

Limelight Networks (www.limelightnetworks.com) is one of the world's largest video hosting companies. Cofounder Mike Gordon says he makes sure there's an entry price offering (about $500 a month) because he wants to keep Limelight open to new and small companies.

He says he'll never forget the day in 2005 when two scruffy-looking guys in their 20s came to him with an idea and modest expectations. Chad Hurley and Steve Chen didn't have an impressive presentation or very much money, but their company, YouTube, became a key client for Limelight and sold to Google for $1.65 billion just 18 months later. Like Limelight, Akamai (www.akamai.com) is a content delivery network (CDN) that delivers your video when you put it up on a host like Blip.tv or Brightcove.

Streamhoster (http://streamhoster.com) is a small host that provides an excellent entry point for small companies and producers who want to serve low volumes of video or longer videos of events. Prices are $15/month for 500 MB of video storage and 5,000 MB of video transfer and $25/month for 1,500 MB of storage and 12,000 MB of transfer. The advantage of going with a smaller CDN like Streamhoster is that you can very flexibly include video in your Web site with the assurance it will be there and available at the quality you define while you keep total control. Streamhoster offers special pricing for events and serves both Windows Media Video and QuickTime.

Paid hosting can get expensive. One solution is to work with a host with technology that lets users pass your video on, sharing the bandwidth cost. P2P networking, which was vilified by the recording industry for facilitating music piracy via Napster, has come of age as a legitimate commercial platform for sharing video. Today's P2P uses a hybrid technology that allows customers to pay for a specified number of streams but minimizes the cost when the video gets popular, using a safe technology that recruits each viewer as a host to serve the video to others.

Set Up an RSS Feed for Your Video

Really Simple Syndication (RSS) provides a way for your viewers to subscribe to a regular feed or podcast of your video. Instead of visiting their favorite video Web sites individually, viewers configure a feed reader to search their favorites and let them know when there's something new to watch. Many hosts' "channels"—including those you can configure yourself—use RSS to organize and deliver the videos.

Viewers can use the aggregator built into Firefox or download and install one from a company like Bloglines (www.bloglines.com). Before you set up your own RSS feed, create an account in Bloglines, and set up your RSS reader in Firefox or use Google's personalized home page or My Yahoo to make a list of all your feeds.

Create a free account with Brightcove and upload a video. The Brightcove player provides an RSS feed of your video. Click the menu to add an RSS feed to Bloglines, Google, Yahoo, and Newsgator.

You can also use RSS stand-alone software to create an RSS manually with XML. Extralabs (www.extralabs.net) offers free downloads of Feed Editor, which is an RSS editor that also includes features to transfer your feed via FTP. Feedvalidator (www.feedvalidator.org) is a free Web-based validator where you can check your files. You can also create RSS feeds with Adobe's Dreamweaver Web development software, but you'll need to download a third-party plug-in, RSSdreamfeeder (www.rnsoft.com/en/products/rssdreamfeeder), to make it easy.

A better option is to look for a host that provides the feed for you, as many of those mentioned in this chapter do. Look for the XML or RSS button on the host's players.

PROJECT

Create a Version of Your Video for the iPhone

Making your video accessible for mobile viewers can increase your audience. YouTube videos can be viewed on the iPhone, so that's one option. Another is to format your videos for the iPhone and upload them to iTunes.

Under their H.264 output options, both Adobe Media Encoder and Final Cut Pro's Compressor provide the option to format your video for iPhones and iPods (**FIGURE 8.12**). Compressor also includes settings for Apple TV. (Adobe Production Premium CS3 also includes a utility called Design Central that allows you to tailor and preview your video for a multitude of cell phones and other mobile devices.)

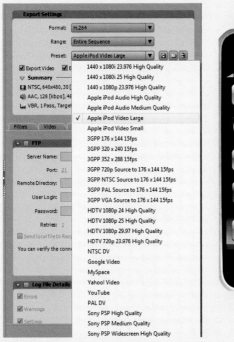

FIGURE 8.12 Adobe Media Encoder offers a full complement of iPod and iPhone compression options.

You can also encode with QuickTime Pro, an inexpensive upgrade from the free QuickTime Player (**FIGURE 8.13**). iPods and iPhones will play back only video encoded with MPEG-4 or H.264 compression (H.264 is an advanced version of MPEG-4 called AVC; usually, when video producers refer to MPEG-4, they mean an early version called MPEG-4 Part 2). H.264-encoded videos show up with better quality. Your soundtrack should be in AAC or MP3 format. Keep your video size small: 320x240 for the iPod, 480x320 for the iPhone. Use the smaller format if you want it to work on both.

FIGURE 8.13 iPod encoding settings in Apple QuickTime Pro.

You can also use your editing software to knock down the video's frame rate to reduce the file size. If your video was shot in wide-screen (16:9) format, you'll want to crop it to a full-screen (4:3) aspect ratio for viewing on the original video iPod (the more recent iPhone and iPod touch models feature 480:320 wide-screens, so if you're encoding exclusively for one of those devices, go with 16:9). Both Adobe Media Encoder and Compressor have visual interfaces that will let you see what you're doing. Once you have the video encoded, you'll upload the XML file to your Web server. You'll still need a video host to make this work.

A much easier solution is to upload your video to your video host, your video host, which will take care of the encoding and send you back a link. Try it.

CHAPTER 9

MAKING IT PAY

9   MAKING IT PAY

Often the best price for your Web video will be free. Doug Gayeton did his remarkable Second Life animation *Molotov Alba* without a sponsor, but the buzz persuaded HBO to pick it up. Brian Conley depends on donations to support *Alive in Baghdad* but Sky News and the BBC have purchased footage from him. *Funny or Die* inspired a comedy tour and got picked up by HBO. One of the most popular viral videos, *Diet Coke and Mentos*, made some money from ad sales and led to profitable gigs offline for its producers.

Just because viewers don't pay to watch your video doesn't mean you can't profit from it. Once you have a large audience, your viewers' attention is a valuable commodity. Advertisers will pay for their "eyeballs"—marketing-speak for their attention. Advertising supports much of the video on the Web, just as it has supported most television broadcasts for decades. You can sell advertising on your Web site, share revenue with a distributor such as Revver, or find a host such as Blip.tv that will match you with a sponsor.

Another way to make money is to take a job producing Web video. Today's options include a few highly sought after opportunities to produce your own work financed by a studio. Companies such as ON Networks and 60Frames produce high-quality professional Web video. You can also make money if you can find a niche where viewers will pay. Lynda.com is one of the most successful, providing training videos to subscribers.

But most people will make their rent working for large commercial operations. Fortunately, the networks are adding thousands of jobs in new media. Advertising agencies and other media outlets are looking for thousands more. Newspapers, magazines, radio stations, foundations, hospitals, schools, museums, and corporations all produce Web video today.

Stay tuned for job-hunting tips, insider job sites for Web videomakers, and the best places to meet people and make the contacts that lead to jobs. And finally, I'll talk about how Web video can pay off in a host of indirect ways, from strengthening your reputation to helping you spread the word about something you believe in.

Understanding Your Audience

The key thing to keep in mind as you read this chapter is how important it is to understand your audience. All the benefits and rewards that come from making Web video start with capturing and keeping your viewers' attention. That's what advertisers want and what you want too, even if your only goal is to make the world a better place.

Everyone in Hollywood knows Web video has the potential to make a lot of money for a lot of people. Screenwriters even shut down Hollywood with the biggest strike in recent history to make sure they get their cut. But where does the money to pay producers come from? Mostly ad revenues. Viewers may not like watching ads with their Web video, but soon they might not have a choice.

Like their television network counterparts, many Web video hosts are superimposing ads over video. The best ones feature options that allow viewers to opt out. These devices might give viewers a sense of power over the ad, but the ad typically doesn't disappear until more than half of it plays. Is this deliberate? Advertisers aren't talking (**FIGURE 9.1**).

FIGURE 9.1 Note the advertising opt-out box on the lower right of the screen.

At a recent business conference in New York, Madison Avenue execs were positively gleeful at the prospect of glomming up five-minute Web shows with billboard ads that play before a viewer gets to watch and after, with multiple overlays while viewing video, and with product placements. As with television, our options are narrowing. Viewers now pay for cable TV *and* are forced to watch ads between shows and ads on top of shows, and sadly there's no Web video equivalent of TiVo to soften the pain. As the tools that measure Web video audiences get more accurate, there will likely be more ads. Even the most creative ads get old quick, a problem exacerbated on the Web, where enterprising providers sometimes force viewers to watch the same ad again with each new video selected because they have so few advertisers.

All of this is likely to change as advertising on Web video becomes more sophisticated. There are new tools for statistical analysis that show not only what a viewer watches but also for how long. Advertisers will soon have a clearer understanding of what works and be able to better target Web video ads.

Although there is no one answer to which ad strategies will work on Web video, advertisers know that matching the programs to advertisers that viewers might actually have an interest in lowers viewer dissatisfaction and improves the effectiveness of the advertising.

Making Advertising Work for You

Diet Coke and Mentos producers Fritz Grobe and Steven Voltz call their experience the quintessential example of viral spread. But the two Web entrepreneurs, collectively known as EepyBird, didn't wait until the video was popular to check out options for making money from it. "As we were getting ready to put the video online, we had a lot of discussions about where's the best place to put it," they say. They considered putting it on YouTube but decided instead to put it on Revver. "Let's try it," they said. "Let's see if we can make some money.'"

When they signed with Revver, the site was new and didn't have much of a track record. Looking into Revver's financials gave EepyBird the confidence to sign on. They say, "It ended up being a fantastic decision."

From the start they made decent money on *Diet Coke and Mentos* in a 50/50 split with Revver. The video gained popularity fast. Within a few days it was getting hundreds of thousands of views a day. To date the video has earned them about $40,000. Would they do it again? Maybe. Although they found Revver was great to work with, that $40,000 represents millions of viewers. Until those numbers go up, they say, "Don't expect to be able to quit your day job, even if you have a big success."

It's difficult to anticipate in advance whether your video will be a hit and which host will generate the most income for you. The exposure you get on popular Web sites may end up being more valuable than the money you can make revenue sharing. If you have a live act, as EepyBird does, the more views you have, the more you'll get booked, and that can translate into more money than you'd earn online. Grobe and Voltz say it's great to see companies like YouTube moving toward a revenue-share model.

Getting Paid for Ads

Revver (www.revver.com) started with a great idea: host user-generated Web video, and when it gets really popular, share ad revenue with the video creators (**FIGURE 9.2**). So far they've had hits with *Ze Frank*, *Ask a Ninja*, and *Diet Coke and Mentos*. Revver reports that it paid out more than $1 million last year to content producers.

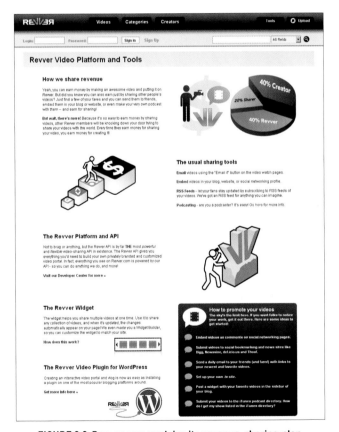

FIGURE 9.2 Revver.com explains its revenue-sharing plan.

Finding a Niche, a Sponsor, and a Distributor

Dina Kaplan, Chief Operations Officer, Blip.tv

Blip.tv is a favorite among independent producers. Ze Frank moved his popular show to Blip.tv before retiring. Blip hosts *Alive in Baghdad, Wallstrip, Geek Entertainmenttv, Treehuggertv, The All-For-Nots*, and many other successful Web shows. Blip COO Dina Kaplan graciously agreed to talk about how Blip works with producers and about revenue opportunities in the current market.

How do you know when one of your producers is ready for an advertiser or a sponsor?

We have a joke around the office. People complain, "I have 500 views and no sponsor." It just doesn't make sense for a big brand like Kraft, Pepsi, or Microsoft to [buy an ad to] reach 500 people, even if all 500 go out and buy the product. Once you're at the point of reaching 50,000, 100,000, or 500,000 a month with your show, then you're ready for sponsorship.

There are some exceptions shows like Beet.tv—run by the fabulous Andy Plesser—which is all about trends taking place in Web video. That show reaches a good-sized audience but not a huge audience. However, it's very valuable for some companies that want to target people running Web video companies like an Akamai, or a Limelight, or an Adobe. In that case, you can do a brand match where you have a company that's doing something, maybe a kind of B2B-oriented [product] and a show that directly reaches the people running those companies. It's a terrific match for the advertiser to market to exactly the audience they want to reach.

Do you keep track of how successful a show is, or does the producer have to come to you with evidence their show is doing well?

We're constantly looking at the list of the top shows on Blip and making sure we're actively going out and looking for sponsorships for the shows that have high numbers and want sponsors, because there are shows that don't want sponsors, and we respect that. If you have someone that's percolating up or a great show that's just about to move to Blip from another network, we actually appreciate it when they say, "Hey, we're moving over. Do you think there's a good sponsorship match for us?" If that person is going to get 500 or 1,000 views, it's just not going to make sense for us to go out and sell it.

Do advertisers look at the show's production values?

The quality of the shows that are hosted on networks like Blip.tv is dramatically increasing, and that's really exciting to watch. In terms of sponsorships, though, I'm not sure how much it matters. We've had some great sponsorships of shows like the *Ze Frank* show. It was really well produced, and he's unbelievably talented. But that was essentially Ze Frank—a talented guy and a camera in his living room or somewhere. I think if the show is good—however you want to define that—and it has an important audience for an advertiser, then that show can get a sponsor. It doesn't have to be a show that's shot in HD.

Does the word professional even apply in Web video?

More and more production companies based in Hollywood are producing Web-only shows. I'm talking about companies like 60Frames, which is an offshoot of UTA—a terrific talent agency. They shoot incredible-looking shows, and they're just for the Web. Maybe we should say that's professional content that just happens to be airing on the Web instead of television.

What constitutes success for Web video shows?

We sent out several five-figure checks this month for Web shows for campaigns that were less than a month. Some people are earning over $10,000 for campaigns that lasted just a couple of weeks. Eventually what you want is for the top Web show creators to make enough money that they can do what they love full-time.

Are we there yet? Not reliably, but I do see us earning more and more money for more Web show creators. And I think once the standards are set for advertising on the Web—when we know how big an overlay should be and it's the same size on Blip as it is on Daily Motion, YouTube, Revver, MetaCafe, etc., that a pre-roll should be a certain length, and a post-roll should be a certain length so that it's easier for a big brand to make a cross-network buy—I think the amount of money being spent on Web video will soar.

▶▶

Right now, every campaign needs to be tailored to every site. On Blip, a brand needs to make their creative look a certain way and on other video sites it needs to look a different way, so it's very difficult and expensive right now to do cross-network buys. When we make that easier, we'll see a lot more money going toward it.

Are producers breaking even?

Breaking even is tough to talk about when most of the shows are done for almost no money. It's tough to say "break even" when we're talking about very different levels of production costs. Are some people making money? Yes, but very few. A lot of it is luck, and a lot of it's personal connections. It will continue to be tough this year. It will be easier in 2009, but we're looking to 2010 for things to be a lot easier in terms of making serious amounts of money for shows.

What's working: pre-rolls, post-rolls, overlays?

The ideal campaign right now is similar to what *Wallstrip* [a daily finance show] has been doing, a pre-roll, or billboard saying "*Wallstrip* is brought to you by Options Express," within three or four seconds, with the logo of the brand on a slate and the logo of the show. Then you could reinforce the brand's messaging: "Options Express is great because..." on an overlay that pops up for five or ten seconds on the lower third of the video, then reinforce the message with a post-roll full-motion ad or slate saying "This episode was brought to you by Options Express. Thanks."

I also think humor is great. If you can ask the show creator "What's the best way to reach your audience, and by the way, do you want to make this ad?" you're always going to do better than just saying "I'm the brand; here's our ad. Put it up there, and let's hope for the best."

Does success mean crossing over to broadcast television?

Having a Web show cross over to TV is a goal for some producers, and it's not a goal for others. I don't want to speak for the *Ask a Ninja* guys, Kent [Nichols] and Doug [Sarine], but I think they've been offered some TV opportunities that they've turned down because they want to continue to own their brand (they recently accepted a $300,000 deal with ad network Federated Media). There are other shows that think of their Web shows almost like a pilot. They'll have more than one episode because you have to do that on the Web. *Wallstrip* sold, but they made a lot of money, so that's great. The financials have to be there because they are giving up control, they are giving up their independence, and they are giving up the potential upside for staying on the Web.

Using Google's AdSense, contextual advertising is another way to make advertising revenue on your video Web page. To qualify, you must own your domain name and provide information for payment, and your site has to be active and easy to navigate. After you qualify, Google sends spiders to crawl your Web page and delivers ads relevant to your audience and your site. You can customize the look and feel of the ads and choose picture ads or both pictures and text. There are two ways to earn using Google: pay-per-click and pay-per-thousand. If you don't yet have a site, you can use Blogger (http://blogger.com) to create one. Google also makes creating a site easy with Page Creator, a wizard that walks you through developing a simple Web page.

There are a few basic restrictions. You can't encourage clicks or have racist, violent, or other Google-prohibited content including gambling, profanity, or knockoff designer goods on your site. Google takes its advertising seriously, and it knows when you're trying to trick it, so don't bother adding a lot of irrelevant key words or try any other workarounds. As long as you follow the rules, you can just put the code on your site and wait for a check. If you have the right content and a lot of traffic, Google ads can be very lucrative.

When your show gets very popular, you'll have other options. Andrew Baron used eBay to auction off the ads on Rocketboom. The winning bid, $40,000, included an ad produced by the Rocketboom team. But the publicity was worth far more.

Even though the final form of Web video advertising is not yet clear, TV networks are betting hundreds of millions that ad sales will be profitable and are already streaming most of their shows. Anyone can post immediately to Revver or Magnify.net (www.magnify.net) (**FIGURE 9.3**) and get an immediate share of ad revenue.

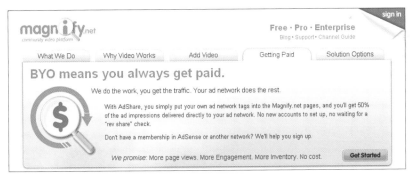

FIGURE 9.3 Magnify.net provides Bring Your Own ad network revenue sharing on its network.

You can create a simple Web site, enable Google AdSense, and collect immediately. But as you learned in Chapter 8, *Getting Your Video Noticed*, easy success in viral video is a myth, unless you're improbably lucky. A handful of people earn as much as a corporate video producer. It takes more skill than luck to make a profit producing independent Web video—unless you've developed a lucrative niche audience.

Selling Your Web Video

Bands make money selling records; movies make money in the theaters although some go direct to DVD. Motivational speakers and preachers have long sold their tapes. Cable video-on-demand is growing rapidly. It's logical to think that Web video producers could earn a living this way, but to date there have been few opportunities. But that's changing.

ON Networks (**www.onnetworks.com**) has created a library of high-quality short-form Web programs by paying producers (**FIGURE 9.4**). Titles include videos for a wide range of tastes including golfers, yoga practitioners, and parents. They look good even when blown up to full-screen. ON Networks' lineup includes shows with clearly defined audiences such as *The Parent Code*, offering advice for parenting kids of all ages; and *I am Blackness*, which looks at the diversity of the Black experience.

FIGURES 9.4 ON Networks' shows target an audience beyond 18 to 24 year olds.

The programs are shot well with high-quality production values including music tracks and professional graphics. You can answer surveys such as how often do you shop for clothes or subscribe to magazines while you watch, but you don't have to. The tattooed host of *Dinner with the Band* keeps things interesting while teaching how to make a milkshake with equal parts rum, chocolate ice cream, and seltzer.

ON Networks is looking for producers with a proven track record, who shoot in HD. If you meet these qualifications and have an idea for an episodic series, you can point them to a URL or send a demo reel by snail mail.

Another approach is to compete for Web video success on the Independent Film Channel's Media Lab Studio Web site (`http://medialab.ifc.com`). IFC made a commitment to Web video shows after rapper R. Kelly's opera *Trapped in the Closet* drew 4.1 million page views.

Web video hosts' ability to pay producers is tied in part to their own ability to make money. ON Networks, for example, is backed by AT&T. Others, like Akimbo, which started with a pay-per-view model, have been forced to adapt to survive. Very few people have been willing to spend money—either pay-per-view or by subscription—to watch Web video, and most of those who do want Hollywood originals. In 2003, Akimbo set out to offer a million of the world's best video and TV programs for sale on the Web. The site had backing from Cisco, AT&T, and top venture capitalists, as well as a robust server system designed to handle the high volumes they expected.

By 2007, they had gone through $30 million and didn't have enough customers to keep going. They scrapped nearly everything, brought in new management, and are trying to survive by selling other Web sites the powerful tools they had developed.

If you haven't visited Lynda Weinman's online training site lynda.com (`http://lynda.com`), take a look. Weinman perfected the art of teaching software in her successful series of books, DVDs, and live classes. On the Web site the classes are broken down into hundreds of short QuickTime movies available by subscription. The tutorials on the Web break down each topic into tiny bites and teach expertly. You can find tutorials on almost any software application you'd want to learn, with heavy concentration in multimedia and video. There are loads of free samples to whet your appetite. A very fair subscription model lets you opt in for a small monthly or annual fee. The premium subscription includes downloadable files to practice with.

Most Web-video-for-pay projects that have succeeded are offshoots of popular sports, like Major League Baseball and NASCAR. Extreme sports have found a niche, and the adult entertainment industry has created some of the most effective subscription technology online. Nearly all the companies who've positioned themselves as "distributors" of paid content are gone, unable to compete with Web video's prevailing "free" model.

▶ Creating a TV Network for the Web

Jen Grogono, Chief Content Officer, ON Networks®

How do you measure success at ON Networks? Hits? Comments? Focus groups?

We try very hard to remove as much subjectivity from our business as possible. We measure success primarily through data we collect through our Flash Player, or through our partner's set-top boxes. The data is used in aggregate so there are no privacy issues. It shows us precisely how a show performs with its desired audience in a totally nonbiased way.

What are you looking for when you evaluate program submissions, both in the idea and in the quality of the talent bringing it to you?

Utility of programming or value of talent. If utility is high, then talent can be lesser known, unproven to some degree, but still must be engaging. If programming is low on the utility front, then the talent makes all the difference.

Web formats are short-form, and writers say it's harder to write short good stories than long ones. Is that also true of Web video programs? Are there ways in which making short-form video programs is harder?

I think the Web in general makes storytelling more difficult because we are less patient in this medium. In short- or long-form original programming, the pace and tempo must be such that a lean-forward viewer is consistently engaged. That's hard to do. Educating and entertaining people in a smart and compelling—but not elitist—way is, in my opinion, the hardest challenge.

How much do you play to viewer's expectations of what Web video should be, and how much of your programming represents wild cards you take a chance on?

We try to do shows on topics that others don't cover, or we try to cover common topics in an original way through original talent or new formats. In that sense, I think we take a chance on almost everything since, by and large, our programming is "original."

You seem to have a wider demographic than many video sites. How would you define your target audience, or should I say audiences?

We target the high-value consumer segments that TV has left behind. We currently target eight segments that we have uniquely defined and that we uniquely understand how to engage: cultureds, modern femme moms, urban chic, smarty kids, etc.

How do you work with producers? Do you have a stable of technical talent, or do they bring their own?

We work both ways. Some producers are all-in-one, and others team up with resources of ours or folks we pair them with.

Is there a set budget for all productions, or is it a sliding scale based on production costs? How long is the contract?

It's a sliding scale, with contracts depending on variables like talent, proven expertise, subject-matter expert, etc.

Online video has been around for about 10 years, but what people are calling Web video seems to be a very specific popular genre with a young target audience. How do you define what you're doing?

We are not going after the 18- to 24-year-old audience only, like so many other Web video concerns. We are all screens, and our programming spans many audiences. Our TV VOD and private network partnerships represent a large and growing distribution group. Plus, we've always had a fundamental belief that everyone—particularly digitally savvy, information-age consumers—are our audience, and they are not as young as everyone believes. Austin, Texas, is a perfect microcosm of this type of consumer—smart, intellectually curious, and interested in seeking out information and entertainment on their own. These people primarily read because there is rarely anything worthwhile for them to watch.

Beyond Advertising

The Internet changes everything, including how much it costs to distribute video. From the producer's point of view, if you put a video up on YouTube, it costs you exactly the same if 3 people watch or 300,000. Suddenly, you're in an economy of abundance. Your ability to distribute content to your audience is limited only by how many people you can attract. The result is you can reach a very big audience for very little money.

Although the audience doesn't pay money, they do offer their attention. You can sell that attention to advertisers, as we discussed earlier. This is the most common approach to monetizing Web video content, but many producers have found other ways to benefit financially from having their work noticed by so many people.

Instead of selling the video itself, sell your talents as a performer. EepyBird entrepreneurs Grobe and Voltz tell us that they make more money from performing than from advertising and revenue sharing.

Prove Your Talent

New York and Los Angeles are full of actors and actresses earning their living in restaurants. Many of them spend years doing unpaid performances, and near-infinite numbers of casting calls, to get their break. Amanda Congdon was an only occasionally employed actress until she became coproducer and anchor of Rocketboom on the Web. She didn't make much money from the Web video, but it led to a generous contract at ABC.

Amber Lee Ettinger's modeling career took off after she did the viral *Obama Girl* video (**FIGURE 9.5**) on www.barelypolitical.com. *Obama Girl* is the brainchild of the founder of BarelyPolitical.com, Ben Relles. Buxom on-camera Obama Girl Amber Lee Ettinger is an actress, lip-synching for Leah Kaufmann, who wrote and sang the soundtrack for the video. It's a crowd-pleaser that was shot music-video style with a full music track. The video generated more than 8 million hits on YouTube and interest in Kaufmann's music.

Sell T-Shirts and Other Tie-Ins

Rock bands sell T-shirts, and so do EepyBird and Ask a Ninja. EepyBird has added an album and even gift certificates. The Ninjas will sell you a hat or a ringtone.

You can also use your video to create buzz for your other work, perhaps a book. An inexpensively produced short Web video might persuade a studio to fund you to complete the work for TV, if it proves that your story and skills are strong.

"I Got a Crush...On Obama" By Obama Girl

This is a video response to Super OBAMA GIRL: The Lost Episode

FIGURE 9.5 The *Obama Girl* video made model Amber Lee Ettinger a video star.

Many Web video producers create their work without expecting compensation. True Believers—people doing video about religion, politics, and other beliefs—don't expect to make a penny off their work and are happy to spread their ideas and beliefs. GodTube (**http://godtube.com**), a religious video-sharing Web site, is one of the Web's great successes. It raised $30 million in its first year and is now valued at a whopping $150 million.

Selling Your Skills

You'll have to deal with the harsh realities of show business when you look for a job producing video for the Web. Web video is fast becoming central to the entertainment industry, a welcome sign of growth. But as in traditional media, there are far too many applicants for each job. It's a tough field, and you'll need solid skills and a good strategy to find a job.

When I went to film school, every student wanted to be a director. I got my start as an editor and soon learned that some of the best producers and directors started out in the editing room. One way to get a job making Web video is to sharpen your skills. Although it might be difficult to sell your ideas, your talent as a camera operator, lighting expert, sound technician, writer, or editor may be very much in demand once you sharpen your skills.

The Art of Creating Video for the Web

Michael Szpakowski, video artist and co-curator of DVblog.com

Artist Michael Szpakowski says he doesn't want advertising on his videos or on DVblog, a site he co-created for fellow artists. He happily pays the server bills on his personal site, Scenes from Provincial Life (**www.somedancersandmusicians. com/vlog/ScenesOfProvincialLife.cgi**), and shares the cost for hosting video on DVblog.com (**http://dvblog.com**), the art video site he co-curates. Szpakowski, who has made hundreds of online videos, got his start putting short QuickTime movies online. For him, it's important that there be outlets for noncommercial work on the Web. A panel of artists reviews submissions on DVblog.com (**FIGURE 9.6**). "We post what we like," he says of the selection process.

FIGURE 9.6 DVblog.org, a site created by and for artists, explores the creative potential of Web video. A video by Matt Smithson is featured here (**www.manvsmagnet.com**).

"There's no question people will always find ways of doing non-market, non-corporate-driven, human-based artwork," says Szpakowski, who lives in London. His Web video has brought him international attention and invitations to show his work at Lincoln Center in New York, at the Pompidou Center in Paris, and at galleries and film festivals in other parts of the world. Play is an essential strategy for creating interesting work, says Szpakowski, who is concerned that the current crop of Web videomakers are far too concerned with the newest equipment and making money to experiment.

Szpakowski, who makes video with his cell phone and cheap MP4 recorders, enjoys testing technology's limits. "I'm quite interested in using deliberately crude and cheap techniques," he says, adding that just pushing technological limits without intelligence and creativity is simply uninteresting. He uses an old Sorenson codec, for example, to deliberately reduce resolution. He believes the results have a painterly effect.

Producing under deliberately imposed technical limitations sparks Szpakowski's interest. He's produced 50 videos for the Lumiere project (http://videoblogging.info/lumiere), initiated by videomakers Andreas Haugstrup and Brittany Shoot, who published a manifesto that encourages videomakers to produce and publish work created under the conditions faced by film pioneers the Lumiere brothers in 1895. "We believe that everyday video brings together a collective consciousness," write Haugstrup and Shoot. "We believe in video as a tool for contemplation."

Szpakowski's video is sometimes meditative, sometimes experimental, and often makes you see things from a new perspective. His short animated operas scored with children's voices are entertaining and fresh (**FIGURE 9.7**). Other works, such as *Peloponnesian Landscape with Poppies* (**FIGURE 9.8**)—a 2.9 MB, two-second loop recorded on a tiny MP4 recorder—are pure art.

FIGURE 9.7 One of several video operas Szpakowki scored with children's voices.

FIGURE 9.8 A short, meditative art video loop from Michael Szpakowski's site.

on the WEB

The Artistic Side of Web Video

There are some great resources available to artists (**FIGURE 9.9**) who want to share their videos on the Web. Videoart.net, for example, provides a searchable online archive and connects artists with curators, producers, and the public (**FIGURE 9.10**).

FIGURE 9.9 (Left) A frame from Carletta Joy Walker's animation "Moving Cool." (Right) Walker cowrote the score for the video opera "Smart and Tart Juicing."

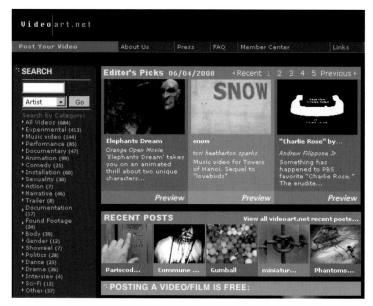

FIGURE 9.10 Videoart.net Web site featuring a gallery of art videos.

Finding a Job in Web Video

Everyone hates looking for work, but with a little luck you may be able find a job you love and gain experience working with Web video professionals and some great equipment. Start by looking at yourself and your work the way prospective employers will. Make a list of your skills and the projects that demonstrate them. Unless you're looking for an entry-level job as a production assistant or an unpaid internship, you'll need to bring some skills to the table.

Make sure your work is online and easy for an employer to check out. Google yourself and see what's there. If your video doesn't show up, go back and work on the key words on your video and on your Web site. While you're at it, put in a little dreamtime. Define your dream job and why you're qualified to be hired for it. Next, think of what you *don't* want to do, and define it as clearly so you'll know it when you see it.

Collect information about the companies you admire and start networking. Sixty percent of jobs are filled informally, via friends, contacts, and family. Start by making sure the people you know are keeping an eye open. Do everything you can to meet people in the field. Don't be shy. People involved in industry groups are usually encouraging to new people. Here are some more suggestions for getting your foot in the door.

Some Strategies That Often Work

To stand out from the crowd of applicants, start with something personal about your skills and why the company or job is right for you. Many people just send their standard letter and résumé, and these usually make it rapidly to the circular file. The first thing employers look for is whether you've done similar work previously so that your experience is relevant. If you have skills relevant to the job, make that one of the first things they see.

Of course, look at the big job sites, like Yahoo Jobs, Monster.com, and Careerbuilder.com. I was surprised when researching this chapter to find how many jobs came up when I typed in "Web video." Companies like NBC-Universal list dozens of jobs. There are more jobs in big cities, but I also found positions in Rochester, New York, with the U.S. Navy and Lexington, Kentucky, with a local graphics design shop. Do check several services. Some jobs were listed many places, but most were not. Also check thebiz.variety.com, which has thousands of listings in the entertainment business, including 264 in Texas as I write this. They range from sales assistant to vice president. Only a few are natural for a Web video person, but it takes only a few minutes to check. You might find entry into a good company or perhaps a perfect position.

Don't be afraid to use Craigslist (www.craigslist.org). I hired an excellent assistant for a shoot in Stockholm on Craigslist, and many of the "cool companies," including Google, use it regularly.

If you have substantial experience, find the places the pros use. At this writing, Paidcontent.org has listings for a senior vice president, Digital Media, Playboy Enterprises; producer, MTV Interactive; and two dozen more, including product and marketing manager positions.

If you're in New York, Los Angeles, or San Francisco, connect through the guilds. The Producers Guild of America New Media Council (www.pganewmedia.org) is very welcoming to newcomers and has strong events.

In other towns, find the local industry pros and write them directly for advice about what's possible in your city. Many enjoy helping newcomers and talking about their own work.

Follow what's going on in the industry. Read blogs like New Tee Vee (www.newteevee.com), Dan Rayburn's business of video blog (http://blog.streamingmedia.com), and Paid Content (www.paidcontent.org), where Liz Gannes and Rafat Ali are doing great journalism. Check magazines like *Streaming Media* (www.streamingmedia.com) and *Videography* (www.videography.com). If you see an item about a corporation raising money or starting a new project, they may well need someone with your skills. Being current on what's going on will help you during interviews as well.

Attend trade shows like NAB (Las Vegas, April) and Streaming Media (East Coast show, May; West Coast show, October) (**FIGURE 9.11**). Most have free or inexpensive exhibit passes, especially if you check the show Web site in advance. The big shows can be intimidating. Start by going first to the booths of products you know and use and asking some questions. The annual "Supermeet" sponsored by the Los Angeles Final Cut Pro Users group at NAB draws a great crowd.

You should also check your college placement bureau. Staying in touch with alumni from your college is one of the most effective strategies for finding work. Advertise your successes in alumni publications and read them so as to keep up with people you know in the industry.

Check government training programs for free technical training. Sometimes the programs can give you an extra boost by paying for you to take courses in local universities or industry schools. Professors and vocational teachers often know who's looking and will help students. Local TV stations have been the starting point for many successful careers, including Oprah Winfrey's. Most stations are producing for the Web and might have a spot.

FIGURE 9.11 Streaming Media, Inc., runs two annual trade shows for the Web video industry, Streaming Media East (New York, May) and Streaming Media West (San Jose, October).

You might also try a personal letter asking for advice from someone senior in the industry. Not everybody will respond, but some might be generous and steer you in the right direction.

Accept an unpaid internship if you must and if you can afford to. It's a way to get experience and meet people. You may find opportunities that work to your advantage. Don't take the first thing that comes along. Talk with others who have interned for a company to get a clearer view of what will be expected of you and whether it's worth your unpaid labor.

Look for a different type of job at a company you'd like to work for. Once you're in the company, you may find a chance to switch to the work you want to do. In particular, good marketing and product management people are in short supply. If you have relevant experience, you'll find many opportunities.

Industry Groups and Events for Networking

Some folks have old friends that can help them find a job; others have family connections. Many jobs are never advertised or are advertised only after they've been filled. So don't give up on the "informal job market." Start making your own connections wherever industry people get together. A good industry group has interesting people discussing relevant topics. Volunteering to help an industry organization can help you meet members. Organizers are often looking for ways to grow the organization and will appreciate the help. Get up your courage to introduce yourself to people, including the leaders. Mention the kind of a job you are looking for, and ask whether they know anyone hiring.

In New York, several hundred people come together for the Video 2.0 meetup (**FIGURE 9.12**) (http://web.meetup.com/13). Everyone is welcome, and the cost is $10 or less, mostly to pay for the meeting space. Some are pros trying to keep up and meet their peers. Many others are just starting out. A few minutes are set aside during each meeting for folks to announce they are looking to fill or find jobs. NYC Women in Media & Technology (www.wimlink.com) is another industry group whose main purpose is "connecting women media professionals and innovators." There are also Final Cut Pro User Groups around the country and dozens of other guilds and associations that might be helpful.

FIGURE 9.12 New York's Video 2.0 has 1,700 members, including some of the top Web video producers in the business.

Let Your Work Open the Door to New Opportunities

Now that you know what it takes to create great video on the Web, you've taken the first step to creating a career producing Web video. Improve your skills by making lots of Web video. When your work gets good, employers will often find you on the Web. There is no substitute for the confidence that comes from experience. But remember different venues have technical requirements specific to the way they work. Don't be too quick to try and wow the hiring committee with your new knowledge. Paying attention to a potential employer's needs is the best strategy for getting ahead. Their operation may require that you use different software or polish new skills.

One of the most convincing things you can do to demonstrate your expertise is produce your own work on the Web. Market it in interesting and intelligent ways that demonstrate your understanding of social networking and building Web audiences. Do whatever it takes to generate lots of visitors and keep track of your visitor stats. When it serves your purposes, make them visible on your Web site. Show potential employers you are skilled at producing the kind of work you'd like to get paid for, and you're more likely to land a job.

Making Great Video

Learning what makes video work on the Web from the best in the business has been an exciting journey. I come away from writing this book inspired and with admiration and respect for the many producers who shared their stories. A few things come into clear focus as I look back over the powerful examples they shared: how important each producer's unique and individual perspective is to shaping their work, the importance of crafting a good story to tell, and the pivotal role planning plays in creating good work.

As you develop expertise in the technical aspects of Web video, you'll have more tools to share your own point of view. Developing good skills in shooting, lighting, editing, and creating buzz to get your work out to the world will give you more opportunities to tell your video stories. You'll get to keep doing the work you love, and you'll learn the mark of a true professional. Keep learning, and keep getting better at what you do.

One last word of advice: get started today, and don't let anything stop you. Learn what you need to know while you make video. Experiment, explore, and don't be afraid to take chances. You'll learn faster and bring more imagination to your work if you bring the spirit of play to making video instead of working at it. I wish you joy in the process and lasting success. I'm looking forward to seeing your videos on the Web.

PROJECT

Identify and Target Your Audience

Look up the stats for a clip you've created while working through the projects in this book to find how many hits your video is getting. Change your key words and video descriptions see whether new titles and tags generate additional views.

Identify your audience. Who do you think would like your video? Identify a demographic. Include age, sex, ethnic identification, education, and interests.

Visit Web sites popular with your demographic. In your Web browser, use View > Page Source to look at the HTML, if available, and identify the key words for the site. Not all pages are designed in HTML, so look for a site with this option. See whether any of the key words are appropriate for your site. If they are, add them to your own key words.

Next you will compare your view of your audience to Google's. To do this, you'll need to set up Google AdSense for your site. Before you add AdSense to your site, make sure you name each page in your site and carefully select key words for each page that clearly identify your site's content.

Use the instructions in this chapter to add Google AdWords to your video Web page (**FIGURE 9.13**). Check periodically to see what ads Google serves. Use the ads served to deduce who Google thinks is the target audience for your video and your site.

For example, if Google serves ads for parents and Pampers, you can bet they think 25- to 40-year-old parents are your demographic. Compare Google's idea of your audience to the one you're trying to reach. Adjust your key words and your content to focus your target audience.

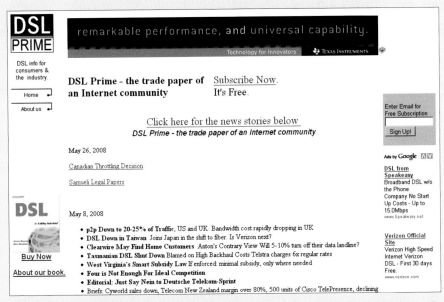

FIGURE 9.13 This Web site has a traditional banner ad at the top and Google text ads on the right.

Do a quick-and-dirty test marketing for your video Web site. Solicit honest reactions to your site, starting with friends. Ask them to look at your site, choose a video to watch, and watch it. Observe them while they do this. Don't hang over their shoulders; sit at a discreet distance. When they're done, ask questions. Make changes to your site's navigation and content based on their responses. Then find people who are in you defined target audience, and ask them to look at your site. A good way to get people to test your video and your site is as a member of a user group or interest group related to your video. Producing sailing videos? Ask members of your local sailing meetup.

Listen to their responses to see whether you're getting through to your target audience. Make sure you ask what they like online and what kind of video they watch. Their answers will better help you reach viewers like them in the future.

PROJECT

Network!

ind two networking groups, one for Web video and another in a topic area you're likely to create videos about. Meetup.com is a good starting point for finding networking groups. Attend one meeting of each group.

Create and practice an elevator pitch, a 90-second summary of your current project. Have some business cards printed with your current e-mail address and phone number, and make sure your Web site is up and working.

Listen during your first meeting and identify the thought leaders in each group. Try to get a sense of the members, their interests, and their level of expertise. After each meeting, introduce yourself to at least three people. When they ask who you are or what you're doing, try your elevator pitch. Pay attention to their response.

Ask questions to get a conversation going at networking events: almost everyone in technical fields enjoys talking about their work. Asking about a new contact's work, rather than launching into a list of your needs, will help break the ice. At subsequent meetings, raise your hand, and identify yourself before asking a question that also demonstrates your knowledge during the Q&A.

Pay special attention if there is a jobs segment at the meeting you attend. After the meeting, watch to see whether there is any immediate response to job requests. You'll know a pitch was effective if there are several people waiting to talk with the job seeker. Craft an announcement for future meetings that describes what you're looking for succinctly. At the next meeting, identify yourself and present your requirements. Follow up with anyone who responds. If the job isn't for you, pass it on to someone you think it's right for, or make a connection by introducing the employer to someone who might fit her needs. Keep the person as a contact in your database, and touch base when you have something of genuine mutual interest to share.

During interviews don't ask for basic information that is available on the company's Web site. Learn as much as you can about the companies you'd like to work for. That way, when you introduce yourself to the person sitting next to you, you're more likely to recognize the name of the person you most need to meet.

ADDITIONAL RESOURCES

Here are a few recommendations for good books, conferences, and additional resources to help you discover more about Web video.

Books and Films

Video Shooter: Storytelling with DV, HD, and HDV Cameras, by Barry Braverman (2006, CMP Books)
This is the best book we know of for an amateur video maker who wants to work like a pro. Braverman has decades of experience, from shooting feature films to no-budget videos, and the book lends a valuable perspective for even the most experienced video makers. Braverman actually covers much more than shooting, giving useful advice on everything involved in a production. Because we liked the book so much, we sought out Barry for an interview in Chapter 2, *Shooting for the Web*.

Single-Camera Video Production, Fourth Edition, by Robert B. Musburger (2005, Focal Press)
The information you need for setup, lighting and most of your practical shooting is in this book. There is little flair, but if you want to get better at shooting the information is here and well-explained. While the title is "single-camera," most of the information applies to almost any video shooting situation.

How to Shoot a Movie Story & Video Story; Technique of Pictorial Continuity, by Arthur L. Gaskill and David A. Englander (1985, Morgan & Morgan).
This short book taught us valuable lessons about continuity. Revised and enlarged, this new edition includes a section on breaking into the field.

The Five C's of Cinematography: Motion Picture Filming Techniques, by Joseph V. Mascelli (1998, Silman-James Press)
Web video is very different from the films Joe Mascelli wrote about in the 1960s but "The Five C's" (camera angles, continuity, cutting, close-ups, and composition) are still essentials of our craft. Mascelli's clear exposition of basic principles remains right on target and is in print again for about $20. Arthur C. Miller's introduction begins, "While production of motion pictures has changed considerably since I photographed *The Perils of Pauline* in 1914, some aspects—particularly those involving story telling—are still the same as they were half a century ago." Yet another half century later, that remains true.

Screenplay: The Foundations of Screenwriting, by Syd Field (2005, Delta)
Field's remarkable book sums up the full range of clichés that define popular movies. While that may not appeal to intellectuals, the screenwriters of an extraordinary range of motion pictures credit Field. His work was crucial to *Gorillas in the Mist, Like Water for Chocolate, Terminator, Silence of the Lambs, Y Tu Mama Tambien, Harry Potter and the Prisoner of Azkaban*, and an amazing number more. His book contains practical material about building conflict, audience expectations, and more.

Hitchcock, by Francois Truffaut and Helen Scott (1985, Simon and Schuster)
This is a book-length interview with two masters explaining their craft.

What is Cinema?, by André Bazin (2004, University of California Press)
Essays by the mentor of Jean-Luc Godard, François Truffaut, Éric Rohmer, Claude Chabrol, and Jacques Rivette, this book contains powerful ideas about the French New Wave filmmakers who were the acknowledged inspiration of Coppola, Spielberg, and Lucas.

In the Blink of an Eye, by Walter Murch (2001, Silman-James Press)
Murch is extraordinarily reflective about his work, which includes *The Godfather Trilogy*, *The Conversation*, *Apocalypse Now*, *The Unbearable Lightness of Being*, and a dozen more extraordinary films. His spirit is generous and his book thoughtful.

Behind the Seen: How Walter Murch Edited Cold Mountain Using Apple's Final Cut Pro and What This Means for Cinema, by Charles Koppelman (2005, New Riders)
Cold Mountain was one of the first major motion pictures edited with Final Cut Pro. This extraordinary book looks at the editing process by one of the industry's greatest editors of all time.

The Art of the Documentary, by Megan Cunningham (2005, New Riders)
This book gives insight on documentary filmmaking techniques by today's most accomplished documentary directors, cinematographers, editors, and producers.

Hillman Curtis on Creating Short Films for the Web, by Hillman Curtis (2006, New Riders)
Hillman let us use some stills from one of his short films on our book's cover. He is one of the most artistic individuals creating short films for the Web today.

Real-World Video Compression (2007, Peachpit Press)
If you need to compress your video for the Web, for DVDs, or mobile, this indispensable guide will give you the information you need.

Vision of Light: The Art of Cinematography
The Cutting Edge: Magic of Movie Editing
These two remarkable films include the best Hollywood pros explaining their craft. Containing short comments and illustrative clips from more than a dozen Academy Award winners, both films are remarkable and show "how it's done."

Software-specific books

For more than a decade, we've been learning from the Peachpit QuickStart, QuickPro, and Adobe Press Classroom in a Book series. The experience the folks at Peachpit bring to these guides almost always produces an excellent book, designed for effective learning.

Final Cut Express 4: Visual QuickStart Guide, by Lisa Brenneis (2008, Peachpit Press)

After Effects CS3 Professional for Windows and Macintosh: Visual QuickPro Guide, by Antony Bolante (2008, Peachpit Press)

Premiere Pro CS3 for Windows and Macintosh: Visual QuickPro Guide, by Antony Bolante (2008, Peachpit Press)

Final Cut Pro 6: Visual QuickPro Guide, by Lisa Brenneis (2008, Peachpit Press)

Adobe Premiere Pro CS3 Classroom in a Book, (2008, Adobe Press)

Adobe After Effects CS3 Professional Classroom in a Book, (2008, Adobe Press)

Online Training

Safari Books Online, http://safari.peachpit.com
Web Video: Making It Great, Getting It Noticed, and almost everything else from Peachpit, O'Reilly, lynda.com and a slew of other good publishers, is available online at Safari. The cost of access to everything there is as little as $22.99/month, which is convenient when you have a lot to learn and it includes books, short PDFs, and video.

Lynda.com Online Training Library, www.lynda.com
Lynda Weinman has built a mini-empire of videos about computer graphics, Web site creation, and more. There are 70 titles on video software and related topics, most of which have five to twelve hours of video instruction.

Edit Well, www.peachpit.com/editwell
Larry Jordan (www.larryjordan.biz), a Final Cut Pro trainer who tours and gives classroom-setting instruction, also edits an online magazine for Peachpit Press called Edit Well. Larry talks about the editing process in this book in Chapter 6, *Editing and Post-production*.

Networking Events

Final Cut Pro User Groups, http://fcpugnetwork.org
Organized in cities across North America, the Final Cut Pro user groups come together for a big party at the NAB Exposition and Conference in the spring.

Video 2.0 and other **Meetups**, http://web.meetup.com
Hundreds of New York video people come to the Video 2.0 meetup once a month, where novices rub elbows with the likes of MTV vice presidents. Meetup.com is definitely worth checking for events in your area.

Videobloggers NY, http://videoblog.meetup.com
A smaller group, but choice and very dedicated to help each other get better. Andrew Baron of Rocketboom is a leader. If you're visiting New York, try to make the monthly meeting.

NAB, IBC, and SIGGRAPH
NAB (National Association of Broadcasters) is in Las Vegas, NV, in the spring (www.nabshow.com), while IBC (International Broadcasters conference) is in Amsterdam in early fall (www.ibc.org). These are both huge shows where every manufacturer shows their latest gear, and they're loaded with free presentations given by interesting presenters. The exhibits are often free if you register in advance and it's a great chance to meet people who can

help you learn the latest. In fact, we met our editor Karyn Johnson in the Peachpit booth at the FCPUG meeting at NAB. SIGGRAPH, the "Special Interest Group on Graphics" (www.siggraph.org) is where the best animators and graphics people gather. TinToy, from Pixar, played SIGGRAPH years before the team made Toy Story and other feature films.

Streaming Media East and West, www.streamingmedia.com

If you want to know about encoding, content delivery, software for networks on the web, and more, Dan Rayburn's event is the place to be. Dan has been in the center of this world for more than a decade, seems to know everything and everyone, and puts together a strong program.

Other Trade Shows

Digital Hollywood, iHollywood's Digital Media event, and DMV's Future of TV, emphasize the business side of digital video. The main action is executives meeting each other; if that's your game, these are all strong events. The three mentioned are well programmed, with prestigious speakers and many experts.

Stores

Check out local Apple Store retailers. They often have seminars by Apple, Adobe, Tricaster, and other equipment and software manufacturers.

In New York we're lucky to have Tekserve, an Apple reseller, as well as B&H, a world-renowned reseller of professional video, camera, and audio equipment. The companies provide training, often by professionals who travel around the country giving workshops on the latest tools.

FIGURE CREDITS

Introduction
Figure 1, Revision3
Figure 2–4 Mark Von Holden Photography

Chapter 1
Figure 1.1 Joanne Colan. Rocketboom.com.
Figure 1.2 VideoJug.com
Figure 1.3 Move Networks
Figure 1.4 Expotv.com
Figure 1.5 Miro Player. Participatory Culture
    Foundation.
Figure 1.6 Illdoctrine.com. Courtesy Jay Smooth.
Figure 1.7 Jay Smooth. Photos by Jennie Bourne
Figure 1.8–1.9 Ken Schneiderman
Figure 1.10 Courtesy Alive in Baghdad
Figure 1.11 Nancy Bennett for Eepybird.com
Figure 1.12 Courtesy Sony
Figure 1.13–1.14 Courtesy Brightcove™
Figure 1.15 ON Networks®
Figure 1.16 Courtesy Marconi Society
Figure 1.17 Courtesy Tube Mogul

Chapter 2
Figure 2.1 Courtesy Sanyo
Figure 2.2, 2.4–2.6, 2.9–2.13, 2.15–2.22 Photos
    by Al Holston
Figure 2.3, 2.7, 2.8 Courtesy Sony
Figure 2.23 Courtesy Focus Enhancements
Figure 2.24 Nebula Awards. Photo by Jennie
    Bourne.
Figure 2.25 Larry Byrd. Photo by Jennie Bourne.
Figure 2.26 Mai Ly. Photo by Jennie Bourne.
Figure 2.27 Photo by Jennie Bourne
Figure 2.28 Photo by Al Holston
Figure 2.29 Courtesy Bogen Manfrotto
Figure 2.30 Christo "Gates" images, © Mimk42,
    Sloth 92 and joycevdb at Dreamstime.com

Chapter 3
Figure 3.1–3.3 Courtesy Web Video Summit.
Figure 3.4 EMS Wreath. Photo by Danny Burstein
Figure 3.5 Courtesy Sennheiser USA
Figure 3.6 Jennie Bourne, Amy Goodman WBAI
Figure 3.11 Courtesy Sennheiser USA

Figure 3.14–3.15 Photos by Al Holston
Figure 3.16 Courtesy Litepanels™
Figure 3.17 Courtesy Lowel

Chapter 4
Figure 4.1 Courtesty Ze Frank
Figure 4.2 Courtesy Roxanne Darling
Figure 4.3–4.4 Courtesy Annie Leonard
Figure 4.5 Courtesy Rocketboom.com
Figure 4.6 Joanne Colan. Photo by Jennie Bourne.
Figure 4.7 Rocketboom studio. Photo by Jennie
    Bourne.
Figure 4.8 Courtesy Irina Slutsky
Figure 4.9 Courtesy Alive in Baghdad
Figure 4.10 James Mastrangelo, Ray Beauty
    Supply. Photo by Jennie Bourne
Figure 4.11 Cantata PR. Photo by Jennie Bourne
Figure 4.12 Photo by Steven Nathans-Kelly
Figure 4.14 Josh Wolf. Photo by Dina Boyer.
Figure 4.16 Courtesy Expotv.com
Figure 4.17 Lure Lim, Jade Lim, and Mai Ly. Photo
    by Jennie Bourne.
Figure 4.18 Parade. Photos by Jennie Bourne.
Figure 4.19 Jade Lim. Photos by Jennie Bourne.

Chapter 5
Figure 5.1 The Burg. Courtesy Dinosaurdiorama.
    com
Figure 5.2–5.6 All-for-Nots. Courtesy
    Dinosaurdiorama.com.
Figure 5.7 Cinergy Script Editor. Courtesy Mindstar
    Productions.
Figure 5.8–5.9, 5.11 Courtesy Celtx
Figure 5.10 Courtesy Storyboard Pro
Figure 5.12 Courtesy Denke, Inc.
Figure 5.14 Auralex SonoSuede™. Courtesy
    Auralex Acoustics.
Figure 5.15 Courtesy Sony
Figure 5.16 NewTek TriCaster™ Courtesy NewTek,
    Inc.
Figure 5.17 NewTek LiveSet™ Courtesy NewTek,
    Inc.
Figure 5.18 Courtesy Sennheiser USA
Figure 5.20 Jef Raskin. Photo by Aza Raskin.

Figure 5.21 Risers at Pulver.TV. Photo by Jennie Bourne.

Figure 5.22 C-stand. Courtesy Matthews

Figure 5.23 Courtesy Kino Flo Lighting Systems

Figure 5.24 Gordon Bourne. Photo by Jennie Bourne.

Figure 5.25 Rosco Colorizer and Steel Gobos. Courtesy Rosco USA.

Figure 5.26 Mai Ly. Photo by Jennie Bourne.

Figure 5.27 Greenscreen. Photo by Jennie Bourne.

Chapter 7

Figure 7.1 *Smart Girls at the Party*. Courtesy ON Networks®.

Figure 7.2 Brightcove Media Manager. Courtesy Brightcove™.

Figure 7.3 Courtesy Expotv.com

Figure 7.4 Courtesy Magnify

Chapter 8

Chapter opener photos: Mentos World Record, Ohio. Bethany Vail for Eepybird.com. Eepybird at Blueman Group. Jaime Tardy, Idaka.com for Eepybird.com.

Figure 8.1 Photo by Jaime Tardy, Idaca.com. Courtesy Eepybird.com.

Figure 8.2, (top) Diet Coke and Mentos. Nancy Bennett for Eepybird.com. (bottom) Mentos World Record Ohio. Bethany Vail for Eepybird.com.

Figure 8.3 Courtesy Zadi Diaz from Epic Fu.com

Figure 8.4 Courtesy Internet Famous

Figure 8.5 Photo by Vu Bui for Rocketboom.com

Figure 8.6 Courtesy Blip.tv.

Figure 8.7 Courtesy Brightcove.com

Figure 8.8–8.9 Scenes of Provincial Life. Courtesy Michael Szpakowski.

Figure 8.10 Miro Player. Courtesy Participatory Culture Foundation.

Figure 8.11 Songza homepage. Courtesy Aza Raskin.

Chapter 9

Figure 9.1 Courtesy VideoJug

Figure 9.2 Courtesy Revver.com

Figure 9.3 Courtesy Magnify

Figure 9.4 Courtesy ON Networks®

Figure 9.5 Obamagirl. Courtesy Barley Political.

Figure 9.6 Dvblog.com. Courtesy Matt Smithson.

Figure 9.7–9.8 Courtesy Michael Szpakowski

Figure 9.9 Moving Cool, Courtesy Carletta Joy Walker. 5 Operas, Courtesy Michael Szpakowski.

Figure 9.10 Courtesy Videoart.com

Figure 9.11 Courtesy www.StreamingMedia.com

Figure 9.12 Web 2.0 meeting. Courtesy Yaron Samid.

Figure 9.13 DSL Prime. Courtesy Dave Burstein.

INDEX

VC-1 Encoder SDK, 233
vectorscopes, 87, 88
Veoh, 25, 29
version control, 194
Viddler, 219
video. *See also* Web video
    adding keywords to, 26, 27
    adding titles to, 68
    choosing format for, 26. *See also*
        video formats
    creating thumbnail for, 27,
        254–255
    creating version for iPhone,
        279–280
    editing. *See* editing
    fixing mistakes in, 61
    formatting for the Web, 247–248
    getting from camera to
        computer, 25–26
    impact of motion on, 79
    job opportunities, 295–302
    lighting considerations. *See*
        lighting
    linking to, 27
    live switched, 168–169
    managing production of, 19–22
    mixing sound and, 166–167
    monetizing, 255, 275, 282,
        294. *See also* money-making
        opportunities
    monitoring popularity of, 29
    naming, 29, 254
    overusing effects in, 185
    paying bloggers to recommend,
        252
    planning shots for, 20
    pre-production, 18–19
    recording sound for, 19
    setting up RSS feed for, 278
    shooting. *See* shooting video
    storytelling with, 54–59,
        197–202
    tagging, 265
    trade-offs when putting online,
        220
    uploading to host, 26–27, 68,
        214
    using transitions in, 199
    viral. *See* viral video
    Web sites. *See* video Web sites
Video 2.0 meetup, 275, 302
video blog awards, 109
video bloggers
    as journalists, 128
    tips for, 13, 111
    Yahoo list of, 111
video blogging software, 130–131
video cameras, 34–40

video compilations, 194
video compression. *See*
    compression
video-editing software
    compressing of video by, 215
    consumer *vs.* pro versions,
        188–190
    creating new projects in, 183
    creating titles with, 199–200
    learning to use, 184, 186, 188,
        190
    student discounts for, 190
video equipment. *See also* cameras
    reviews, xiv
    shipping/transporting, 63–65
    shopping for, 34
video formats, 26, 34, 183, 187, 221,
    226–228
video guestbooks, 76
video hosts
    choosing, 215–221, 272
    compression tools provided by,
        204
    creating account with, 23
    downloading video from, 214
    enterprise-level service, 246
    file-size guidelines/limits, 196
    format considerations, 26, 223
    free *vs.* paid, 218, 276–277
    getting marketing help from,
        271–273
    list of, 24–25
    settings for popular, 226–228
    upload tools provided by, 204
    uploading video to, 26–27, 68,
        246
video marketing company, 252
video news business, 113
video projects. *See* projects
video search engines, 266
video-sharing sites, 273
video-shooting basics, 33
video tutorials, 40, 291
video Web sites
    driving traffic to, 265–267
    examples of good, 261–264
    making money from. *See*
        money-making opportunities
    market-share rankings, 273
    optimizing for search engines,
        267
    tips for creating, 264–265, 269
Videoart.net, 298
Videoblogging Meetup, New York,
    116
Videoegg, 271
Videography, 300
VideoJug, 4, 131, 132

videomaker interviews, x, xiv
    by interviewee
        Baron, Andrew, 116–118
        Braverman, Barry, 54–59
        Darling, Roxanne, 110–112
        Grace, Kathleen, 146–151
        Grogono, Jen, 292–293
        Jordan, Larry, 184–187
        Kaplan, Dina, 286–288
        Raskin, Aza, 268–269
        Samid, Yaron, 274–275
        Smooth, Jay, 10–13
        Szpakowski, Michael,
            296–297
        Waggoner, Ben, 230–233
        Wolf, Josh, 128–129
    by title
        Art of Creating Video for
            Web, 296–297
        Build a Great Team, 116–118
        Creating TV Network for
            Web, 292–293
        Finding Niche, Sponsor, and
            Distributor, 286–288
        Getting Started in Web
            Video, 10–13
        Important Encoding
            Considerations, 230–233
        Keep User Experience in
            Mind on Video Web Page,
            268–269
        Responsibilities of Online
            Journalists, 128–129
        Shooting Dramatic Series for
            Web, 146–151
        Take Charge of Distribution,
            274–275
        Take Viewers on a Personal
            Journey, 110–112
        Tell Stories with Images,
            54–59
        What You Need to Know
            About Editing, 184–187
Videomaker magazine, 152
VidMetrix, 271
viewer statistics. *See* statistics
viral video, 250, 252–256, 259, 282,
    290
virtual sets, 167, 175
visual continuity
    errors, 161
    maintaining, 135
    shaping story with, 197–198
    studying, 136
    ten commandments of, 160–161
visual metaphors, 113, 199
visual storytelling, shooting
    strategies for, 162